# RUNNER'S WORLD®

## COMPLETE BOOK OF

# *Women's*

# RUNNING

**The Best Advice to Get Started, Stay Motivated, Lose Weight, Run Injury-Free, Be Safe, and Train for Any Distance**

BY DAGNY SCOTT

RODALE®

**Notice**

This book is designed to help you make decisions regarding your fitness and exercise program. It is not intended as a substitute for professional fitness and medical advice. As with all exercise programs, you should seek your doctor's approval before you begin.

**Library of Congress Cataloging-in-Publication Data**

Scott, Dagny.
    Runner's world complete book of women's running : the best advice to get started, stay motivated, lose weight, run injury-free, be safe, and train for any distance / by Dagny Scott.
       p.    cm.
    Includes index.
    ISBN 1–57954–118–6 hardcover
    ISBN 1–57954–466–5 paperback
    1. Running for women.   I. Title: Complete book of women's running.
II. Title: Women's running.   III. Title.
GV1061.18.W66 S36   2000
613.7'172'082—dc21                       99–059609

To my mother and father,
*for showing me the starting line.*

And to Arturo,
*for waiting at the finish line.*

# Contents

# Acknowledgments

AMONG THE NUMEROUS LIFE-ENHANCING ASPECTS of running, the people you meet are near the top of the list. Over the years, I've been lucky to get to know many of the wonderful runners, coaches, physicians, and leaders in this sport. Dozens of these people have graciously assisted in the creation of this book, offering their time and knowledge.

First and foremost among them is Maureen Roben—runner, coach, mother, and overall delightful spirit. Never without a smile and a laugh, Maureen is a force of nature who has quietly given back to the sport for years with her Women's Running Camps. She served as the sounding board for this book and helped to devise its workout schedules. Thanks also go to Diane Palmason, who cofounded and codirects the camps with Maureen. Diane's wealth of knowledge on the health of women runners was invaluable to me in my research. My thanks to both Maureen and Diane for allowing me to use their camp as a forum for discussing the issues covered in this book with other women runners.

Thomas Shonka, D.P.M., deserves thanks not only for his assistance with this book but also for his attentive treatment of my own litany of injuries. Thomas is a runner's dream podiatrist: He understands our fervent need to get back on our feet quickly, and he finds time in his busy schedule to see that he makes it so. As a former president of the American Academy of Podiatric Sports Medicine, Thomas provided invaluable help with this book.

Countless other experts contributed their wisdom to this book, among them Henley Gabeau, Judy Mahle Lutter, Lynn Jaffee, Susan Kalish, Lewis Maharam, Jack Daniels, David Martin, Neal Pire, Ray Browning, Amy Roberts, Steven Ungerleider, Carol Otis, Nancy Clark, Susan Kundrat, Jerilynn Prior, Douglas Hall, Jerry Lynch, Roy Benson, and Lisa Callahan.

Special thanks go to the runners and friends who shared their thoughts and tips throughout these chapters: Shelly Steely, Nadia Prasad, Jane Welzel, Libbie Hickman, Kim Jones, Ann Boyd, Lorraine Moller, Anne Audain, JoAnn Behm Scott, Shirley Van

Slooten, Mya Jones, Laurie Mizener, Mary Kirsling, and so many more.

To my coach, Willie Rios, goes a heartfelt thank-you. He was a guiding spirit to me in writing this book. Although I no longer race, Willie will always be "Coach" to me, just as he will always be with me on my runs.

To my editor, John Reeser, I owe a debt of gratitude. Thanks to John's kindness and generosity, this author's first book was a joyous experience.

Finally, I thank my husband, Arturo, for his support while I undertook this project. The rest of the world knows him as a great runner; I am the lucky one to know him as a great man.

# Foreword

THESE DAYS, IN CASE YOU HAVEN'T HEARD, women are running the world. By many measures—shoe company surveys, retail sales, new subscriptions to *Runner's World* magazine, even entries in road races—women runners have reached 50 percent of the total running population. And their participation is growing.

Twenty-five years ago, women made up only 5 percent of all runners. This is a revolution, make no mistake about it. And it has happened because running is the perfect sport for women.

I actually figured this out a long time ago. It was a simple call, really. You didn't need a crystal ball to see it. You just had to think for a moment about women and all the attributes they bring to running.

Many women are disciplined and determined and incredibly well-organized. They have to be to succeed in all the roles society layers on them—job, housework, mother, wife. And more. Running comes easily to these women, because all running takes is discipline, determination, and organization—exactly what women have.

And there's a bonus: Running doesn't require any special athletic skills. You don't have to be able to hit a backhand. You don't have to know a three-iron from a nine-iron, or a slalom from a mogul. You just have to make up your mind that you're going to do it.

Women also excel at running because they understand the importance of patience and following directions. Guys? Not always so bright. My wife cooks meals according to recipes, and they always come out delicious. I make things up as I go along, yet I can't understand why everyone refuses to eat my concoctions.

In running, it turns out, following a plan is the key to success. There's a beginning plan, an intermediate plan, an advanced plan, a first-time marathon plan, and so on. Follow the plan, and you'll do just great at running. Women value plans, and they reap the benefits.

Women also understand the emotional side of running better than men. Men sometimes make the mistake of thinking that running is a never-ending race against the stopwatch. We want to go fast. All the time. As a result, we too often get injured, fatigued, and burned out. Worse, we get depressed when we reach an age where we can no longer run as fast as we did in our youth.

Women like to run fast, too. I'm not saying that they don't train as hard as men, or don't try to make it to the Olympics. But more women than men accept running for what it is—a simple and immensely satisfying fitness activity. A time for solitary reflection, or for group social banter. An opportunity to drain out all of the stress of daily living and to celebrate the joy of good health.

Over the years, I have been lucky enough to run with some famous women. I ran with Joan Benoit long before she became a Boston Marathon and Olympic champ. I ran with Oprah Winfrey long after she became an international TV and movie star.

And here's what I've learned from Joan and Oprah and hundreds of other women runners: You can make your running into whatever you want it to be. You can go for the gold, or you can simply set out to achieve something you never dreamed possible (even if no one else notices).

It's entirely up to you. I know you can do it, because tens of millions of other women runners have done it. In the pages that follow, Dagny Scott, a wise and experienced woman runner, has laid out all the plans and recipes and wisdom you'll need.

The next step is yours.

*Amby Burfoot*

Amby Burfoot
Executive Editor
*Runner's World* magazine

# Introduction

AS I SIT DOWN TO WRITE THIS, I am sweaty, grimy even, from a windy November run that has coated me with dust. Although it's the weekend, I've logged on to the computer in an attempt to capitalize on the fresh mind-set that is the gift of a run—as I so often do.

Today, I saw two friends out on the trail that meanders along the outskirts of town. It is a vast and hushed landscape where the Rocky Mountains give way to the quieter majesty of the endless plains to the east. Beth and Jennifer were with their three dogs, a spectrum of shaggy, golden- and cream-colored beauties. We chatted about the run, the day, yesterday's workout, the dogs. The two mentioned how they looked forward to this time each week, this Sunday ritual. Time away from husbands and boyfriends, from work and home, from tidier pursuits. This is what it's all about, they said. Yes, I said. This is what it's all about. I felt a chill and noticed that I had goose bumps, although the air was not cold yet.

So I watched Beth and Jennifer resume running with their dogs, enjoying their piece of the day. And I tried to figure out why such a simple thing moved me so. Dozens of women were out on the trail today—some in groups, some alone. In fact, there were far more women than men. And then it struck me just how far we've come. A generation ago, women had no such model for companionship. Men alone participated in athletics and reaped its ensuing benefits: the bonds of friendship, the revitalization of time away, the healthy glow from movement. Women's participation in sports—and, in particular, in the hugely popular second running boom—has given us a new paradigm. A refuge in the day that holds only good things. A place in which we develop friendships, love, and trust as solid and uncomplicated as the beat of our feet and the rhythm of our breathing.

When I learned that I would have the honor of writing this book—and it is an honor—I felt a deep sense of responsibility. How could I do service to the depths of feeling that I have for this sport? How could I possibly enumerate all the gifts that running has given me: strength and health; love and friendship; a sense of self, of discipline, of capability and power; and even a profession and a husband?

As I sat down over the course of a year to write this book, my goal was to impart the breadth and depth of what running can mean to women: more than just fitness or friendship or sanity but rather all those things together. I can only hope that this book offers you at least a portion of the strength and inspiration that I have drawn from other women along the way.

I hope to see you out on the roads, the trails, or the track. May your feet and your heart feel light.

# The Need for a Women's Running Book

THERE'S AN IMPORTANT STORY you should know about. It's the story of a million women finding their legs. Along the way, they found their voices, their hearts, and their dreams. This story can be yours, too. All of running's benefits are right here for you to grab.

Why a women's running book? Are women runners different from men? After all, we both put one foot in front of the other, again and again. We both revel as we become fit and strong. We both struggle with days of leaden legs; days of no time to think, much less run; days when a brilliant stroke of motivation means sliding off the couch to order a pizza. In these ways, women runners are no different from their male counterparts.

But wait.

Listen to those millions of women runners. Listen to their quiet breaths as they talk in predawn pairs, before the rest of the family wakes—the lessons and questions they share to the rhythm of steady footsteps. "I never thought I could . . ." "I feel so much stronger . . ." "I'm ready to take on a new challenge . . ." Women develop a special sorority on the roads. This bond is an understanding based on acceptance, an appreciation of how far they have come, a knowing wink that says how much is yet to be gained. And so they talk and share and grow—and run. Singly and in groups, swiftly and slowly, they run.

# THE WOMEN'S RUNNING BOOM

Running has always had some women enthusiasts. But as millions of women have taken up the sport, they have redefined it even as it has redefined them. At the onset of the first running boom, which started when Frank Shorter won the gold medal in the 1972 Olympic Marathon in Munich, female runners were a rarity. Strenuous sports activities were still considered unfeminine and even harmful for women, so most women stuck to traditional activities such as golf and tennis. It was an oddity to see a woman running down the street, and those who did were sometimes asked who was chasing them. The women's movement changed that, and by the 1980s it was no longer uncommon to see women jogging in city parks, on tracks, and on trails throughout the country.

Over the course of those years, running evolved from a fairly obscure activity of hard-core athletes to a fitness activity of the masses. Good for the heart and lungs, easy on the budget, and possessing virtually no learning curve, it grew in popularity as Americans recognized the value of regular exercise. During the 1990s, as fitness evolved from healthy pursuit to holistic lifestyle, the United States experienced a second running boom. Now more than ever, running fills the bill for people with all sorts of goals, providing a social circle, stress relief, personal growth, and more.

This time around, women have driven the resurgence and recharacterization of the sport into a quest for health and fitness. Why women? More people of both sexes have begun pursuing the physical and emotional benefits of fitness. However, time has become a commodity in seemingly ever-dwindling supply, and women have felt especially pressed as they balance career and family while attempting to maintain healthy lifestyles. For increasing numbers of women, running has been a saving grace. A workout for the whole body, running requires a minimum of time, instruction, equipment, and planning. Although many women have entered the sport for its physical benefits, its surprising bonuses are what spur their enthusiasm. Running is conducive to both socializing and time alone, to relieving stress and solving problems, to relaxing and venting. Running has become a simple route to fitness that fits the complicated life of today's woman.

Now, women's enthusiasm for running has carried over into organized events, accelerating the sport's second boom. More and

## TRAINING LOG

So who am I and why did I write this book? After all, you haven't seen my name in the annals of Olympic-gold history. I'm not a hero or a household name, like Joan Benoit Samuelson or Grete Waitz.

No, when it comes to running, I'm probably far more like you. I've had my dreams of athletic glory since I was a little girl. I've come tantalizingly close to some of those dreams over the years—close enough to taste them at times, mostly salty and bittersweet in my mouth. But in the end, I did not become a professional runner. I became a journalist, focusing my pen and thoughts on female athletes and on runners in particular.

Writing and running have woven together to define my life and my career. The two passions have built upon each other, becoming virtually indistinguishable. The lessons I've learned while pursuing my goals of excellence on the track and on the road are the foundation upon which I've built a career as a journalist. The women who have crossed my reporter's path have been an unending source of inspiration.

Throughout these chapters, I share some of my personal running experiences in these "Training Log" sections. It's fair to say that these experiences range from the sublime to the ridiculous—with the ridiculous winning out most often. In running, after all, we learn as we go, bumps and bruises along with the triumphs. At most, I hope you can glean some enlightenment from my journey—at least that you can come away from it with a good laugh.

In the end, I've learned that this journey is what counts. It is a lesson that comes sooner or later to every woman who runs. More than any medals earned or pounds lost or races run, the journey is always the thing. That is why we run. It is what we share. And that is why I wrote this book.

more races, fun runs, and walk/run events cater to women. Women-only events and charity fund-raisers regularly draw tens of thousands of women. It's not unusual for women to make up half the field of a marathon or a 10-K race, once vastly male in numbers. "Back-of-the-packers" are recognized with special awards, as are finishers in their golden years. The cumulative result is a sport that celebrates everyone who participates, not just those who are fleet of foot.

Women have been able to have such an impact in part because of running's egalitarian nature. Join a running club for a Sunday outing, and all are equals: young and old, wealthy and poor, all races, colors, and creeds. And yes, male and female. Friendships that might seem odd in another context are struck up when two strides fall into sync somewhere out on an otherwise lonely road. Even the speedy and the slow traditionally meet at the end, sharing their tales over bagels and coffee. And on race day, the tortoise shares the starting line with the hare, and the jogger can literally follow in the footsteps of her professional heroes. It's within the context of such an open social fabric that women have made their mark on all levels of the sport.

## BRINGING IT ALL BACK HOME

As more women have become runners, the body of research documenting the sport's effect on women's bodies has grown. Now it seems that for every similarity between men and women runners there is a significant difference. For example, although the training principles of gaining speed and fitness remain the same for men and women, fluctuations in women's hormone levels can mean that it's more complicated for them to peak for an event.

On the other hand—possibly thanks to their hormones—women seem better cut out for endurance than men are, because their pain thresholds are generally higher. And though the principles of biomechanics are the same for both sexes, some women are more prone to knee and foot problems than men, because they have wider hips. The female metabolism even seems to react differently to exercise, resulting in different nutritional needs. The list goes on.

In addition to such biological nuts and bolts, many women find that their questions and concerns about running veer in different directions than men's. Yes, the story of women's running is a story of how to become fit, and, should you desire it, even how to get fast. But it is also a story of how to set and reach goals, make time for yourself, make peace with yourself, and more. It is a story of relishing the moment and working toward the future, of appreciating the little things in life and never losing sight of the larger picture. These are the benefits women find today when they become runners—benefits every bit as noticeable as trimmer thighs and faster times.

# 2

# Dress like a Runner

RUNNING IS SUCH A SIMPLE ENDEAVOR. To get ready, you just lace up your shoes and head out the door.

It's so simple that plenty of women think that they can lace up any old shoes. They'll scrounge in the closet for some worn antique of a sneaker and head off happily on collapsed heels and flapping soles. Well, that won't do. Running doesn't require a great investment in gear, but it does require a special pair of running shoes. Not those shoes you used to wear in aerobics class or those five-and-dime canvas cuties but real running shoes, built for running—and ideally used only for running.

Why? Wearing only good shoes can keep a runner training year after year on uncomplaining knees, but the wrong shoes can lead to cranky, debilitated joints, muscle soreness, and even injury. Shoes can mean the difference between an enjoyable experience and one miserable enough to quit the sport. So don't even think of trying to save a few bucks on sneakers. A visit to the podiatrist will cost a lot more than a pair of running shoes.

Just as you shouldn't run in any old shoe, you also shouldn't run in any old bra. For fairly obvious reasons, the right sports bra also can make the difference between misery and enjoyment out on the trail. A few extra dollars spent here won't be a mistake.

And that's really all of the must-haves. Of course, the longer you run, the more accessories you'll start to consider your must-haves. Beyond shoes and bras, you may opt for performance clothing that keeps you cool and dry in the summer and warm in the winter. Or you may notice the watches, sunglasses, hydration systems, and other gadgets marketed to runners. Some are helpful, some less so. Some work wonders but cost a small fortune. Should you buy them?

Ultimately, the amount of gear you end up with is a matter of personal preference. Some runners wear enough of these gizmos to get them through an ultramarathon even when they're out for a 30-minute jaunt. Other runners are ascetics, sticking to simple shorts and a T-shirt and replacing even those items only when they wear thin. Much of the fancy clothing and gear is suited more to the competitive runner who logs many miles than to the three-times-a-week jogger. On the other hand, many recreational runners find that purchasing a treat such as a new jacket or a pair of sunglasses can be just the thing to jump-start flagging motivation.

The bottom line is that before you start running, or if you're an old pro who hasn't paid proper attention to her body, it's time to hit the store. Pick out some shoes and a bra. Beyond that, it's your choice: Knock yourself out on the extras or exit the store with your budget intact. Read on to learn what to look for when choosing any of these items.

## SHOES

Running shoes are high-tech insulation between your feet and the ground. "When you run, your feet might strike the ground between 70 and 100 times per minute, each time with a force two to three times the weight of your body," says Tim Hilden, an exercise physiologist and biomechanics specialist in Boulder, Colorado. "Each time you contact the ground, that force is transmitted up into the body. The right pair of shoes can help to attenuate that force."

Today's running shoes are small scientific wonders, backed by multimillion-dollar research and development labs. Hundreds of different models exist to accommodate different foot and body variations. The shoes are designed to complement your natural structure of bones, ligaments, and tendons—commonly referred to as the body's biomechanics—and therefore minimize damage from incessant pounding. The right shoe for you will depend on several factors, including the way your foot strikes the ground, your gait, your weight, and your running program.

Beginning runners often ask which brand of shoe they should buy. The answer is whichever one feels best. All the major running shoe manufacturers produce a variety of shoes for runners' varying needs. Rykä, Saucony, and New Balance were pioneers in creating

# When Just a Shoe Isn't Enough

**A**thletic shoe inserts are designed to take the place of your shoe's removable insole or to work in conjunction with it. Made in a variety of materials, inserts range from arch supports to heel cups, from half-length to full-length, and more.

For many women, the insoles that come with their running shoes perform perfectly fine. But if your arches deviate from "normal"—meaning they're either very high or very flat—you may benefit from special insoles, says Thomas Shonka, D.P.M., a former president of the American Academy of Podiatric Sports Medicine who has a practice in Boulder, Colorado. The more you deviate from a perfect arch, the more likely you'll benefit from an orthotic device added to the shoe. Another tip-off is the onset of running-related injuries after increasing mileage. "If you develop an injury every time you go over a certain number of miles per week, that can be an indication of an overuse injury that is biomechanically related. Shoe inserts can alleviate that kind of injury," Dr. Shonka says.

First try running in shoes that are well-suited for you without additional accessories. If pain develops in your feet, knees, hips, or back, inserts might be a simple solution. (You can try them without the expense of consulting a physician—a specialist at a running shoe store should be able to help you choose an appropriate model.) If you don't get relief from an over-the-counter model, more aggressive customized orthotics can be crafted from a personalized mold. See a sports physician; podiatrists who specialize in running or sports medicine are best qualified to make running shoe inserts. Expect to pay between $200 and $400.

Here's a rundown of the most common inserts and their functions.

*Arch supports.* Designed for different arch types, these insoles are molded for varying degrees of support. Primarily for overpronators, whose feet collapse inward too much upon landing, they stabilize the foot and ankle. To find a pair that

true women's shoes based on a form with a narrower heel and a wider forefoot, and most companies have now followed suit. More important than finding a woman's shoe, however, is finding *your* shoe. A model that fits one woman like a dream will feel misaligned on another. Since each manufacturer tends to have a "signature" shape and feel, you should try several brands to find the one that fits your foot best.

The easiest and most reliable way to choose a shoe is to shop at a running specialty store. The salespeople there typically are

---

feels comfortable, try them with your running shoes in the store before you buy them. If these don't provide relief, custom-made orthotics might be in order.

*Cushioned insoles.* Although these inserts are used mainly for additional cushioning and comfort, some runners also place them over custom-made orthotics when the orthotics don't provide their own cushioning. Each insert is a flat, thin layer of foam that is either full- or half-length. When used only in the back of your shoe, the insert can raise your heel to alleviate stress on tight calf muscles. The inserts are also easily trimmed into any shape: You can glue trimmed pieces to specific areas of your shoe's insole to build up cushioning where you need it. Play around to find a formula that works for you, or go to a podiatrist for guidance.

*Heel cups.* These look like what the name implies, with the cup cradling and cushioning the heel. Heel cups are typically used to provide relief from the pain of plantar fasciitis (inflammation of the band of tissue on the bottom of the foot), which is felt just under the heel. Heel cups may alleviate the pain but they don't solve the problem, which is usually related to overpronation. Sturdier shoes or arch supports might be more appropriate.

*Metatarsal cushions.* You insert a metatarsal cushion in the front of your shoe under the ball of your foot. It can help alleviate the pounding on the bones that are just behind your toes—and the ensuing pain—by providing both support and cushioning.

*Replacement insoles.* These are beefed-up versions of the insoles that come in shoes. Replacement insoles can provide better, more durable cushioning than regular shoe insoles. They essentially upgrade your shoe without changing its characteristics.

experienced runners who will look at your gait, ask about your running schedule, and then recommend several pairs of shoes best suited to your needs. (This does not apply to large, chain sporting goods stores, which rarely have salespeople trained in specific sports.)

If you must choose shoes without the help of a knowledgeable salesperson, you can get on the right track by doing some research on your own feet. The most important distinction to learn is whether you *overpronate*, *supinate*, or are a normal pronator. That's not as complicated as it sounds. When your arch collapses and rolls inward as you run, you are pronating. Some pronation is a natural part of the shock-absorbing action that takes place as your foot hits the ground and proceeds to roll forward. Ideally, when you are running, your foot hits first on the outside portion of your heel, and your weight shifts toward the inside and front of your foot until finally you push off on the ball of your foot and your toes.

If you overpronate, your foot collapses inward too much upon landing, or you may even land on the inside of your heel. This lack of arch support can result in a myriad of aches and pains.

On the other end of the spectrum, feet that are rigid and don't roll inward enough are also problematic because they don't provide adequate shock absorption for your legs. This condition—less common among women than among men—is called supination.

Runners whose feet do neither of the above are called normal pronators.

There are two simple methods shoe designers recommend to determine which category you fit into.

**Look at an old pair of shoes.** The pattern of wear tells a story. The soles and midsoles of an overpronator's shoes tend to wear down and compress toward the inside. A supinator's shoes tend to wear down and compress on the outside. Women with neutral feet will generally have evenly worn shoes.

**Look at your footprint.** The next time you step out of the shower, stand on a dark mat or towel that shows your footprint. If the middle of your footprint is almost filled so that your arch is barely visible, you have flat feet and are likely an overpronator. If your footprint shows a gradual curve in the middle of your foot,

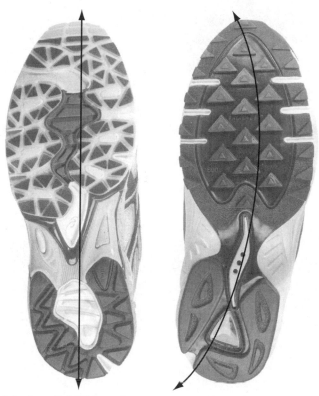

A straight last *(left)* is best for overpronators, while a curved last *(right)* should be worn by supinators. A semicurved last, which is for normal pronators, looks very similar to a curved last.

you have normal arches and are likely a normal pronator. If your arch is very high, so that your footprint is nearly or completely divided into two segments, you're probably a supinator.

Now that you know which category your feet fit into, you must know what kind of running shoe you need. Running shoes generally fall into three categories to parallel the categories outlined above.

**If you are an overpronator, look for shoes that offer additional support.** When you look at these shoes from the bottom, you should be able to draw a fairly straight line from the heel to the toe. You'll also find three other features.

**1.** A rigid device built into the arch or inner heel of the shoe that discourages your foot from rolling in.

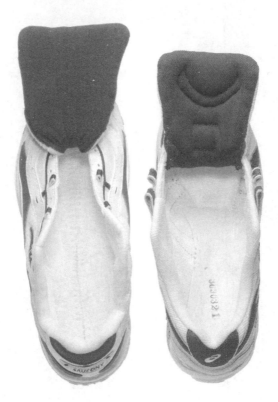

A slip last provides substantial flexibility, while a combination last *(right)* offers stability and flexibility.

2. A built-in combination last. Check for this by lifting out the shoe's inside liner and looking underneath. A firm, cardboard-like material should cover the soft fabric underneath in the rear of the foot from the heel to the arch.

3. A rigid design. Support shoes are generally difficult to twist. Test them by grabbing the shoe at the heel and toe and torquing your hands in opposite directions.

**If you are a supinator, look for shoes that offer flexibility and additional cushioning.** When you look at these shoes from the bottom, the line from heel to toe should be curved. They should have extra cushioning in the midsole, often throughout the length of the shoe. The inside construction should be slip-lasted for greater flexibility. That means that when you look under the shoe's inside liner, you'll find fabric that is sewn together moccasin-style. These shoes are generally easy to twist by torquing the heel and toe in opposite directions.

**If you are a normal pronator, look for neutral shoes.** These shoes feature a semicurved line from heel to toe. They usually have cushioning and support mechanisms, but neither should be extreme. They often have either a slip last or a California slip last, which is a solid piece of fabric in the shape of the foot that is sewn to the shoe's upper.

Once you've determined which category of shoe you need, follow these tips to zero in on the perfect pair.

**Try on a number of styles from different manufacturers.** Each will have a slightly different shape, and one will mold to your foot better than others.

**Run in the shoes.** Walking in a pair of shoes is not a good enough indication of how they'll feel when you're running. Try a few strides down an aisle or hallway. Better yet, if the store allows, take them for a spin outside. Pay particular attention to pinching and slippage. If any part of your foot slides around when you run, you'll eventually get blisters. Also, if any part of your foot feels confined, you can bet that the shoes will make your feet hurt after a few miles of running.

**Wear socks of the same thickness as the ones you'll be running in.** If necessary, ask to borrow a pair from the store.

**Get measured, and have a salesperson check the shoes for proper sizing.** A whopping 90 percent of women wear shoes that are too small, according to the American Orthopaedic Foot and Ankle Society. For some women, improper sizing is a vanity issue. Others simply don't realize that their foot size increases with age, especially after pregnancy. Make sure you allow a finger's width of space between the end of your toes and the shoe; otherwise you'll suffer from jammed toes and black toenails. Also make sure the shoe is wide enough. If the front of your foot feels confined against the edges of the shoe, look for a brand such as New Balance that comes in different widths.

Expect to pay at least $60 for your shoes. And be sure to replace them regularly. Don't judge by the appearance of the tread: Midsole materials break down, often with no visible clues. A good rule of thumb is to replace shoes every 300 to 400 miles. Mark a calendar when you purchase a new pair to help you remember when to replace them.

## SPORTS BRAS

Just like your old tennis shoes, your old bra wasn't meant for running. Sports bras are designed to minimize the bouncing associated with impact sports. The good ones also wick sweat away from your body to reduce chafing and keep you at a comfortable temperature. Athletics are more forgiving for small-breasted women because control is less of an issue and the first priority is overall comfort. Women with larger breasts need more high-tech, supportive bras.

When choosing a bra, try on a few and pay attention to the following:

- The band around your rib cage should be snug but not stifling. You should be able to breathe freely. Try raising your

## smart tips

A running store is your best bet for finding the right gear, especially proper shoes and a sports bra. If you don't have a running store nearby, try one of these specialty catalogs.

- Road Runner Sports sells a wide variety of shoes, bras, running apparel, and any other accessory you could possibly want. The knowledgeable staff can even help you select a pair of shoes over the phone. Road Runner Sports, 6150 Nancy Ridge Drive, San Diego, CA 92121; (800) 551-5558.

- Title Nine Sports offers a super selection of hard-to-fit bra sizes. All styles are tested and approved by the athletic staff. The catalog also sells performance-oriented women's sports apparel. Title Nine Sports, 5743 Landregan Street, Emeryville, CA 94608; (800) 609-0092.

arms above your head, bending them, and swinging them around. The band should not move. If it does, the fabric will rub and irritate your skin.

- The fabric over your breasts should likewise be snug but not stifling. Jump up and down a bit. Your breasts should feel comfortable, and the bounce should be minimal. Remember that any movement you feel now will only be multiplied on a run.

- Look for well-crafted seams. This is where most chafing occurs. Seams should be sewn flat and free of extraneous material—or better yet, they should be on the outside of the bra.

- Make sure the fabric is meant to handle activity and sweat. Look on the label to see which fabrics the bra is made from. Steer clear of cotton in the liner; it will keep sweat clinging next to your body. Instead, look for a label that touts the fabric's wicking properties. This is one case where seeing the word *polyester* on the label is not a bad thing. CoolMax in particular is a good choice for bra liners.

- Expect to pay between $15 and $30.

- Replace your bra when the elastic no longer provides adequate support.

- If you are a C cup or larger, you might find greater comfort and support with a bra that encapsulates each breast separately instead of compressing the entire chest. Two companies that specialize in bras for large-breasted women are Champion and Enell.

## SPORTS WATCHES

Sports watches today are really miniature computers. They can do everything from sounding an alarm at regular intervals to storing your workouts so you can download them into your home computer. Of course, if you're running only 30 minutes a day, you can do without the bells and whistles—and the added expense. No matter how simple or complex a model you decide upon, look for large, easy-to-press buttons and large, easy-to-see digits. These models are easier to use while running. An easily audible beep accompanying each press of the buttons is helpful, too.

Many experienced women runners prefer to avoid so-called women's models. Their petite size means smaller, harder-to-press buttons, not to mention fewer memory features. For most women, the men's models fit just fine and are superior products. Stick to plastic or fabric straps, which are durable and comfortable. When it's time to change the battery, take the watch to a jeweler to have a new one installed. If you try to do it yourself, your watch might become disposable before its time.

## SHORTS AND TOPS

Today's fabrics can help wick away sweat so that it evaporates, keeping you dry and free from chafing. This feature can be especially helpful in shorts. Look for a liner made of CoolMax or a similar synthetic fabric. Shorts are available in a variety of cuts and lengths to accommodate different tastes. Be aware that what you gain in modesty with longer shorts, you'll give up in range of motion. That's not a problem unless you are running at fast speeds and need full leg lift. Expect to pay $15 to $30 for running shorts. Although that might seem steep, you'll appreciate the comfort from the first step.

Cotton T-shirts will get you through most runs just fine. But if you live in an especially humid climate or run for more than 30 minutes at a stretch, you might want to invest in a tank top or singlet made from one of those great synthetic wicking fabrics. Cotton, which tends to hold moisture, can get pretty heavy and cause some nasty chafing when it's hanging on to an hour's worth of your sweat.

## APPAREL FOR RAIN AND COLD

The old elements just aren't what they used to be. Today, a runner can be out in the rain or cold for hours and remain comfortable. High-tech fabrics have been developed specifically for exertion in the rain and snow. These materials repel water from the outside while allowing perspiration to evaporate from the inside.

When buying running jackets and pants, read the label to ensure that they are constructed of a material designed for this one-way moisture transport. A heavy lining will provide more warmth, but if you're going to purchase only one running suit, a more versatile option is to choose items with very light linings (or no lining at all) that can be worn year-round. For rainy days, wear the pants and jacket over a light underlayer of shorts and a wicking top. For colder weather, start with a base layer of tights and a wicking top. If necessary, add a middle layer of insulating fleece. (Cotton should never be used as a layer in cold and damp conditions. It absorbs water and quickly grows heavy and cold.) When choosing a running suit, look for these features.

- The jacket's zipper and/or collar should not scratch your chin when fully zipped.

- The collar should fit fairly snugly around your neck to keep cold air out.

- Sleeves with Velcro or elastic allow easy access to your watch.

- Vents in the jacket's sides, back, or underarms provide breathability.

- A jacket panel can cover your rear end during very cold weather.

- Zippers at the pants' ankles should enable easy ins and outs with your shoes still on.

## SOCKS

Running socks are available in every weight, length, and material. The main ones to avoid are those made of 100 percent cotton. Cotton tends to keep your feet clammy and cold in the winter and cause blisters and chafing in the summer. Instead, look for synthetic blends made from polyester, acrylic, CoolMax, and even Teflon. Wool blends such as SmartWool are good for winter. Wool or synthetic-blend socks will provide superior wicking and lessen the chance of blisters. Double-layer socks are also effective at reducing the risk of blisters.

The thicker the sock, the more cushioning it will provide. Many women prefer thicker socks for easy runs because of their superior comfort and cushioning. For faster runs or races, look for a thinner sock. The reduction in cushioning allows for greater "road feel" and responsiveness.

It's important to try on socks with the shoes in which you will be running. Some thicker socks can require a shoe up to a half-size larger.

## HEART-RATE MONITORS

Until the 1990s, the heart-rate monitor was an obscure gadget used mostly by professional athletes. Today, it has gained widespread acceptance as a useful tool for runners of all levels. Heart-rate monitors can be used to target specific zones of effort on harder runs and to ensure that a run doesn't get too difficult on easy days. Most monitors consist of two parts: the pulse-reading monitor band, which straps around your rib cage just under your bust, and the display unit, which looks and works much like a watch.

Monitors come with a wide range of functions and settings, which can sometimes be more overwhelming than helpful (think VCRs). When buying a heart-rate monitor, look for one that's simple enough that you will actually use it. Most runners prefer a stopwatch feature and an alarm that sounds when you exceed or fall short of your target pace. Expect to pay at least $100 for a monitor with these functions.

## SUNGLASSES

Sunglasses for running are designed to provide protection from sun, wind, glare, and flying objects such as bugs. Some runners won't leave home without them; others never wear them. If you do purchase a pair, look for shatterproof lenses that offer broad-spectrum protection, filtering out both UVA and UVB rays. Although prices on name brands with superior styling top $100, you can find models for less than $20 that have the features you need.

The glasses should fit snugly, so that they don't bounce when you are running, but they shouldn't fit so tightly that they give you a headache. When trying them on, prop them up to see if they'll stay on top of your head: Since weather can change while you're out running, it's an added convenience if they stay put in that position.

## TRAINING LOG

*A*t the risk of sounding like everybody's grandmother, here's an "I remember when" story. I was 8 years old when I started running. That was back around 1970—the Stone Age of the sport. No women's running shoes existed; no children's running shoes existed. Men's running shoes were a relatively new concept, and even those were hard to find. (In those days, tennis shoes and high-tops pretty much covered the sporting gamut.) My parents would buy shoes for me from a man who traveled around to cross-country meets selling running shoes from the back of his van. We'd get the smallest size he had, and I would stuff them with paper towels to fill out the toes.

And so it's with great fondness that I remember my first pair of true women's running shoes. They were baby blue and they were called the Tigress. They fit. They were fast. They looked cool. (For about a week, that is. A rainy day turned their cheery blue into a mildewed green that never quite cleaned up.) Having them made me feel like a certified member of this sweaty, grueling sport, despite the fact that I was "just a girl."

Well, women's shoes have come a long way. Unlike the Tigress, many early women's shoes were just downsized men's models in pastel shades. Many were cheaper-quality as well because, the thinking went, a woman didn't need "serious" shoes. Virtually all of today's women's shoes are truly built for women's feet and are offered in the same range of quality as men's models. Indeed, manufacturers consider the female market a hot segment: They realize that all those women runners mean dollar signs!

So when you go to the store, you'll have the luxury of choosing from a wide range of shoes made just for you. Shoes in every price, shape, style, and size imaginable. May your choice bring you as much joy and inspiration as my first baby blues brought me.

# HYDRATION SYSTEMS

Yes, a drinking fountain will still hydrate you perfectly well. But some runners like to carry water or sports drinks with them on longer runs. A waist belt with a pouch in the back to hold a plastic bottle is the simplest option, but you might find it irritating to have a bottle jostling against the small of your back. Look for a belt with wide webbing to disperse the weight of the bottle. Other hydration systems come in backpack or fanny-pack form, with a bladder connected to a tube for sipping. These are best suited to runners who plan to be out for several hours. For shorter workouts, their extra weight isn't worthwhile.

# 3

# A Beginner's Guide to Frequently Asked Questions

YOU WALK OUT THE DOOR, you start to jog, and you feel . . . awkward. Silly. Clumsy. Fat. Slow. Any number of things. Any number of things, except like a runner.

Stop right there. Before you take another step, remember: Everybody started somewhere. The best of runners began with the same slow steps that you are about to take. Your first run can feel anything but normal. You're full of uncertainties: Can I really do this? What if it hurts?

To start you off, here are answers to novice runners' most commonly asked questions. This quick primer will alleviate your fears and speed you on your way out the door with confidence.

### Q: *Do I really need to get a health check from my doctor?*

**A:** It's the first admonishment you hear when you begin any exercise program: Get a health check. So what exactly is everybody getting checked for?

The primary concern for anyone starting a workout program—particularly an aerobic one, such as running—is heart disease. Every adult woman has some buildup of plaque in her arteries, explains Amy Roberts, Ph.D., exercise science coordinator at the Boulder Center for Sports Medicine in Colorado. That's dangerous only if you have advanced buildup—whether from diet, lack of exercise, or genetics—and suddenly begin exercising heavily. Women under the age of 50 aren't at particularly high risk, Dr. Roberts says, unless they are overweight or have family histories of high blood pressure, high cholesterol, or heart disease. If any of these are the case, no matter what your age, you absolutely must have that health check.

Ultimately, it's not a bad idea to be examined even if you don't have any of the red flags for heart disease. Depending on your age, your physician may check for other conditions as well. Rosemary Agostini, M.D., of the Virginia Mason Medical Center Sports Medicine Clinic in Seattle, explains that minor health conditions can sometimes grow worse with the additional physical requirements of a workout program. Your doctor may investigate your overall nutrition and check for anemia and osteoporosis. If nothing else, finding out your cholesterol level, blood pressure, resting heart rate, and body fat percentage at the beginning of your program can inspire you down the road when those numbers improve. So go ahead and make an appointment for a physical.

### Q: *Should I eat something before running?*

**A:** You should be neither famished nor stuffed when you head out for a run. A good rule of thumb for beginners is to eat a light high-carbohydrate meal or snack such as a bagel an hour or two before running. Rich or high-fiber foods usually cause stomach distress in beginners. Eating immediately before a run is something your system will be better able to handle as your body becomes more used to running.

### Q: *How should I dress?*

**A:** Check the weather outside. The exertion of running will keep you warmer than if you were standing around, so choose clothes that leave you on the cool side when you start out. If you haven't purchased specific running clothes, any pair of athletic shorts or tights will do to start. If it's hot outside, a sports bra and a T-shirt or a tank top will suffice on top. If it's cooler, wear a polyester or polypropylene turtleneck or crew-neck top. Layer a jacket on top for cold or windy weather. A nylon vest will stand in for a jacket in a wide range of temperatures. Check for clouds on the horizon; a baseball cap will save your vision in a sudden downpour. And if it's at all chilly, wear a hat and gloves. Much of your body's

## Debunking the Myth of Pain

For such a healthy sport, running has a bad reputation. "All that pounding!" "Doesn't it give you arthritis?" "I've heard it makes your breasts hurt."

But the fact is, almost anybody can run—comfortably.

Most running horror stories surface from misguided first outings. Any activity you jump into too quickly will leave you with achy muscles and sore spots. (Think of how sore your legs were the last time you played softball at the company picnic.) Because running is so simple, people have a tendency to overdo it on the first try. "The reason that people think they can't run is that when they've started in the past, they've gone kamikaze," says Maureen Roben, cofounder and codirector of Women's Running Camps in Denver and a five-time Olympic Trials Marathon qualifier. By starting a running program smartly—and slowly—you can avoid painful pitfalls.

Sore knees are almost always due to two factors: the wrong shoes and previous inactivity. If you start out slowly with a walk/run program, you should never experience anything more than a mild ache. After 2 to 3 weeks of consistent activity, most soreness will be gone.

Other concerns: "Some women think their breasts are going to sag," Roben says. "I still hear people who think running is going to loosen the uterus!" Other rumored side effects include loose skin, chunky muscles, and exacerbated incontinence. None are true. All stem from the dark ages when women were discouraged from participating.

Also untrue is the association of running with arthritis. Quite to the contrary, women who are regular runners retain greater range of motion as they advance in age. Their bone health actually tends to be superior to that of their sedentary counterparts because weight-bearing activity improves bone strength. Roben, who is 43, tells of a study that she and camp cofounder Diane Palmason, 61, were asked to take part in. Both women, who have competed at world-class levels for decades, showed bone density in their legs comparable to that of 20-year-olds.

heat can escape through your scalp. Also, many women find that their hands stay cold while they're running, even if they're working up a sweat.

**Q:** *Do I have to wear something over my sports bra?*

**A:** Most sports bras can be worn without T-shirts. (The exceptions are some of the bras for large-breasted women that are designed like more traditional undergarments.) Plenty of women are comfortable running without T-shirts, but others wouldn't be caught dead with their stomachs showing. It's a matter of personal preference. Just beware of white bras, which can lose their opacity when drenched with sweat, especially if the fabric is thin.

**Q:** *What if I feel self-conscious?*

**A:** If you do, you're in good company. A bunch of elite women runners I know were chatting when one confided that, during runs, she regularly looked down at her thighs "to see if they looked fat." Expecting ridicule at such a confession, she was instead met with a chorus of "Me, too!" from the group. Some might scoff at such insecurity, but women can be hard on themselves, and taking up a new physical activity can exacerbate such concerns.

Remember that one of the wonderful benefits of running is improved self-confidence. The sooner you start, the more quickly you will become comfortable with your body, your speed, and your stride.

Also, remind yourself that everyone *isn't* watching you. Running today is everywoman's sport. Consider checking out the local jogging path before your first run. You'll see women and men of every age, every weight, and every speed. They're all enjoying themselves too much to be judging the color of your shorts or the girth of your thighs.

**Q:** *Where should I go?*

**A:** If you're lucky, right out the front door. For convenience, many women run from home. Try to find a nearby park, bike path, or trail. Soft surfaces are easier on your joints than pavement or concrete surfaces are, and they'll reduce your next-day soreness. If a soft surface isn't available, a road is fine, but look for the following for safety and enjoyment.

- Minimal traffic
- Minimal stoplights
- A wide shoulder
- A soft running surface (gravel is softest, followed by asphalt and then concrete)
- Low speed limits

If local roads are not conducive to a safe and pleasant run, it might be worth a short drive to a park or trail. Another option is a track. Most high-school tracks are open to the public, as are some college tracks. Tracks can be fun for beginners who want to know how far they go each day. Most tracks are 400 meters (roughly ¼ mile) around.

## Q: How fast should I run?

**A:** Speed shouldn't be a concern. It's impossible to go too slow, and it's risky to go too fast. Start by walking for 5 to 10 minutes to warm up, then break into a shuffle. If you wish, increase your pace slightly until you find a stride that feels comfortable and natural. If other runners are around you, don't compare speeds. The sooner this lesson is learned the better. Even professional runners have easy training days when they barely break above a shuffling speed, no matter what the competition is doing nearby. On your first runs, maintain a pace at which breathing remains comfortable. If you find yourself growing tired or breathing heavily, slow down or walk.

## Q: How should I breathe?

**A:** Breathe through your mouth. Your nose can't deliver enough oxygen for your body when you're running. Long, deep breaths will help you take in more air and prevent side stitches, which are caused by a buildup of lactic acid. For now, run at a pace at which you can breathe easily. (A good test is whether you can carry on a conversation.) If you're gasping for breath, slow down or walk if necessary. "Most people will be short of breath when they start an exercise program," says Dr. Roberts. Shortness of breath that is caused by running isn't particularly troublesome, but tightness in the chest or pains that shoot from the chest are symptoms that should be checked by a physician.

**Q:** *What if it hurts?*

**A:** If you're wearing the right running shoes for your foot type and starting off slowly, nothing should hurt at first. But beginning runners can soon expect to experience minor discomfort, usually in the knees, shins, feet, or chest. Faint soreness is due to your body adapting to a new source of stress, and the irritation will dis-

---

### IN YOUR OWN WORDS

## First Running Memories

*When we were in elementary school, my sister and I ran a mile to a beach. I started out sprinting and got ahead of her. With a few blocks to the end, I could see her closing in. I overcame this by picking up stones and whipping them at her.*

**Ann, 35, Ann Arbor, Michigan**

*I remember loving the feeling of my first runs as a child with my dad. I loved to emulate a horse. I'd charge other neighborhood kids money to learn my "secrets of galloping correctly"!*

**Heather, 27, Los Angeles**

*When I started running at the age of 65, my endurance was practically nil. On my first runs, I would jog to one telephone pole and walk to the next, slowly increasing my distance. Gradually, my runs became longer and my walking time became shorter until I was running my goal of 5 kilometers. It took me about 10 months to reach that goal.*

**Mary, 76, Albuquerque, New Mexico**

---

sipate over the next few weeks. On the other hand, a sharp pain is always a sign to stop. Walk for a bit and see if the pain diminishes. If it resumes upon running, cut the run short and walk home. Ice and rest will take care of most minor sore spots; more serious injuries call for a trip to the doctor.

## Q: *What if I have to go to the bathroom?*

**A:** Welcome to one of the realities of running. There's something about the activity that makes some women have to go. A little proactive precaution goes a long way toward ensuring a pleasant run. If you want to drink anything before your run, do so at least a half-hour before you set out. This will give you time to go to the bathroom before your run and reduce the chances of a potty call. Don't eat any later than an hour before your run, and stay

*It was a hot summer day in Detroit, and I ran with my dog the half-mile around the block to my grandmother's house. My grandmother saw me run by, and she came out of the house and asked me what I was doing. The next day, the dog sat down in the middle of the run and refused to budge.*

**Renee**, 35, Silver City, New Mexico

*I was 29 and had just moved from Northern California to Pennsylvania. The run was horrible because it was hot and humid, and I wasn't used to that combination. But I was determined to get some exercise. At the time, it seemed like I was running a marathon, but actually, I probably went 2 to 3 miles.*

**Jane**, 34, Quakertown, Pennsylvania

*When I was a kid, I used to go out and run around the school fields in the weeks following the Boston Marathon. (I grew up in Hopkinton, where the race starts.) The first time I actually went for a run with the intention of training, I ran 3 miles, from my parents' house to the gun club and back. I was wearing Jack Purcell tennis sneakers, cutoff dungarees, and a halter top. I was very impressed that I was able to run that far. I was 19 years old.*

**Jane**, 43, Fort Collins, Colorado

*Growing up in the thick forestland of northern Illinois, my older brother and I would race around our yard as if it were a cross-country course. There was the 50-yard dash down the driveway and the 1000-meter race around the yard's perimeter. I raced my little heart out, each time thinking this might be the day I would beat Dane—but I never did. I didn't know it then, but those sprints were my introduction to a lifetime of running. They also ensured that I would never know the self-consciousness that comes with taking up the sport as an adult.*

*As it turns out, that's a good thing. When it comes to new sports, I've developed the track record of a chicken. I shied away from golf for years, thinking that it was a requirement to whack the ball onto the green in one shot. I avoided mountain bikes, too, not realizing that it was acceptable, when faced with a slope of loose rock, to simply get off and walk.*

*Even an uncomplicated sport such as running holds mysteries and challenges. Over the years, I've been awed by the women I've met who were taking up the sport: some battling cancer, some struggling with obesity or the pains of advancing age, still others seeking strength to start new passages in their lives. All have stood at a crossroads and taken those pivotal first steps, becoming more fearless with every day. If I had to do it now, I could only hope that I would exhibit the same courage and grace.*

away from high-fiber foods, such as fruit or granola. If you do need to go while you're running, by all means stop and find a place to do so. There's no rule that says you must finish your run without a break, and you will be far more comfortable afterward.

### Q: *How far should I go?*

**A:** As a beginner, don't be concerned with the distance you cover. For now, just listen to your body and think in terms of total time rather than miles. This eliminates pressure to perform at a certain pace. Your first run should be a comfortable combination of walking and jogging to introduce your body to the activity. For most women, a total of 30 minutes of activity is a good start. Warm up by walking for 5 to 10 minutes, then alternate jogging and walking so that your breathing and your legs remain comfortable. Cool down with another 10 minutes of walking. For a full beginning running program, see chapter 5.

Okay: You have your clean bill of health in hand and new shoes on your feet. You're ready and raring to go. So relax. Remember to breathe. Start off at a brisk walk. When you're ready, let yourself break into a jog. Now you're a runner.

## Q: *Does fitness affect sexual performance?*

**A:** Anecdotal evidence suggests that some runners experience increased sex drives as their fitness levels increase. "In women, sex drive is far more psychological than hormonal," says Mona Shangold, M.D., director of the Center for Women's Health and Sports Gynecology in Philadelphia. Some research has shown a temporary increase in women's levels of testosterone—which contributes to sex drive—during a run. But the effect is short-lived, Dr. Shangold says, and it's unlikely to contribute to increased libido. Increased feelings of well-being and improved body image, however, can make a world of difference. Since runners often report these positive side effects, it is quite possible that you could feel a surge in sex drive as your fitness improves.

# 4

# The Principles
# of Training

WHY DO YOU RUN? Simple question. A thousand possible answers. The reasons run the gamut: time alone, time with others,
fitness, sanity, freedom, health, to eat more without gaining
weight, to worry less, to stay young, to push limits, to eliminate
limits.

Although there's really only one way to run, there are many
ways of being a runner. When you pinpoint why you run, you focus
your goals, which will determine how you train. Each day you head
out the door, you are faced with choices: how far, how fast, and
how hard. Your decisions will depend on your goals.

If you've had a hard day at work, for instance, and you're
looking for some stress release, you might amble along while you
contemplate the beauty of nature. On the other hand, if you're
feeling competitive and want to beat your partner in an upcoming
5-K, you might decide to hammer out some speed repeats on
the track.

Setting goals is the first step on your path to fulfillment as a
runner. Learning the basic principles of training is the second step.
Combine the two, and you can determine the level at which you
wish to run and the type of training schedule that's most appropriate for you.

# WHAT DO YOU WANT FROM RUNNING?

Having goals enriches any endeavor. By having goals, you become more keenly aware of what you have accomplished and what you still wish to attain. But goals can be frightening, dangerous things, too. Some people avoid them at all costs. Why? Because by acknowledging a goal, you face the possibility of that awful "f" word: failure. You can make setting goals less frightening if you keep the following two points in mind.

**Goals are not immutable.** They can and will change over time. Your life is a complex tapestry of work, love, family, hobbies, and obligations. One year may bring freedom and lightheartedness and a zest for adventure, while another brings tough challenges and a longing for security. Your goals—for work, running, or anything else—will likely shift at these times, even if you have not attained your original hopes. This brings up the next point:

**Not meeting a goal is *not* failure.** In fact, if success were a certainty, you wouldn't have much of a challenge to begin with. There is little point in setting an easily attainable goal. Goals are meant to stimulate you and inspire greatness. A goal that is obviously attainable is without value. That means that any worthy goal comes with the implication that you might not meet it. Learning and growth come only in the struggle to attain your goal.

# YOUR PERSONAL RUNNING PROGRAM

There is one fundamental truth about running that can spare you much frustration when it comes to setting goals: Your potential speed, aerobic capacity, and body shape are greatly determined by genetics. Some women can run for years and never turn into the sleek, petite whippets they envisioned they would become. Others take up the sport at 60 and find themselves, to their own astonishment, walking away with age-group trophies.

That's genetics. And no, it's not fair. But here's the good part. No matter who you are or what your starting point is, you can and will improve. Your heart and lungs will become better conditioned. Your legs will grow stronger. Running can help you achieve the greatest possible health for your body type. Also, hard work and determination can go a long way toward expanding your possibilities. One elite women's distance coach I know has turned away talented runners, saying, "Give me a runner with heart over one with talent any day."

So don't despair or bemoan your genetics. Rather, recognize that your physical makeup is the luck of the draw. Instead of wasting time trying to change it, learn to work with it. You can learn to take advantage of your strengths and work on your weaknesses. Don't compare your running with that of others or become self-critical if you aren't progressing as quickly as you thought you would. Such comparisons can lead to frustration and demoraliza-

# smart tips

You usually won't reach your running goals within days or weeks. Instead, it typically takes months or years. Although a beginning runner will improve virtually overnight, both progress and setbacks can continue for a lifetime. Because of that, it's a good idea to set short-term goals that help motivate you along the way to reaching your long-term goals.

Set short-term goals so that you can easily attain them within a certain time period, and then set some more once you achieve them. Reaching these intermediate objectives can, in turn, keep you inspired and on target for long-term goals. Here are some tips for both short- and long-term goals:

● Choose short-term goals that seem attainable within one season—such as being able to run for 30 minutes straight by the end of the summer or taking 30 seconds off your best 5-K time.

● Choose long-term goals that span the course of a year or more—perhaps running your first marathon or breaking 40 minutes for a 10-K.

tion—as well as to inappropriate training that will only compound physical problems.

Just as every runner progresses at a different rate, every runner responds differently to training, nutrition, and all other aspects of the sport. The workout that one runner swears by as her secret training weapon will leave another runner broken down. The vegetarian diet that gives one runner energy will seem Spartan to another, leaving her weak.

Books and coaches often promote a single "winning formula" that they say will yield guaranteed results. That sounds great, but there's no such thing. It's not that such programs are always com-

● Set goals that will help you develop the strengths you value. If you're not concerned about going fast, don't set a goal based on your 10-K time. Instead, set a goal of running with friends at least once a week for the duration of the summer. Other examples are learning 10 new routes by the end of the year or losing a modest amount of weight in 2 months.

● If you do set goals for a personal record (PR), set both short- and long-term marks.

● Write it down. Note your goals in a diary, training log, or calendar. Having concrete evidence of your goals is a wonderful motivator. In the future, it will also serve as a fun reminder of how far you've come.

● Reevaluate your goals once a year. Choose whatever date you wish: New Year's Day, your birthday, the beginning of spring, the anniversary of the day you started running. Look at how far you've come in the past year, and use this time to set new goals or recommit to old ones.

pletely wrong, but they simply can't be applied universally. While garnering advice from any source—including this book—remember your individuality, and weigh the advice as it relates to your own situation. To apply advice successfully, you need to know yourself, body and mind.

Listening to your body is the foundation for a successful and enjoyable running program. It's also surprisingly hard to do. Self-knowledge becomes more evident over time and miles. It is an accumulation of learning that never stops, since your body continues to change. Self-knowledge can be as literal as learning that you need water every half-hour on your runs or that you're the kind of runner who can run indefinitely without feeling dehydrated. It can also be evident in less tangible factors: Time might teach you, for example, that you push yourself too hard when you run with a group, so you need to run alone on days when you want to take it easy.

As you get to know your body's capabilities, you develop a valuable sense of confidence. You learn when to push and when to

## Should You Use a Heart-Rate Monitor?

**P**lenty of runners and coaches love to use heart-rate monitors, but are they right for you? Heart-rate monitors provide an easy, high-tech method of taking your pulse. By displaying your heart rate, they give you instant feedback on a run, essentially telling you how hard you are working. You can then adjust your effort by running faster or slower to reach the rate you desire.

Proponents appreciate this objective measure of a workout. After all, numbers never lie. So why doesn't everybody take advantage of the feedback that a monitor can offer? Some runners love the sport because it puts them closely in tune with their bodies. For these athletes, it is a challenge—and a joy—to learn to read their physical responses during training. Mechanical input can be seen as an intrusion on what should be a natural and flowing effort.

There is no right or wrong when it comes to heart-rate monitors. Runners of all levels benefit from their feedback; likewise, runners of all levels succeed in training without them. Should you try one? It all boils down to your personality.

back off. You can predict how you will feel if you notch up the intensity of a run and just how long you can last at a given pace. You learn what builds confidence and what is destructive. In short, knowing yourself results in the ability to create a personalized training formula. And in the end, no book or coach can provide such information. It's a matter of logging the miles and paying attention while you do so.

# THE RULES OF RUNNING

Putting one foot in front of the other isn't exactly rocket science. But just as you can make your runs as hard or as easy as you wish, you can make your training as complex or simple as you wish. Ultimately, your reasons for running will determine how much of the science of training you need to know.

If your goal as a runner is to relax, have fun, and maintain your health, you may never want or need to run more than 30 to 40 minutes at a time. Many women find running at this recreational level to be a great stress reliever and fitness booster. They don't need to test their endurance, and indeed, they would rather not undertake anything so strenuous that it becomes another energy drain. These women are perfectly content never to know what it feels like to enter a state of oxygen debt.

For other women, fitness is just the beginning. They derive pleasure from pushing themselves and their limits. They are driven by wanting to know how fast or how far they can possibly go. To investigate the boundaries of potential, these runners will need to push beyond levels of comfort.

Regardless of the level at which you wish to run, some principles of training and improvement remain the same. If you sidestep or shortcut these rules, you'll experience burnout, discomfort, and injury. But if you understand them, you will be able to do more than simply follow the workout schedules in this book; you will actually be able to customize a schedule to fit your specific needs and goals. You'll know "how far, how fast" each time you head out for a run.

**1. Do the minimal training needed for optimal results.** "If I'm improving this much by running 30 miles a week, think how much better I could be by running 50 miles a week!" What could be wrong with that logic? Plenty. Finding your optimal training schedule—for fitness or for racing—is not a matter of cramming in as many miles as your legs can possibly handle. Instead, it's about finding the optimal number of miles and training days per week to help you reach maximum fitness while still feeling energized and strong. Just because a friend is running 6 days a week doesn't mean that you should. Perhaps she has a more advanced fitness background, or maybe she has a desk job and you work on your feet. For a myriad of reasons, different runners thrive on different workloads.

Anyone can fall victim to the "more is better" disease. Although it's something that advanced runners need to worry about more than beginners, anyone can overtrain. Overtraining happens when you exert yourself past the point of positive returns. The price you pay might be exhaustion, burnout, or injury. For runners who wish to improve, training smart is just as important as training hard.

**2. Balance your hard efforts with rest.** You don't get faster or fitter on the days that you push yourself. Improvement comes during your rest *after* the days when you run hard. "The benefits of stressing the body come during recovery," explains Jack Daniels, Ph.D., exercise physiologist at the State University of New York College at Cortland. He illustrates the principle with this extreme example: Imagine yourself running as hard as you can one day, then again the next day, and the next. Sooner or later, you'd barely be able to run at all. In this scenario, "you'd never be giving your body a chance to recover, to strengthen itself, to ward off injury, or to just feel good again," Dr. Daniels says. During recovery time, he explains, your body is busy: repairing muscle fibers, building new blood vessels into your muscles, increasing your muscle fibers' ability to process nutrients and oxygen, and eliminating waste products from them. On off days, your body can repair muscle damage, fortify your immune system, and prepare for the next onslaught. If you don't give your body a chance to recover, over time, you will tear yourself down.

This rule of rest holds true for runners of all types; only the level of effort and rest change. Recreational runners will balance their running days with days of complete rest, meaning no running.

More serious runners will rest from their hard workouts by running a short distance slowly or by cross-training on off days. For competitive distance runners, a 10-mile day may serve as a "rest" day. Even these runners, however, benefit from the occasional day *completely* off to rest their muscles and tendons.

**3. Expect peaks and plateaus in your running.** Just because you lopped 5 minutes off your 10-K last summer doesn't mean it will happen again this summer. Dr. Daniels calls this the principle of diminishing returns. If you stress your body by running 20 miles a week, for example, you will improve until you eventually reach a fitness level that this amount of work allows. Your 10-K time might drop by 5 minutes over the course of one summer spent this way, but when you increase your training to 40 miles a week, you won't double your fitness or necessarily cut your time by 5 minutes again. In general, your greatest improvements come as you begin your running career. Although improvement can continue for years thereafter, the pace of improvement will likely slow down.

Not only will the pace of improvement slow, but also you will hit peaks and plateaus along the way. Your body adapts to the demands you place upon it, and it will be at varying levels of stress and recovery depending on where you are in your training. Dr. Daniels cites studies in which researchers measured adrenaline secretions in runners and nonrunners to gauge their stress levels. When study subjects who ran 10 miles a day had trained for a certain length of time, they had the same adrenaline levels as nonrunners.

Although a plateau is probably a good indication that it's time to increase your training intensity, more advanced runners must read plateaus with caution. Ironically, they can also be signs of overtraining. "The people who are training really hard and don't notice improvement might have an opposite scenario," Dr. Daniels explains. "These people are probably training too hard and need more recovery."

It's a good idea to pay attention to your peaks and plateaus, especially if you train hard. But you shouldn't obsess over them. They are a normal part of the running experience.

**4. Be consistent.** Sorry, last summer's workouts won't keep you trim and fit this spring. If you stopped running over the winter, you'll have to start almost from scratch, slowly building up to the level at which you left off. Don't make the mistake of trying to jump in where you were 6 months ago—you'll find yourself out of breath, frustrated, and sore as can be. The good news is that fitness tends to come back more quickly the 2nd, 3rd, or 10th time around. On some level, your body remembers those "miles in the bank."

That's why persistence is crucial to your success as a runner. Ask coaches what the one most important factor is in training, and most will answer, "Consistency." That applies to runners of all levels. Recreational runners won't see improvement if they run once a week, because that's not often enough for the body to make physi-

## TRAINING LOG

*Why do I run? Over time, the answer to that question has evolved, as have my goals.*

*When I was a child, I ran because it felt good. By the time I reached high school and was competing on athletic teams, I ran not out of joy but because of pressure for results from adults. Because of that, my enjoyment was limited to rare glimpses of triumph when others felt I had done well. I stopped running in college because I no longer felt any connection to the thing that had once given me such pleasure.*

*When I turned 30, I began running to keep my bottom from drooping onto my thighs. I was a journalist married to a desk, and running was a way to defy gravity. But something happened along the way: My legs and trunk became stronger, my heart and lungs grew powerful, and I rediscovered my child's delight in the sport.*

*By my mid-thirties, it seemed as if I had learned to fly. I ran to feel my feet skim over the ground, to feel my heart swell in my chest, to feel invincible. I ran to be free; I ran to avoid pain; I ran to feel pain; I ran out of love and hate and anger and joy. Somewhere along the path, running became the canvas upon which I documented my life.*

ological changes. Likewise, more serious runners won't improve if they regularly run hard for a week but then take the next week off.

Consistency *doesn't* mean never missing a day out of foolish stubbornness, no matter the cost. If you feel a cold coming on, for example, it's better to miss a day or two and allow yourself to get healthy than it is to keep running until you're extremely sick and forced to take several weeks off.

**5. Practice patience.** Your body is an amazing machine. It adapts to the stresses of working out by becoming fitter and stronger. Even at an advanced age or after years of neglect and abuse, your body can regain strength and endurance. Getting in shape is a gradual

*For a brief year during that time, I ran to see how fast I could be. The more I believed that I was approaching my limits, the less I understood what those limits were—and the less I knew whether they had to do with legs and lungs at all but rather with heart and head. That's when I realized that I was no longer running to see how fast I could be, but instead to learn what other stuff I was made of.*

*I now work more than I run, which means I no longer wish for my running to be work. I run to feel the slap of cold air on my face or the heat melting into my bones. I run for the sunsets, for the way the shadows play over the mountains, to keep pace with my beloved in a silent contest that only running partners know.*

*The way I see it, I've had at least four different running careers over the last 25 years—and I'm nowhere near done. During each stage, the training most appropriate for the time has been different, and I have adapted accordingly: different workouts, different training partners, different sources of joy and accomplishment. Over time, my running has faithfully and graciously adapted to suit my circumstances. Through it all, each morning has patiently asked me, "Why do you run today?" And over the course of the years, one simple answer has quietly become more clearly heard than all the others: because I must.*

process, however. And no matter how much of a hurry you might be in to lose weight or run faster, you can't shortcut the process of fitness. Piling on the intensity in your running program at the start of your training, after a winter layoff, or to break through a plateau won't get you in shape faster. It might get you injured, though. Increase any training gradually. Get comfortable before increasing quantity or quality. A good rule of thumb is the 10 percent rule: Don't increase your workload in time or distance by more than 10 percent a week.

**6. Train your entire body.** It takes a whole body to make a running stride. Although hamstring muscles might seem like the workhorses of running, you ignore the rest of your body at your own peril. Tendons and ligaments, for example, are integral to the running process, yet they adapt and strengthen very slowly. That's why many running injuries involve these connective tissues. The small muscle groups of your feet and legs come into play with each stride, as do your arms, shoulders, trunk, and back. Respect these parts of your body. Strengthen and stretch them. Gradually, you'll see the difference in your running. (For more on total-body stretching and strengthening, see chapter 18.)

Over time, you will come to understand these training principles as you see them in action. You will feel the bounce in your step after you take your off day; you will become aware of the microcycles of improvement in your running from month to month; you will recognize when you push too hard or when you are being inconsistent and your training suffers accordingly. Pay attention to these principles and to the messages your body sends. Eventually you will find that you can tailor a training program to your own needs, no matter what type of runner you are.

# From Walking to Jogging: Training for the Beginner

**THE BEGINNING OF YOUR RUNNING PROGRAM** is a time of immense excitement, progress, and growth. You'll see your legs in a new light, as powerful and capable. You'll take pride in one day's accomplishment and use it to motivate yourself the next day, when temptation is tugging you to slow down. You'll feel triumphant at the end of your first steady runs.

But the beginning is also a time of challenge and discomfort. You'll discover sore spots and worry about them. You may tire quickly and feel discouraged. You may have days when the kids are sick and the phone won't stop ringing, and before you know it, you'll have missed your workout and feel like all progress is lost.

When you start running, you will experience both extremes. That much is guaranteed. For some women, this stage will be relatively easy and pass rapidly. For others, it will require more patience. These ups and downs are part of the process of conditioning your body and mind in a new way. The tough days might not be fun, but they are the days on which you make real progress—physical and mental. The easy days when the pavement skips lightly underfoot, well, those are the days that make all the work worthwhile!

# RUNNING STYLE

Beginners often worry about how to run. How should I carry my arms? they ask. How high should I lift my feet? Should I look down or ahead?

It's best not to worry too much about all of that. Every runner has a unique style that she will fall into naturally. Most coaches agree that it's not a good idea to stray too far from the form toward which your body innately gravitates.

On the other hand, vastly improper form can be taxing, causing you to tire early and sometimes leading to soreness or injury. Generally speaking, the best running style is the one that is most efficient. You should strive to avoid wasted motion. Since running is primarily a forward-driving action, no part of a runner's body should display excessive side-to-side or up-and-down motion.

The following guidelines will help you develop an efficient running style. These are generalizations that work best for most runners, but if something feels uncomfortable, don't force it. Also, don't concentrate relentlessly on your form, or you'll wind up tripping over your own feet. (And you certainly won't enjoy your run.) Instead, consciously practice these points for a minute or so during your runs. Eventually, they will become second nature.

**Maintain erect, but not stiff, posture.** Don't bend forward or lean backward at the waist. Hold your neck and head erect as well. Most runners prefer to look at a spot on the road several strides ahead.

**Relax your shoulders.** Don't hunch them forward or up near your ears.

**Swing your arms loosely at your sides.** Your elbows should be bent at approximately a 90-degree angle. Let your arms come slightly across your waist in a natural motion. Your hands, held in loose, relaxed fists, should swing no higher than your chest and should not cross the center of your body.

**Raise your legs a few inches off the ground.** There is no benefit to lifting your knees and feet in an exaggerated motion. Start with something slightly more animated than a shuffle. As you develop more power, you will naturally take longer strides.

**Land lightly on your heels.** Your foot placement is highly individual and depends greatly on the structure of your feet. Beginning runners, however, shouldn't run on their toes, as so many ill-advised gym teachers insist. Generally, your foot should strike somewhere on the outside portion of your heel and roll forward until your toes push off.

**Relax.** From time to time as you run, take stock of your body. Is your jaw set? Is your face screwed up tight? Are your fists clenched? Relax, relax, relax. One of life's little paradoxes is that sometimes when we strain hard, we accomplish less. This is certainly true in running.

## SET YOUR OWN PACE

I'll assign your very first running goal right now: You want to be able to run for a half-hour without stopping. The aim of the schedule offered here is to gradually integrate running with walking so that in 6 weeks' time, you'll meet this goal.

● Begin a cooldown program of regular, light stretching after your runs to avoid muscle tightness. Gently stretch your legs, arms, and torso without bouncing. Hold each stretch for about 20 seconds.

● Strengthen your back and abdomen by exercising these muscle groups two or three times a week, after a run. A common pitfall for beginning runners is to hunch over when their midsection tires. A strong midsection will help you retain proper form and keep you running longer.

● Take stock of your nutrition. The bagel-and-salad diet that many women stick to lacks protein and fat. These nutrients are more important now that you are revving up your muscles regularly. Try to include at least a small amount of protein in every meal. You should be getting between 20 and 30 percent of your calories from fat.

● Participate in a fun-run event. Races are no longer just for hard-core runners. Sign up with friends to jog in a low-key 5-K a month from now. The party atmosphere, the food and drink, and the women of all abilities and backgrounds are sure to jazz your workouts for weeks to follow.

You've probably heard of people who start running programs only to quit within the first couple of months. Why? Typically, they try to accomplish too much too soon. Instead of working up to a half-hour of running, they try to do it all on day one. This leads to an array of problems: side stitches, shin pain, breathing discomfort, lethargy, and so on. Ideally, running should never hurt when you are a beginner. If it does, you're trying too hard.

The walk-to-jog transition program in this chapter assumes that you can already comfortably walk 30 minutes three or four times a week. This base of walking activity ensures that your heart, lungs, and legs are ready for the additional stresses of running. If you've been especially sedentary or if you aren't sure of your fitness level, first work up to a half-hour a day of walking several times a week.

As you make the transition from walking to running, you will continue to exercise in 30-minute sessions, but you will incorporate jogging into your walks. Each week, you will extend the length of time spent running and reduce the amount of time spent walking. Plan to exercise in this manner 3 to 5 days a week. Fewer than 3 days will not be enough to condition your cardiovascular system. More than 5 days might not give your muscles the rest they need.

Knowing when to run and when to walk is the tricky part for beginners. The two most common pitfalls are pushing too hard and not pushing at all. The first will leave you hurting; the second will mean that you won't see much progress. Maureen Roben, cofounder and codirector of Women's Running Camps in Denver and a five-time Olympic Trials Marathon qualifier, tells beginners to run until they are slightly uncomfortable, then try to keep running for another 30 seconds or so. "I tell them, 'When you think you can't go any farther, go a bit farther.' You get more benefit that way, and it gets you out of the habit of stopping the second that running becomes uncomfortable," Roben says. "And when you walk, don't stroll. Pump your arms, and really work to keep that heart rate up."

The sample schedule given in this chapter is meant to offer a comfortable, conservative transition to running, but each woman's body will react differently. The 6-week plan is just a guideline. You

## By the Numbers

If you decide to run with a heart-rate monitor, you can use it to determine when to walk and run during your 30-minute sessions. A beginner should stay at between 60 and 75 percent of her maximum heart rate, according to Roy Benson, a running coach and expert on heart-rate training in Atlanta. (Your heart-rate monitor's instruction manual should tell you how to determine your maximum heart rate. To calculate your 60 and 75 percent limits, multiply the maximum by 0.60 and 0.75 respectively. Then program the numbers into your monitor.) The method is simple: Just jog until the monitor registers your 75 percent limit, then walk until your heart rate drops to the 60 percent rate. At that point, begin jogging again until you hit 75 percent, and so on.

might want to go more slowly, taking twice the time, or you might want to advance more quickly. You should never feel pressed beyond your limits based on how much somebody else is running or what somebody else tells you to do. Books, coaches, and friends can offer suggestions and advice, but in the end your body will tell you how hard to push.

When listening to your body, it's important to understand that you can't separate your running from the rest of your life. If you're tired from other activities, it can and will affect your running. You might find your energy drained from a family problem, a bad night's sleep, or office stress. You can't fight the impact of those things, nor should you ignore them. Factor them in when gauging how hard to push in your workouts. Running at this stage should remain a positive, enjoyable complement to the rest of your activities.

If any day proves too challenging—your legs hurt or your breathing is uncomfortably labored—back off. Walk as much as you need in order to finish. Take the next day off, and repeat the previous workout until you can complete it comfortably. Do this as many times as necessary.

But be honest. Don't create excuses to fold up on the couch any time you're the least bit weary. If you haven't exercised before, you'll soon find that running gives you more energy than ever. To get to that point, however, you must go through a phase of several weeks or even months when your body will protest while adapting to the increased activity.

If, on the other hand, the workouts feel unchallenging, increase the jogging portion more rapidly, by a minute or two more than the schedule shows. Don't overdo it, though: Your body's aerobic capacity usually adapts more quickly than your muscles and tendons do. You might feel fine while you are jogging, but your muscles will pay the price the next day in increased soreness if you do too much too soon. The idea is to increase slowly enough that you never experience significant soreness the next day. Remember that speed is not important. The point is to get your body used to the activity of jogging.

## SIX-WEEK SCHEDULE

Use the following schedule as a guideline for your transition from walking to running. You'll notice that no distances are listed. For now, don't worry about miles. They can be a pain for beginners to measure, and knowing how far you've gone each day can create unnecessary pressure to improve each time you run. Remember, if any day feels too hard, take a break, and then repeat that workout until it feels comfortable.

*Week 1.* Walk 10 minutes to begin and end each 30-minute session. Alternate between walking and running for the middle 10 minutes, starting the week with running segments of a minute or less and working up to 2-minute segments.

*Goal by week's end: 2-minute running segments.*

*Week 2.* Walk 8 minutes to begin and end each 30-minute session. Alternate walking and jogging during the middle 14 minutes, starting the week with 2-minute jogging segments and working up to 4-minute running segments.

*Goal by week's end: 4-minute running segments.*

*Week 3.* Walk 5 minutes to begin and end each 30-minute session. Alternate walking and jogging during the middle 20 minutes, starting the week with 4-minute jogging segments and working up to 6-minute running segments.

*Goal by week's end: 6-minute running segments.*

# The Beginner's Challenge

*My greatest challenge when I first started running was overcoming the stares I would get. I began running in 1967, and no other women were out there. I ran around a track and it was so uncomfortable because the men would make comments and I didn't like how they would look at me. I overcame it by running without my contact lenses and pretending the guys weren't there.*

**Renita, 55, Sarasota, Florida**

*I had been an aerobics instructor for years, and I was used to thinking ahead to the next move. When I started running, there was nothing to occupy my mind, so all I could think about was how much it hurt or how long it seemed. I over-came this by learning to use my runs as a time to let my mind focus on things that needed to be pondered, like the next paper I was going to write for grad school or some problem that I needed to solve.*

**Jane, 34, Quakertown, Pennsylvania**

*When I started running, I was very young, and the greatest challenge was over-coming my fear of competition, which I did by just competing a lot. Having a goal or choosing an event, whether a 5-K or a marathon, to work toward helps to keep me motivated. My work schedule is such that I can easily find an ex-cuse not to run; having a goal helps to eliminate the potential for giving in to excuses.*

**Nancy, 31, Boulder, Colorado**

*I didn't pick up running until almost age 32, and I was still smoking cigarettes. My greatest challenge when I started was just to keep running without stop-ping to walk. In my first race, I just set a goal of running the 5-K without walking. Having that goal helped me to keep going.*

**Kelly, 36, Bloomington, Minnesota**

**Week 4.** Walk a few minutes to begin. Run 7 minutes. Walk until rested. Run 7 minutes. Walk the rest of the half-hour. As the week progresses, extend the running portions by 1 minute at a time, aiming for 10-minute runs by the end of the week.

*Goal by week's end: two 10-minute running segments.*

**Week 5.** Walk 3 minutes, then run 12 minutes, then repeat. By the end of the week, walk 3 minutes, run 15 minutes, walk until rested, then run the rest of the session.

*Goal by week's end: a 15-minute running segment.*

**Week 6.** Walk 5 minutes to begin and end the workout. Run the 20 minutes in the middle. As the week progresses, cut back on the walking portion at the beginning and end.

*Goal by week's end: 30 minutes of continuous running.*

## TRAINING LOG

*I* remember the day I learned to jog. It all came about rather backward for me, since I had grown up competing in junior high, high school, and college. Workouts were a matter of grave intensity, hardly the stuff of stress relief and sunsets. In fact, jogging was the "j" word, and whenever somebody used it, teammates and I were quick to point out that we didn't jog, we ran.

Then I got busy with a career, and running became something that I used to do as a girl. Until, after several sedentary years, quite out of the blue, the urge struck. It must have been the first hint of spring in the air. I trotted off along the lakefront path into the bright Chicago morning, feeling like I hadn't skipped a day. Momentarily. The first block or two of exhilaration quickly turned into oxygen debt, as my out-of-shape body struggled for breath. I slowed. I walked. I stopped.

That's when I noticed the lake. The landscape had been transformed overnight. What had only yesterday been a dull, frozen expanse was now sparkling, steaming, and churning with life. Overnight, winter had crystallized into spring. The sun's warmth had thawed Lake Michigan, turning the shore into a rolling crash of miniature icebergs.

As I marveled at such hopeful beauty, I realized that I never would have noticed the spectacular day had I been running as I used to. When I took off again, I was jogging. I did so deliberately, joyously, at a pace that my out-of-shape body could comfortably maintain while taking in the wonder of it all.

# THE NEXT STEP

Many beginners find it motivational to sign up for an organized run when they start out. A 5-kilometer walk/run a month or two down the road, for example, can be a fun event to participate in with friends and a good celebration of your 30-minute run accomplishment. It doesn't matter if you don't finish the 5-K in a half-hour— simply walk the rest. You might, however, surprise yourself with the adrenaline of the event pumping through your veins and run the entire way. If a race sounds intimidating, choose one of the many women-only or charity events; these are designed specifically to be fun for beginners.

Once you've accomplished your first 30-minute run, a next logical step is to build up to running 30 minutes regularly and comfortably. For at least a few weeks, alternate your 30-minute runs with 30-minute walk/run sessions. When that feels comfortable, try running 3 days a week, but still do 1 walk/run day during the week. When you can comfortably run for 30 minutes three to five times a week, you'll be ready to take on more rigorous workouts if you want to.

# 6

# From Jogging to Running: Training for the Intermediate Runner

WHEN DOES A JOGGER become a runner? Here's a hint: It has little to do with going faster. There is no cutoff speed per mile, no magic number of miles per week, no firm starting point at which the moniker is bestowed.

The difference between the two exists primarily as a mind-set. While some women are content with jogging as a fitness activity, others find that running gets under their skin and becomes a part of their fiber. Much like playing an instrument or keeping a journal, what you get out of running is not determined by how good you are at it. The joy of participation is not an exclusive commodity reserved for the elite runner any more than it is for the concert pianist.

Women turn from joggers into runners for different reasons and at different stages. For one woman, the transformation might occur when she realizes that she no longer runs to keep her weight down but rather to keep her sanity. For another, it might be the night before a trip, when, as she is packing, she realizes that she must take her running shoes because she can't bear to miss a week of workouts. For still another woman, it might be that her schedule barely allows her a morning jog, yet she surprises herself when she finds that she describes herself as a runner.

Once a woman becomes a runner, she finds that the sport is woven into the fabric of her life. Whereas running might have been only a vehicle before—to fitness or to weight loss, for example—it now becomes that rarest of things: a means *and* an end. To a runner, running is still a means of strength and health, of exploration and socialization. But unlike the jogger, who seeks only external results, the runner finds that the very act itself is enough; running is the thing she craves. Within it is a new sense of wonder at the power of movement—whether labored or light—over ground, the rise and fall of breath in her chest. When a woman knows *this* feeling, she knows that she cannot do without running. And thus is born a runner.

## LONGER, STRONGER, FASTER

Many women feel the urge to improve their running, and that can mean many different things. Some simply want to get faster. Some want to be able to run for longer periods of time so they can enjoy new routes or challenging trails. Others want to increase their fitness levels in order to join new groups of running friends. Some wish to go faster just for the feeling it gives them.

"I've been plodding while I run, and that's fine, but in another way, it's frustrating to run 9.5-minute miles, because I know that my body is capable of running faster," says Jean, 37, an accomplished climber and outdoorswoman who runs for fitness. Jean has been running since she was a teenager, but in the last 2 years, she has developed a yearning to reach a new level in the sport. For Jean, speeding up has nothing to do with competition. It has to do with recognizing her potential. "I want to use my body in that way because it's a beautiful feeling, like you're free and flying and using the machine you have in an efficient way. I've felt that way a few times when running—and it's when I'm running a little bit faster."

Running more often, running for longer periods of time, becoming more comfortable with running, becoming more fit, running faster, finding more running friends, expanding your running routes, training more intensely, and beginning to race: If you have any of these goals, it's clear that you're becoming more serious about running. Yet many women get stuck in beginner mode because they don't know how to proceed to the next step.

"I feel as though I don't know how to take my running to the next level. There's so much information about what to do and what not to do that I become overstimulated and do nothing," jokes Katherine, 31, who has been running since she was 20. "I end up sticking to my tired, less-than-challenging routine and not experiencing the growth and progression of which I believe I'm capable. It really compromises the motivation factor."

She's not alone. Some runners get stuck in a rut when they find that they are comfortable at a certain level of training. Each day's workout is easy, familiar, and safe. Even if they want to

---

### IN YOUR OWN WORDS

## Why Become a More Serious Runner?

It's not as if it's a concern to go faster, but rather, it's an enjoyment. I wanted to test my ability in any given situation, whether racing or training. A good friend saw potential in me and has helped me with training, running form, and track workouts.

**Maggie, 46, Boise, Idaho**

I like the feeling I get from pushing myself. It makes me feel strong and capable in other areas of my life.

**Andrea, 24, Evanston, Illinois**

Going fast, being fit, and having fun all work together for me. I've always been "serious" about my running in that regard. The faster you run, the faster you want to run.

**Linda, 49, Ketchum, Idaho**

I want to be able to enjoy doing what I do to keep fit because that keeps me doing it. I have done a lot of different things to get fit, but running gives me the greatest sense of accomplishment. When I get faster, I know I am getting better. I'm not satisfied simply doing; I want to do and get better.

**Gwen, 40, Fort Worth, Texas**

improve, they don't know how, or they're intimidated by the idea of taking on more. The reaction is to overdo it or to not change anything. But taking your running to the next level needn't be complicated or painful. It can and should be a gradual transition.

You'll probably be pleased to find that the workout schedule offered in this chapter is, above all, simple. The new workouts you'll be doing are playful and nonrestrictive. There is no need for regimented track workouts at this stage or for marathon long runs. Will you have to work harder? Of course—that's how you improve. But you needn't fear or dread it.

As you become more serious about your training, you should follow a simple and logical progression of steps to improvement, just as when you first started running. In making this transition, the principles that got you to this point still apply. But this is precisely where many runners throw the rules out the window. Raring to go, impatient to improve, they toss caution to the wind. ("Well, my friends were doing that 10-mile trail run, so I thought I'd just jump in . . .") The result is typically extreme discomfort, discouragement, or injury.

Don't rush. Mastery of any endurance sport is an exercise in patience. Change happens gradually at every level. Improvement in running is a slow process of adaptation, and it can't be rushed. Never bump up your training to a new level overnight. In your quest for a new level of expertise, you are essentially a beginner again, with challenged legs, lungs, and mind.

## NEW LIMITS

Until now, you have stayed in your comfort zone, which was good. If you had pushed too hard or too fast as a novice, you could have wound up injured and discouraged. But now you have a strong foundation. The muscles in your legs are used to running. So are your heart and lungs. You're ready for more.

In order to take on more, you'll need to train your brain as well as your body. Pushing yourself to new limits is as much mental as it is physical. If you didn't grow up playing sports or exercising, pushing yourself may feel frightening and strange.

Simply put, it hurts. As you increase your pace, you'll breathe harder and pick your legs up higher. You'll get acquainted with oxygen debt—the feeling that you can't breathe fast enough to supply your body with the oxygen it needs. You'll sweat. And at

## *now* is a GOOD TIME to ➤

● Try a new running route, preferably one that takes you to a place of beauty. Once a week, drive to a local park or trail for your run. The scenery will be good for your soul, and the change of location will help keep your running fresh. Also, running on dirt or grass at least once a week is good for your feet and legs. The softer surface reduces the impact on your joints, and the uneven terrain helps to develop tiny muscles and tendons to strengthen your feet and ankles.

● Check out your local road runners' club. These clubs attract runners of all abilities, ages, and levels of experience. You're sure to find someone at your level to run with as well as someone to inspire you to new levels.

● Incorporate flexibility and strengthening exercises into your fitness routine. Stretch lightly for 10 to 15 minutes after running. It feels great, wakes up your body, and will keep your muscles from tightening as you physically challenge yourself.

● Start a tradition: Jump into a race with friends for a festive day of fitness. Many towns have races to celebrate anything from the season to a holiday. The Fourth of July, Thanksgiving, and New Year's are just some of the holidays you can celebrate in healthy fashion with friends. Some runners like to choose one such local event and make it an annual family tradition. It's a great motivator, and it helps get others involved in your pastime.

● Cross-train once a week. By swimming, biking, or hiking 1 day out of the week, you can keep your muscles and mind fresh and engaged.

● Consider attending a women's running camp or clinic. Women of all ages, experience levels, and abilities attend these. Participation in a camp or clinic virtually guarantees that you'll be inspired, motivated, and challenged. Plus, devoting a day or a week to nothing but your health and fitness is a worthwhile indulgence. To find a camp, consult your local university or running store, or check out *Runner's World* magazine's Web site, www.runnersworld.com, which posts a listing of camps in late spring.

first, you may even feel some postworkout soreness in your ribs, thighs, and even abdomen.

It sounds dreadful. But the right mind-set can turn negatives into positives.

It helps to understand that discomfort is a given. Discomfort is your body telling you that it is working hard to achieve the challenge you have set for it. This is progress. Although the old saying "no pain, no gain" is exaggerated and misguided, it is true that you must stress your limits in order to expand them. If you are following the rules about gradually increasing your training distances and speed, then the discomfort you feel will be a normal part of the improvement process.

As you progress to new levels of training, your mind takes on a more important role. As a beginner it's fine to let your mind wander on runs, to chat with friends, to construct shopping lists in your head—in short, to make each run as painless and as pleasurable as possible. This type of mental distraction is called dissociation, and it can be extremely helpful at times. Your internal dialogue while running up a tough hill might go something like this: Look at those pretty flowers over there. I didn't realize spring was coming along so quickly. Boy, I'd better start watering my garden. . . .

When you're disassociating, you're doing your best to focus on anything but the task at hand, specifically *that* hill.

Dissociation will still work on your easy runs. When your goal is to pick up the pace or to improve your form, however, it won't do you any favors. It's far more helpful to train your mind to enter into a partnership with your body. How so? You can use your mind to monitor your every step and to dispense feedback. You can pay attention to your breathing and your form, staying relaxed and positive. Your internal dialogue on that same killer hill might go something like this: Okay, hold together here. This hill isn't all that tough. Just another few hundred yards. How's my posture? Oops, I'm hunched over at the waist. Stay upright; that's it. Now my legs are lifting more easily. Nice and steady. Even breathing. Here's the crest—good job! Now relax and recover on the downhill.

That's a big difference in approach. It takes concentration to run a notch harder than what you're used to; your body would love nothing more than to slip into its old, comfortable pace. Stop paying attention for a moment and it will do just that. Several studies have shown that when runners let their minds wander, their bodies actually slow down. The mental concentration required to maintain a tough effort doesn't come naturally or easily. On your early attempts, you may be surprised to find your mind working against you: I'm so tired, I'll never make it up that hill. I want to stop. Why am I doing this anyway?

Yikes! With a mind like that, who *wouldn't* rather daydream about the landscape? It's crucial that your feedback remain positive; otherwise, you'll use your brain's powerful impact to talk you right out of a workout.

Concentration is most important during your more challenging workouts, but it's a good idea to develop it by practicing on other runs. After all, it's easier to work on maintaining a positive attitude during a comfortable run when everything is going well. Try doing regular "check-ins" to monitor your form, breathing, stride, and mental attitude. Use these periods to gently correct yourself: Drop your hunched shoulders, take a few deep breaths and exhale slowly, lengthen a stride that has turned short and choppy, stop any negative thoughts midstream. If you get used to this process on easier runs, you'll be more prepared when all the challenges come lumped together at the end of a long run or other tough stretch.

Like anything else, training the brain takes time. Become aware of your dialogue, and when it turns negative, consciously correct yourself kindly, reaffirming that you are up to the task at hand. Over time, you'll naturally develop a more positive association between body and brain.

## TRAINING CONSIDERATIONS

You're now ready to explore workouts that are longer and more involved than the short, steady jogs you're used to. "It's good for women to start on something other than slow jogging as soon as they have the necessary base," says Maureen Roben, cofounder and codirector of Women's Running Camps in Denver and a five-time Olympic Trials Marathon qualifier, who works with many beginners making the leap to a higher level. "When you do the same thing every day, you use the same muscles and develop the same systems. Adding some variety to the program is healthy."

As you add more intense workouts to your schedule, you'll need to keep the emphasis on smart training. Here's how.

**Add distance first.** When increasing your workload, never boost distance and intensity at the same time. The combination can overload your body, leading to injury or fatigue. In this training schedule, your distance will increase first, in order to improve your general fitness. Only then will you add workouts of a greater intensity. As always, take the necessary time to get comfortable with the training program. If you find that a certain week is particularly difficult, keep training at that week's level until it becomes comfortable.

**Run for time, not miles.** At this stage of your training, it's still most practical and useful to run "by the clock"—for set amounts of time as opposed to distance. So that's how the workouts in this chapter are structured.

Some runners will be curious to see how far they are going, though, or to see how fast they are covering a route of a certain distance. Many bike paths and park trails are already measured and marked. If your routes aren't, you can measure them using either the odometer in your car or one that's set up on a bicycle. At each mile point, note a landmark that you'll remember, such as a mailbox or a tree. Although this isn't a perfectly precise mode of measurement, it's good enough to get an idea of your distances.

Avoid the temptation to measure every route you use, however. As you become more serious about running, you may find yourself tempted to time every mile on every outing and to compare them from day to day. That's one sure way to press too hard in your training and to set yourself up for disappointment. Most runners find that they enjoy leaving some runs unmeasured; it helps them avoid pushing too hard on easy days.

**Keep easy days in the mix.** To effectively increase your training level, this schedule requires that you apply the "hard-easy" approach. Since you'll be running harder or longer on some days, it goes hand in hand that you'll also need recovery days. If you need to depart from the suggested schedule, be sure to keep the hard-easy approach intact.

Never schedule your more challenging workouts on consecutive days. (For now, a challenging workout is anything longer, faster, or harder than your typical 30-minute run.) In general, your week should alternate one longer or harder run with days of easy 30-minute jogs or a day off.

Also, run no more than 4 days in a row. After running this many days at a stretch, take a day completely off. If you crave some form of exercise, try swimming, inline skating, or something else that is less demanding on your joints.

## VARIETY AND INTENSITY

These workouts are designed to increase your strength, endurance, speed, and overall fitness. They are essentially simpler, scaled-back versions of workouts that advanced runners do.

*The long run.* The long run can sound intimidating, and indeed, some advanced runners will eventually hit the pavement for up-ward of 3 hours during one of these workouts. But fear not. Your long run won't start out that long. Pick a day that works best for you, and gradually increase your time running each week until you build up to an hour. (Typically, runners do this workout on week-ends since that is when they have the most time.) Don't bump up the length of this run too quickly. Follow a progression like the one in the sample training schedule on the opposite page, increasing your long run by 5 minutes maximum each week.

Your long run will build your endurance, enhance your fitness, and get your body comfortable working for a longer period of time. Speed is not important on your long-run day. Run at a comfortable pace, walking every now and then if you need to. Once you can run for an hour, keep your long runs at that duration for several weeks or months until you are comfortable with it.

*Fartlek.* This strange-sounding word is a Swedish term that means, roughly, speed play. And indeed, these workouts can seem like child's play, interspersing fast bursts with slower recovery jog-ging. More advanced runners will do a fartlek workout in a regimented style, sometimes including a set number of timed intervals so that it resembles a traditional speed workout. But for the intermediate runner, fartlek can be simply a fun, unintimidating introduction to faster running.

To do fartlek, vary the speed and intensity of your pace, creating work and allowing recovery without stopping. Warm up by starting your run as you ordinarily would, jogging at a comfortable pace for about 10 minutes. Then, for a set period of time (see "Intermediate Training Schedule"), "play" by alternating slow, medium, and faster paces for short periods of time. These timed intervals can be anywhere from 30 seconds to 3 minutes. You don't even have to look at your watch. Try running each seg-

## Intermediate Training Schedule

|  | MON | TUES | WED | THURS | FRI | SAT | SUN |
|---|---|---|---|---|---|---|---|
| **Week 1** | Off | 30 min | Off | 30 min | Off | 30 min | 35 min |
| **Week 2** | Off | 30 min | Off | 30 min | Off | 30 min | 40 min |
| **Week 3** | Off | 30 min | Off | 35 min | Off | 30 min | 45 min |
| **Week 4** | Off | 30 min | Off | 35 min | Off | 30 min | 50 min |
| **Week 5** | Off | 30 min | Off | 35 min | Off | 30 min | 55 min |
| **Week 6** | Off | 30 min | Off | 35 min | Off | 30 min | 60 min |
| **Week 7** | Off | 30 min | Off | 40 min | Off | 30 min | 60 min |
| **Week 8** | Off | 30 min | Off | 45 min | Off | 30 min | 60 min |
| **Week 9** | Off | 30 min | 20 min | 30 min | Off | 30 min | 60 min |
| **Week 10** | Off | 30 min | 20 min | 35 min | Off | 30 min | 60 min |
| **Week 11** | Off | 30 min | 20 min | 40 min | Off | 30 min | 60 min |
| **Week 12** | Off | 30 min | 20 min | 45 min | Off | 30 min | 60 min |
| **Week 13** | Off | 30 min | 20 min | 45 min (middle 20 fartlek) | Off | 30 min | 60 min |
| **Week 14** | Off | 30 min | 20 min | 45 min with hills | Off | 30 min | 60 min |
| **Week 15** | Off | 30 min | 20 min | 45 min (middle 20 fartlek) | Off | 30 min | 60 min |
| **Week 16** | Off | 30 min | 20 min | 45 min with hills | Off | 30 min | 60 min |

ment by picking out a different landmark: Run harder to the fifth telephone pole, for example; then recover by jogging to the pine tree at the end of the street; then pick up the pace again. Follow faster bursts with slower ones for recovery.

Never go so fast that you are sprinting. Alternate tempos so that the overall effect is one of breathing more heavily than you're used to but so that you can still recover within a minute or so for your next "burst." Fartlek will begin to train your mind and your body to shift gears, to feel the difference in paces, and to recover efficiently. So although these workouts can indeed feel like playtime, pay attention to what you are feeling: You can learn a lot.

*Hills.* Ask any runner about her least favorite terrain and she's likely to talk about hills. Hills slow you down, and worse, they hurt. So mythic is their reputation that particular hills in races and on training courses have even acquired names: Heartbreak Hill, the Beast, and so on. In order to overcome such monsters, runners tend to attack them head-on, intentionally training on hills for a tough workout. Typically, this has meant finding a hill and sprinting up it as fast as possible, then slogging down, and doing it over and over again. No wonder runners have come to hate hills.

There is a less regimented way to train on hills, especially at this stage of the game. And yes, it's better to train on them than to avoid them. Running on hills is one of the fastest, most efficient ways to build strength. Plus, they will make you better-rounded as a runner, so you won't need to fear any course or terrain.

Roben explains her kinder, gentler approach to hills this way: "I tell women to find a hilly course or park to run and then, every time they hit an incline, to pick up the pace. If it's a short hill, run a little harder. If it's a long, extended hill, don't go quite so fast. This workout is much more fun and less intimidating than doing hill repeats. Plus, it tends to put less stress on the joints during the downhills."

So instead of going up and down the neighborhood on-ramp, look for a route that includes rolling hills. As you run each hill, concentrate on maintaining good form. In particular, do not slump forward at the waist, which makes it more difficult to lift your legs. Pick up the pace until you reach the top of the hill, then relax and ease back to your regular pace until the next hill. You'll reap all the benefits of running hills, and you may even have some fun along the way.

## 16-WEEK PLAN

The Intermediate Training Schedule will help you reach the next level safely and comfortably. Although the schedule covers 16 weeks of training, remember that this is only a guide and that every woman responds differently to training. Move along more slowly if your body dictates. If a certain week proves particularly difficult, repeat that week's training before progressing to the next week. In fact, every 4 weeks, it's a good idea to repeat the last week's workouts until you feel comfortable at that level. If you feel very sore or are sick, be sure to take a few days off. Resume training where you left off; don't ever jump ahead without taking the incremental steps. Don't worry if you take several extra weeks or months to get through the entire program.

In Weeks 1 through 8, this schedule concentrates on building distance, particularly during your long run and on one other day of the week. Week 9 adds a day of training, bringing you up to 5 days a week. Finally, Weeks 13 through 16 increase the intensity of one workout per week.

You can alter this schedule to meet your own personal needs. If you want to run only 4 days per week, for example, that's fine. You can still work your way through the rest of the schedule. Just repeat the Week 8 workout for several weeks, until you feel comfortable at that level. Then head into Week 9 and subsequent workouts, deleting the fifth day's 20-minute run so that you remain at four runs per week.

## THE NEXT STEP

When you reach the end of this program, it's a good idea to stick with the schedule for a while before attempting anything more strenuous. If you did your 16-week buildup over the spring or summer, for example, continue this level of training—5 days a

*T*he runner's path isn't necessarily a straight one. More often it's a bell curve: A new runner becomes more serious and steps up her training for years until she has maximized her improvement; then she tapers off her mileage and intensity with the eventual demands of age. My own curve hasn't been so predictable. It continues to develop peaks and valleys that make no particular sense, except within the ragged rhythm of my own life.

And so it is that now, despite more than 15 years of experience, I find myself at the intermediate level once more. This time around, it's work and family that have encroached on elite ambition.

When I first withdrew from hard training, my body and mind rebelled. But now, after several months, I've settled into my stride at this new and perhaps more sane level of training. I run as time allows, usually four or five times a week. Once a week, I try to fit in one long run of more than an hour, usually heading off into the mountains on Sunday with my husband. During the week, I also try to fit in one harder effort, with fartlek or a sustained faster tempo. Other than that, it's catch as catch can.

I've learned to appreciate the beauty of running according to how I feel each day, rather than sticking to a regimented schedule. On days when I'm truly worn out from stress, I allow myself to dally, taking notice of the storm systems coming to pass, the newborn foals in the field, the neighbors' latest lawn ornaments. And at those serendipitous times when it all still comes together, I allow myself to fly, the sweet strain of effort leaving no room in my mind for anything but the sensation that is running.

When I first cut back on my training, I thought that I would slip backward, but I have found that there is no such thing when you are a runner. Between the growing pains of the beginner and the growing pressure of the advanced runner, I've rediscovered a beautiful stage of running freedom. To know that you have the strength to run however long and hard you wish, to know that you have the choice of when you will do so—therein lies the sweet spot of running.

week, with a long run of an hour and one other difficult workout—over the winter. Get to the point where hills and fartlek workouts feel truly comfortable. Don't think about increasing your workload again until the following summer.

If you don't want to engage in advanced training for racing but you do want to maximize the fitness benefits of running, the end point of this schedule is a good base from which to work. You might eventually want to bump your long run up—by only a few minutes each week—until you reach 90 minutes. You can also increase your easy midweek runs from 20 or 30 minutes to 45 minutes or an hour.

# From Running to Racing: Training for the Advanced Runner

IF YOU WANT TO EXPLORE your running potential, you've turned to the right chapter. That doesn't just mean the speedster who breaks 40 minutes in a 10-K or the woman who's always the fastest in her group. In running, we can only truly measure ourselves against ourselves. Every woman can work toward becoming her best running self within her own realm of capability. If that's what you wish to do, this chapter is for you, whether your goal is to break a certain time in a 5-K or 10-K or just to see how fast you can go.

That said, this chapter will concentrate mainly on runners who wish to race competitively. Beginning and recreational runners can and certainly do race, too, and I strongly recommend racing for runners of all levels, for its social and goal-setting benefits. This chapter will focus on runners who wish to race up to their potential.

Before you attempt the level of training outlined here, you need a strong base of training to physically prepare yourself for the more intense program. That means you should have at least 1 year of running experience behind you. You should also be at a plateau. In other words, you should have maximized your improvement within the intermediate running program in this book before moving up to this one. "As long as you are improving your racing with aerobic training—and when you're starting out, you can continue to do so for several years—you should continue with that program," says Lorraine Moller, of Boulder, Colorado, a four-time Olympic marathoner and winner of the bronze medal in the 1992 Olympic Games. "It's when you start to plateau that you should start to incorporate changes." Bear in mind that even with an advanced workout program that includes track sessions and sustained hard runs, you won't see your best results until you've been doing this training for several years.

Why race? Why take on the extra work and dedication that an advanced training program entails? After all, most of the sport's general health benefits peak at the intermediate level of training—in which you work out about five times a week, between 30 minutes and an hour each day. Running more than that is not about health. It's not even about superior fitness, which could be achieved with supplementary cross-training. No, the bottom line is that anyone who is training at an advanced level is pursuing something more than health and fitness. She may be pursuing excellence. She may be testing herself. She may be investigating limits. She may be doing all of the above. In short, runners race to see what they are made of. Some runners feel that the training and racing process contains a microcosm of life's challenges and that through the one they learn about the other.

Taking on the commitment to become the best you can be is a bold move. It entails hard work, time, dedication, triumphs, and setbacks. It almost certainly entails frustration and, just as certainly, spectacular fulfillment. Specific results, however, are never guaranteed. Most runners eventually find that it's the journey, and not the destination, that provides the greatest value. In the end, the ultimate reward does not reside in the number of minutes and seconds on a watch, but rather within that process of work, learning, and discipline.

## BE YOUR BEST

The process of becoming the best runner—or the best at any other pursuit, for that matter—involves discipline, dedication, and mental fortitude. One of the benefits of pursuing serious training is that it helps develop these attributes, which can in turn come in handy in other areas of life.

In advanced training, you will need to run more miles, more intense workouts, and more days per week. You must push yourself constantly. That takes increased time and an increased energy expenditure from your body. In order to accomplish your goals, you'll need to be smart, listen to your body, and make wise choices.

The more miles you put in, and the more intense your workouts, the more stress you place on your body. Runners who do large amounts of training are more susceptible to cold and flu, due to their strained immune systems. They are also more susceptible to injury. Obviously the goal is to minimize those troubles, which are counterproductive not only for running but in the rest of your life as well.

You can minimize negative effects by training smart. For advanced runners, that's perhaps even more important than training hard. Most injuries can be avoided by following the rules of wise training. That means never increasing either quantity or quality too quickly and adjusting your schedule at early signs of overtraining or extreme fatigue. It also means giving proper attention to your body's biomechanics. Because any misalignment will be exacerbated by greater training loads, it's doubly important that you wear the proper shoes and replace them often when training at this level.

You'll also have to make choices about how you commit your time and energy. "At a high fitness level, you're going to have to work a whole lot more just to get a little more benefit," says Jack Daniels, Ph.D., exercise physiologist at the State University of New York College at Cortland. It comes down to the principle of diminishing returns. Basically, you see your greatest improvement when you start running. At each subsequent level, you have to work harder for what will almost undoubtedly be a smaller increment of improvement. In order to reach your potential, you will train extraordinarily hard to shave what might amount to seconds or a minute off your time in a race. The question then arises whether the amount of work needed to get to the next level is worth it.

Because of all there is to gain in the pursuit of excellence, for plenty of women the answer is yes. But that answer will likely require some rearrangements in your personal life. The rest of the world isn't set up to work around your tough training schedule. It might mean using up some of the free time you currently spend on other pursuits. It might necessitate shifting a work schedule around in order to meet with a training group.

When intrusions become tempting, remind yourself of your goals and the benefits you get from pushing yourself. View your commitment not as a sacrifice but rather as an investment in yourself. Finally, allow yourself to break form every once in a while—to skip an easy run to go hiking with friends, for example. The change of pace will help keep you from going stale. As always, balance is key.

## MASTERS OF BALANCE

Ask most coaches and elite runners what the single key to success in the sport is and they'll answer, "Consistency." Do the work day after day, month after month, year after year, and improvement is virtually guaranteed. Consistency has many enemies, however: injury, boredom, and lack of discipline among them. Consistency can even be a cannibal. Some of the most focused runners—those who will never, ever, under any circumstances miss a workout—are the ones who discipline themselves right into a debilitating injury, one that could have been avoided by taking a few days off early on.

Former world-class runner and coach Benji Durden, of Boulder, Colorado, believes that the truly great runners are masters of balance. "Ultimately, the best runners are the ones who are willing to work very hard but who have a little bit of a lazy streak in them," he says. What he means is that these runners will be prone to take a day off when they feel worn out rather than pushing through fatigue even when their bodies cry out for them to back off.

Only you can determine your optimal balance between pushing and backing off, between consistency in training and necessary breaks. Master that formula and you've mastered running at the expert level.

So how on earth do you master the balance? Above all, it's a function of time. The longer you have been running, the more information you will have gathered in order to make those decisions. You will have learned the difference between laziness and true exhaustion, between minor tweaks and serious pain in need of attention.

## Too Much Running

**H**ere's one of the most perplexing contradictions about running: More isn't always better. Yes, you must put in more miles and run more intensely to get faster. But there is such a thing as running too much. Scientists call it overtraining.

When you overtrain, you feel sluggish. Your times slow down, no matter how consistent your workouts are. Training partners with whom you ordinarily keep up pass you by easily. When this happens, most women's logical response is to train harder. Wrong answer.

Overtraining can create a nasty little cycle that leads to frustration and debilitation. The last thing that serious runners want to admit is that they might have limits, so overtraining often goes unrecognized. Coaches and training partners can be helpful in spotting the signs.

Pay attention to the following symptoms of overtraining:

- Chronic fatigue
- Loss of appetite
- Trouble sleeping
- Irritability
- Elevated heart rate
- Lack of motivation
- Slowing times
- Frequent illnesses (typically, cold and flu)

Overtraining should not be taken lightly. Some runners who overdo it become chronically tired and ill. It can take months for your body to recover when it's been pushed past the point of healthy training.

But it's also a function of mindfulness. Some women can run for years and never learn to listen to their bodies. Others have an uncanny sense of how hard to push. You can develop this mindfulness just as you would build your muscles—by exercising it. That means paying attention when your body talks to you.

## CLIMB TO YOUR PEAK

To race well, you need to understand peaking. You can maintain peak fitness only for a few weeks, so that's when you want to race. Then you want to rest before building up again. Professional runners might plan to peak several times in a year—for example, for

Although formal evidence is lacking, many runners and coaches believe that there is even a point of no return, from which runners who have pushed too hard for too long can no longer return to their former strength. "You see a lot of people who should have made it but didn't because they pushed themselves too hard and weren't patient enough to progress," says Ann Boyd, an elite runner and coach in Ann Arbor, Michigan. "They have success for a short while, but then they disappear from the racing scene and never come back to that level." Shelly Steely, a four-time World Championship cross-country team member who coaches in Albuquerque, New Mexico, agrees. She says that overtraining is the number one pitfall of serious runners of all levels. "Everyone who starts training consistently sees some improvement, so then they think that more work must be even better," Steely says. "Then, when faced with a little injury or exhaustion, they're already hooked, so they can't imagine taking a day off."

Steely urges her runners to realize that with such behavior, they have the opposite effect of their intentions. "They are, in fact, not investing in long-term consistency at all," she cautions.

If you suspect that you have been overdoing it recently, take a week or two off to allow for a full recovery. Get extra sleep, eat well, and do something other than running if you feel the need to exercise. If you've been pushing too hard for a long period of time—say, for a few months or more—you might want to take several weeks to a month off and run only easy distances until you recover. The payoff will be worthwhile: a stronger, healthier, more resilient you.

track season, for a fall road race, and then for indoor track over the winter. For most other runners, this science is a little too precise, so it's more realistic to peak just once a year. Because most races are held in the period from spring to fall, and because the weather can create a challenge to training in the winter in much of the country, the seasons can help guide your program.

Start by choosing one major event in which you hope to run an optimal performance. This is the race you should peak for. You can and certainly should run other races along the way, but bear in mind that you might not be in your best shape, and therefore you might not run up to your capacity. You'll probably want to "train through" these interim races, which means you won't taper your training before them. Otherwise you won't be able to train consistently enough to reach your peak. Interim races are useful to learn about your fitness at the time and to experiment with pacing and racing tactics.

If you've never raced before, choose a shorter race that you can easily tackle. A 5-K is a typical starting point, not only because you can go the distance but also because the shorter the race, the fewer mistakes can happen. If you go out too fast and find your pace woefully slowed, for example, you won't have that far to run to finish the race. But if you attempt a half-marathon before you can correctly gauge your pacing, you could be in for a very long final 5 or 6 miles. Plan to run a few 5-Ks and 10-Ks before attempting the half-marathon.

Next, break your training into four segments: base building, strengthening, sharpening, and tapering.

*Base building.* Traditionally done during the winter, base building consists of easy distance running. You can certainly add some hilly runs and fartlek, but overall you should concentrate on logging miles. "This phase gives you a good opportunity for development of all the things that happen as a function of time spent running, as opposed to intensity," says Dr. Daniels. Muscle cell adaptation, an increased capacity for your blood cells to deliver oxygen to your body, and other physiological improvements occur during this phase of long, slow distance.

Since building a base is the least exciting, least "glamorous" part of training, it often receives short shrift. Runners will run track sessions all winter, for example, or they won't log enough miles because of cold weather. But the importance of this phase of training can't be understated. Think of your base as the foundation on which you build the rest of your training program—the broader and stronger it is, the higher a peak you will ultimately be able to climb.

*Strengthening.* During this phase you build up your strength with longer intervals, tempo runs, and harder long runs. "At this point, you're working on your running economy, improving lactate threshold and aerobic capacity," Dr. Daniels says. This stage typically takes place during the spring and can last several months.

The terms to which Dr. Daniels is referring are crucial to running performance and bear further explanation.

*Lactate threshold* is the point at which lactic acid, a waste product created during exertion, builds up in your system faster than your muscles can flush it out. This happens when your cardiovascular system can't process enough oxygen to get rid of it, a condition called anaerobic ("without air") threshold. If you've ever run too fast too early in a workout and felt as if your legs had become wet noodles, you've felt the effects of surpassing your lactate threshold. By training near the threshold, you can extend it. These workouts are often referred to as tempo runs or as lactate or anaerobic threshold runs.

*Aerobic capacity* refers to your body's ability to process oxygen. Not all the oxygen we inhale is used when we exercise. The amount used depends on your max $VO_2$, or maximum oxygen uptake, the amount of oxygen your body is able to deliver to your muscles while exercising. Though this figure is partly determined by genetics, training can help you maximize your potential aerobic capacity. Such training is typically done in track workouts in which you run close to or slightly faster than your usual 5-K pace.

*Sharpening.* As you approach your goal race and want to build speed, it's time to start sharpening. Interval workouts focus on shorter distances, and workouts in general should develop your speed without leaving you overly fatigued. Your mileage might drop off slightly at this stage to speed leg recovery. Your body will be able to store reserves, and you will feel bouncy and ready for the race efforts to come.

*Tapering.* Depending on your race distance, 1 to 2 weeks before your race you should reduce your mileage drastically. This final reduction will allow any sore spots to heal and help your body store an optimal amount of fuel to use during the race. (For more on tapering before a race, see Chapter 8).

These phases are not entirely exclusive of one another. For example, you'll still do easy distance runs during your strengthening phase, and you might still run a few strength workouts while you are sharpening. The point is that the overall focus of the training shifts over time.

After your big race, it's not a bad idea to take a few weeks off to let your body recover and to give your mental concentration a break. Some runners swim or cross-train during this break, while others prefer to be completely sedentary. Once you start back, you'll want to begin again at the base-building phase. (The sample training schedules on pages 81 to 83 start at the strengthening phase.)

## OPTIMIZE YOUR TRAINING

Here is a look at some of the most important considerations that should go into your running program at the race preparation level.

● Hook up with a team or a group of friends for hard workouts. For most people, intense training sessions seem easier and more enjoyable when they are run with others. Some friendly competition can also push you to a better effort.

● Begin keeping a training log if you're not already doing so. A record of your workouts will help you determine what works and what doesn't work for you. Besides your workouts, you might want to record what you eat, how you sleep, various stressful events, when you buy new running shoes, and anything else that might affect your training.

● Run a race for time. Set a realistic goal based on your past performances. Choose a race at least 2 months out, then follow an appropriate training schedule for your training level. (For an optimal performance based on a full peaking schedule, you'll want to have 4 to 6 months. If you already have a sufficient base of easy miles, you can begin at the strengthening phase outlined in this chapter's workouts.) Regardless of whether you hit your goal, remain positive and choose another target race. Analyze what went right and wrong in the race and how you can improve your training for the next time around.

● Consider consulting with a coach. He or she can help determine your individual strengths and weaknesses and can tailor a training program just for you. At this level, it can be very beneficial to have someone who can serve as a sounding board.

## Flexibility

The harder you train, the more important it is to listen to your body and make the necessary changes. Your body talks to you all the time, but you don't always pay attention. Try to recognize the difference between niggling soreness and pain. Do the same with the general tiredness from a busy schedule versus the exhaustion that signals overtraining.

When you find clues that you're heading down a destructive path, take action. Take a few days off, have a massage, get a good night's sleep. Don't be so obsessive that you won't miss a workout.

● Invest in racing shoes. If you're training this hard, you deserve to have every advantage when you compete.

● Evaluate your diet—again. It's crucial to get enough calories and the right kind. As women grow more serious about their running, they often start to cut corners on their diets to keep their weight as low as possible. Consider seeing a nutritionist at your local health club to see whether you are eating adequately for your training level.

● Be sure that you're getting enough sleep. Now is not the time to stress yourself in other areas of your life. If you are in the midst of a busy work schedule or have particularly tough family demands, you may want to reschedule your heavy training for another time.

● Get sports massages. Tired, sore muscles can benefit from therapeutic massage. Consider scheduling a regular session, anywhere from once a month to once a week.

● Have your form analyzed. Sports-medicine centers and sports physicians offer form analysis, which can help ensure that you are running as efficiently as possible. If you don't know where to get one in your area, your local running club or running specialty store can help. Or you can simply have a friend videotape you while you run and then watch the tape on your VCR. While you watch, look at your feet to make sure that they are not rolling in or toeing out. See whether your arms are crossing too far over your chest. Are your shoulders hunched? Is your head poked forward?

If you begin a hard workout, such as a track session or tempo run, and find that you are "dead"—you can't stay focused, or you're just physically exhausted—take the day off or go for an easy jog instead. It's far better to be proactive than to miss weeks or months down the line once you've driven yourself too hard. Bear in mind that you can't make up for lost time. Don't try to cram in missed workouts or put hard workouts back-to-back after taking time off. If you skip a hard workout, try to do it the next day if you have several easy days scheduled after that; otherwise, skip it altogether.

## When to Push

Some coaches ask runners to "give their all" every day in training. They are liable to wind up with runners who have nothing left to give on race day.

"There is racing energy and there is training energy," says Moller, "and you don't want to use racing energy up in training. There's only one time when you should use that kind of energy, and that's in a race." In track sessions and tempo runs, though it's important to run hard, you should not run to exhaustion. That energy is in limited supply, and as Moller says, it should be conserved for racing. A good rule of thumb is that you should be able to run your last repeat in track sessions as fast as your first one. If you are getting slower with each repeat, you are running too hard. Likewise, in tempo runs, when you finish, you should feel able to continue running at the same pace if you had to. If you complete the workout and collapse at the finish line, you are using up your race energy.

## A Mental Edge

It's important to ensure that your program builds your confidence, and not the opposite. Some women thrive on hard training; others wind up feeling demoralized and insecure about their abilities. To reach your potential, you must begin every workout and race with utter faith in your coaching and training.

If your program is not inspiring this kind of confidence, think of ways to change it. That might mean a new coach, new training partners, or a different location. Details count, too. Run your quality workouts—the interval sessions, tempo runs, fartlek, and long runs—at a pace that is reasonable for you (as outlined in chapter 6). Don't overextend yourself in order to train with a group that competes beyond your current ability. Don't ruin your workout by either slowing down or speeding up based on how somebody else is running. Make sure that you are getting enough rest between hard workouts. All these little things add up, either building into a ladder of successes that will give you confidence for your race or slowly eroding your belief in your abilities. Ultimately, you are responsible for this process, so don't be afraid to take control of it and make changes in your training if necessary.

## Days Off

You'll benefit from days of complete rest. Typically, that means taking 1 day off each week or every 10 days. This rest will allow your legs to more fully recover for upcoming hard efforts. It can also fend off injuries that might be creeping up. If you're the obsessive type, you can use your off day as a cross-training day, but choose an exercise such as swimming that doesn't tax the legs with impact.

## Two-a-Days

The purpose of running twice a day is to add miles with a minimum amount of stress on your legs. For example, let's say that you are already running 6 afternoons a week, up to an hour each day with a long run on weekends, and you want to gradually increase your miles. Instead of going even longer than an hour, add a short run in the morning on 1 day. Start at 20 minutes and build up to 30 minutes. You'll find that doing so is a lot easier—physically and mentally—than a long, 90-minute run in the middle of the week. When you are comfortable with your additional run on 1 day, you can increase to 2 or 3 days of "doubling." Only professional runners should run twice a day more than a few times a week.

If you have been training at an advanced level for several years and feel ready to try two-a-days, limit them to your hard workout days during the week. (If you double on other days, you'll be making your recovery days too difficult.) Add 20 to 40 minutes of easy distance for your second run. Make sure that you have at least 6 hours between runs, preferably more. Finally, take care to eat enough on these days; otherwise, you stand a chance of running out of energy on your second outing. After your morning run, eat a substantial meal right away. That will leave enough time to digest your food before your second run.

### Effort and Recovery

The harder you run, the more recovery you need. Hard workouts are the bread and butter of an expert runner. These are the days when the real training is accomplished. But without recovery days, hard workouts are worthless: There must be easy runs in order for the training effect to be felt.

Most serious runners will do either two or three hard workouts per week. Newer runners will want to start at two hard efforts and perhaps eventually build up to three. Older runners typically come upon a time when they have to drop from the three workouts they are used to down to two. What really determines this number is the number of recovery days your body requires between hard efforts. If you do a track session on Tuesday and an easy run on Wednesday, for example, you will need to be fairly well recovered in order to do a tempo run on Thursday. If you haven't recovered enough, you might need 2 or even 3 easy days between these efforts. The sample schedules on pages 81 to 83 show what a training program may look like at the beginning and advanced competitive levels.

The principle of effort and recovery applies not only on a daily basis but also over the long haul. Just as you need recovery days, you should have recovery weeks as well. For every 3 to 5 weeks of hard training, you should cut your mileage and your quality back for 1 week. This proactive approach can keep you from over-training, injury, and burnout.

### Quality versus Quantity

Although I've alluded to this in many places throughout this book, it bears spelling out especially for runners who are training at an advanced level. Doing the *right* training is more important than doing the *most* training. Increasing your weekly mileage is not a certain recipe for success. Some runners do successfully run 80, 90, or 100 miles a week over long periods of time, but they are rarities who seem to be genetically blessed with the ability to avoid injury or illness. And there's no guarantee that they are running any faster; they might even be hurting their performance with chronically tired legs.

For runners who are not competing professionally, most performance gains can be maximized at a level of 40 to 60 miles a week. Even some elite runners succeed on far fewer miles than their peers who boast of large numbers in their running logs. So don't feel pressured to run more miles because your friends or training partners are doing so. If you are able to improve on less work, consider yourself lucky.

# STRENGTH AND SPEED DEVELOPMENT

The quality workouts you'll be running in this training program are meant to prepare you for the effort of racing. You'll concentrate on both strength and speed.

The other runs during the week should be considered recovery workouts and run at an easy pace. This means that you shouldn't worry at all about time on these runs. Go with whatever effort feels comfortable to your body.

## Long Runs

Before starting on this program, you should already have built your long run up to about an hour in duration. Now you'll work on increasing that time and distance. For the 5-K, the 10-K, and even the half-marathon, 90 minutes is the maximum time necessary for this workout. (For marathon training, see chapter 9.) Incrementally extend your long run by 5 to 10 minutes each week until you reach 90 minutes.

When you are comfortable with this amount of time on your feet, mix some intensity into your long run. Whenever you pick up the pace in your long run, do so gradually—anywhere from 30 to 60 seconds per mile faster than your easy pace. You don't want to be sprinting when you still have 45 minutes to go. Here are some long run variations you can try:

- Surges. Pick up the pace slightly for short periods of time in the middle of your run. Warm up by going easy for at least the first 20 minutes. Then surge for a total of 15 to 25 minutes of harder running. The surges can be loosely structured ("I'll pick it up until the next big tree") or timed segments of planned duration. Between surges, return to your standard pace. Start with shorter surges the first time you attempt this, and build up to several minutes. Play with variety, for example, running a ladder of surges of different duration—say, 2 minutes, 4 minutes, 6 minutes, 4 minutes, and 2 minutes.

- Segments. Divide your long run into longer segments, running the middle or latter portion at a faster pace. For example, run 30 minutes at your usual pace, 30 minutes slightly faster, then 30 minutes back at your usual pace. Or divide the run into 20-minute chunks, gradually picking up the pace with each one. With these segments, the shift in pace should be very slight, or you'll find yourself unable to complete the workout. As you'll discover for yourself, you'll not only be training yourself to run at a faster pace, but you'll also be getting an invaluable lesson in pacing and in your body's tolerance of different speeds.

- The fast long run. Of course, one way to increase the intensity of the long run is to run the entire workout faster. This can be a very demanding workout and generally should not be done every week. Start conservatively to ensure that you can complete the workout strongly, picking up the pace rather than slowing down over the course of the run.

### Tempo Runs

Also called lactate threshold or anaerobic threshold runs, these workouts are as close as you'll come to simulating competitive conditions. You'll be running at a certain tempo—namely, close to your racing pace—for a prolonged period of time. Ideally, these runs are conducted a little bit slower than your anaerobic threshold, in which lactic acid accumulates in your muscles faster than your body can flush it away.

If you've ever suffered the dreaded "leaden legs" or "bear on the back" feeling after starting out too fast on a run, you know what it means to surpass your anaerobic threshold. By running just under that threshold, your body develops its ability to process lactic acid more efficiently, which essentially raises your threshold and allows you to run harder. In addition to these physiological benefits, tempo runs also help you develop a sense of pacing as well as a confidence in your ability to maintain a strenuous pace for longer duration.

Tempo runs can last for a predetermined amount of time or distance. It's best to start with a short time or distance and move up from there. For 5-K and 10-K races, you'll eventually want to build up to a 3- or 4-mile tempo run. For half-marathons, these runs might reach 6 miles. Always plan to warm up before and cool down after your tempo run with an easy 2-mile or 15-minute jog. Look for a relatively flat place to do this workout; changes in terrain defeat the purpose of your attempt to maintain consistent pace. Gently rolling hills, especially if you know you will be racing on hills, are acceptable. Run the same course each week in order to track your times.

Your pace should be somewhat slower than your 10-K race pace. It should feel brisk but not exhausting. Willie Rios, of Boulder, Colorado, who specializes in coaching women distance runners, likes to describe it as "fresh" pace: a point at which you could talk if you absolutely had to, but you really don't want to. Ideally, your pace should remain the same throughout the duration of each tempo run. When you bump up the distance of the tempo run, don't be surprised to see your pace drop accordingly. As you grow more fit, however, you should be able to increase the distance you can run while maintaining your goal pace.

## Track Sessions

Track workouts are similar in form to fartlek workouts, in that they alternate hard efforts with a recovery pace. But track workouts add the dimension of regimentation: You'll be on a perfectly flat, measured surface. That's why these workouts are invaluable for learning a sense of pacing. They also make it easier to compare times from one repeat to the next, in order to gauge consistency, and from one session to another, in order to gauge your fitness and performance levels.

Track sessions are typically called interval workouts. They consist of repeated hard efforts of a specific distance (commonly called repeats)—alternated with periods of rest (commonly known as the interval). The lengths of the repeats and intervals vary depending on the purpose of the workout and on where the workout falls within the overall training schedule. The track sessions in this chapter's training schedules consist of distances ranging from 200 meters to 1000 meters (2½ laps around a typical 400-meter track).

Run your track repeats around or slightly faster than your goal 5-K race pace. You want to become comfortable running at this pace, and you want to become familiar with the effort so that you can duplicate this pace in a race. Either jog very slowly or walk during your rest interval, but don't sit or lie down; that will leave you stiff for your next repeat and won't allow your system to flush out lactic acid efficiently. A 400-meter jog should be sufficient rest for repeats of 400 meters and up. A 200-meter jog should suffice when you are doing repeats of only 200 meters.

The point of these sessions is not to replicate a race effort. "People think that the minute you put your feet on the track you have to go as hard as you possibly can, preferably until you puke," jokes Women's Running Camps cofounder Maureen Roben. She cautions that most runners could stand to run these workouts more conservatively, especially the ones who are always struggling to complete a given session. You should aim to complete your final repeat as fast or faster than your first. If you find that you are fading throughout the session, you are starting out too fast.

Start your track workouts with a warmup of about 2 miles of easy jogging. Stretch thoroughly, then do some strides to get your body prepared to move at a faster pace. A good method is to choose a straightaway on the track and do "pickups," starting out slowly and gradually picking up the pace until you are striding at around your 5-K pace by the end of the 100-meter stretch. At that point, slow down, stop, rest, and repeat. Do six to eight of these before the track session. Finally, always finish with a sufficient cooldown. Jog slowly for about 2 miles after your repeats. This will help reduce any muscle soreness that might set in the next day.

# RACE PREPARATIONS

The first two workout schedules presented here will prepare you for either a 5-K or a 10-K race.

Use the Beginning Competitor Training Schedule if you want to race more seriously but have been running at an intermediate level for only a year or so. This will allow you to gradually increase the

*(continued on page 84)*

## *Beginning Competitor Training Schedule*

|  | MON | TUES | WED | THURS | FRI | SAT | SUN |
|---|---|---|---|---|---|---|---|
| **Week 1** | Off | 30 min easy | 40 min (middle 20 fartlek) | 40 min easy | Off | 40 min easy | 75 min with two 8-min faster segments |
| **Week 2** | Off | 30 min easy | Track: 4 × 400 m with 400-m jog | 40 min easy | Off | 40 min easy | 75 min (middle 15 faster) |
| **Week 3** | Off | 30 min easy | 40 min (middle 20 fartlek) | 40 min easy | Off | 40 min easy | 75 min (20 min or 2.5 mi faster segment in middle) |
| **Week 4** | Off | 30 min easy | Track: 4 × 400 m, 400-m jog; 4 × 200 m, 200-m jog | 40 min easy | Off | 40 min easy | 75 min (25 min or 3 mi faster segment in middle) |
| **Week 5** | Off | 30 min easy | Track: 10 × 200 m with 200-m jog | 40 min easy | Off | 40 min easy | 75 min (middle 20 fartlek) |
| **Week 6** | Off | 30 min easy | 40 min easy | 30 min easy | Off | 20 min easy with strides | Race (5-K or 10-K) |

# Advanced Competitor Training Schedule

| | MON | TUES | WED | THURS | FRI | SAT | SUN |
|---|---|---|---|---|---|---|---|
| **Week 1** | Off | 60 min (10 × 2 min fartlek) | 45 min easy | Tempo run: 2 mi warmup, 2 mi tempo, 2 mi cooldown | 45 min easy | 30 to 60 min easy | Long run: 75 min (15 easy, 45 faster, 15 easy) |
| **Week 2** | Off | Track: 6 × 800 m with 400-m jog | 45 min easy | Tempo run: 2 mi warmup, 2 mi tempo, 2 mi cooldown | 45 min easy | 30 to 60 min easy | Long run: 90 min easy with surges |
| **Week 3** | Off | Track: 6 × 800 m with 400-m jog | 45 min easy | Tempo run: 2 mi warmup, 3 mi tempo, 2 mi cooldown | 45 min easy | 30 to 60 min easy | Long run: 75 min at slightly faster than easy pace |
| **Week 4** (recovery week) | Off | 60 min: 15 easy, 30 easy fartlek, 15 easy | 45 min easy | Off | 45 min easy | 45 min easy | 60 min easy (or interim race) |
| **Week 5** | Off | Track: 2 × 800 m, 2 × 400 m, 2 × 800 m, all with 400-m jog in between | 45 min easy | Tempo run: 2 mi warmup, 3 mi tempo, 2 mi cooldown | 45 min easy | 30 to 60 min easy | Long run: 90 min easy with 10 surges in middle |
| **Week 6** | Off | Track: 4 × 400 m, 400-m jog; 8 × 200 m, 200-m jog; 2 × 400 m, 400-m jog | 45 min easy | Tempo run: 2 mi warmup, 3 mi tempo, 2 mi cooldown | 45 min easy | 30 to 60 min easy | Long run: 75 min at slightly faster than easy pace |
| **Week 7** | Off | Track: 4 × 400 m, 400-m jog; 8 × 200 m, 200-m jog | 45 min easy | 60 min (15 × 1 min fartlek) | 45 min easy | 30 to 60 min easy | Long run: 80 min easy |
| **Week 8** | Off | Track: 4 × 400 m at goal race pace, with 400-m jog | 30 min easy | 30 min easy with 10 × 100-m strides | Off | 15 to 20 min easy with easy strides | Race (5-K or 10-K) |

# Half-Marathon Training Schedule

| | MON | TUES | WED | THURS | FRI | SAT | SUN |
|---|---|---|---|---|---|---|---|
| **Week 1** | Off | 60 min (6 × 4 min fartlek) | 45 min easy | Tempo run: 2 mi warmup, 3 mi tempo, 2 mi cooldown | 45 min easy | 30 to 60 min easy | Long run: 75 min (15 easy, 45 faster, 15 easy) |
| **Week 2** | Off | Track: 3 × 1000 m with 400-m jog | 45 min easy | Tempo run: 1.5 mi warmup, 4 mi tempo, 1.5 mi cooldown | 45 min easy | 30 to 60 min easy | Long run: 90 min easy with surges |
| **Week 3** | Off | 60 min (8 × 3 min fartlek) | 45 min easy | Tempo run: 1 mi warmup, 5 mi tempo, 1 mi cooldown | 45 min easy | 30 to 60 min easy | Long run: 90 min easy |
| **Week 4** (recovery week) | Off | 60 min: 15 easy, 30 easy fartlek, 15 easy | 45 min easy | Off | 45 min easy | 45 min easy | 60 min easy (or interim 10-K race) |
| **Week 5** | Off | Track: 6 × 800 m with 400-m jog | 45 min easy | Tempo run: 1.5 mi warmup, 4 mi tempo, 1.5 mi cooldown | 45 min easy | 30 to 60 min easy | Long run: 90 min easy with 10 surges in middle |
| **Week 6** | Off | Track: 2 × 800 m, 2 × 400 m, 2 × 800 m, all with 400-m jog | 45 min easy | Tempo run: 2 mi warmup, 3 mi tempo, 2 mi cooldown | 45 min easy | 30 to 60 min easy | Long run: 75 min, slightly faster than easy pace |
| **Week 7** | Off | Track: 8 × 400 m with 400-m jog | 30 min easy | 60 min (15 × 1 min fartlek) | 30 min easy | 30 min easy | Long run: 60 min easy |
| **Week 8** | Off | Track: 6 × 400 m at goal race pace, with 400-m jog | 30 min easy | 30 min easy with 10 × 100-m strides | Off | 15 to 20 min easy with easy strides | Race (Half-marathon) |

intensity of your workouts. Try this schedule in the spring, after a winter of building your base at an intermediate level, as you train for your first serious 5-K or 10-K.

Use the Advanced Competitor Training Schedule once you have spent a racing season completing the Beginning Competitor Schedule. Rebuild your base over the winter, and implement the advanced schedule in the spring.

## TRAINING LOG

*I once found myself engaged in office chitchat with a woman who was curious about my running. She was asking me to explain my—at that time—slavish devotion to my workout schedule and my obsession with racing. After I spoke for a minute or so about what I perceived as the benefit of those things, she replied, "Well, I run for the love of the sport." Within that sideways retort was a smug commentary: Hers, it was implied, was a purer version of running, having nothing to do with the unyielding world of times, miles, and goals. Competition, it was implied, was a dirty word.*

*How odd, I thought. Because I, too, ran for the love of the sport. So I tried to explain. I tried to explain what I found so beautiful about a simple footrace, the oldest game in the world. I tried to explain that for me, the love of the sport at that point in time included the test to see how far I could push myself. That it was in fact the very thing I sought from the sport: to know that I had gone as far as I could possibly go. That I sought refuge in the one corner of my life that was cut-and-dried: a time on a watch, a number on a page. So simple, so unquestionable, compared with the editorial mumbo jumbo of the rest of my life.*

*Now that I'm no longer training at that level, I miss the feeling of being at my absolute physical peak. I miss feeling that I could run through a mountain if I had to, because that's how tough I knew I was. I love my running today, but in a vastly different way, as a mother loves each child utterly for her own unique gifts. That's a beautiful aspect of this sport: It is what you make it. The recreational runner is no greater or less than the competitive woman, and vice versa. And there should be no apology required for either pursuit.*

The last workout schedule is for training for a half-marathon. Plan to race some 5-Ks and 10-Ks before you attempt this distance.

## THE NEXT STEP

As you progress, you may want to continue to notch up your training. If you do, always be aware of the issues raised at the beginning of the chapter. Improvement at this level will require a great amount of effort. Your risk of overtraining and injury increases. Be careful to monitor your body at all times and back off when warning signs hit.

The rules of training won't change much over the course of time. You can use the same workout program presented here whether you've been running hard for a few years or for 10; the only difference is that your speed will change with your level of fitness. The level of effort should remain the same.

If you wish to continue to compete in races of up to a half-marathon, your overall mileage needn't increase greatly. You may wish to do some doubles, adding some easy miles in a second run on your tempo-run days and track days. You can add a few more repeats to your track workouts, but in general the quality portion of each of these workouts should never amount to more than 10 percent of your total weekly mileage. Concentrate on quality rather than quantity, aiming to become faster in the same workouts than you were the year before. Remember, more isn't always better. Many world-class runners do the same workout programs year in and year out with good results.

8

# On Racing Well

**SOME RUNNERS ARE GREAT RACERS.** They perform consistently, delivering solid results even when the stakes are high and the pressure is on. Other runners—equally talented ones—never seem to perform up to their potential. All the promise of their workouts fades in disappointment when, time and again, they fail to run up to expectation during a race.

The difference between the two sometimes results from obvious factors. Training too hard, though it's likely to result in some impressive workouts, can leave you depleted when race day dawns. Inadequate tapering can likewise drain your reserves.

But the difference between a great race and a subpar performance can also be the result of less tangible factors. The best training in the world will not produce results if you are not mentally ready for a race. You must master the seemingly antithetical arts of concentration and relaxation. You must learn to both pace and push. You need confidence. You also need prerace planning, physical preparation, a positive attitude, self-control, wise choices, and, yes, a bit of dumb luck.

The good news is, you can learn all of these elements—except for luck. "Racing is a learned skill," says four-time Olympic marathoner Lorraine Moller, of Boulder, Colorado. "It's like anything else in running: You can practice it."

# MENTAL READINESS

The only thing you can control in a race is your performance. It sounds obvious, but plenty of women toss that concept out the car window when they pull into the race parking lot.

"Some women will look around at the competition and actually decide before the race begins where they will fall within the race," says Ann Boyd, an elite runner and coach in Ann Arbor, Michigan. "They'll say, 'So-and-so's here and she can beat me and so can she, but I can beat her and her. Looks like I'll finish . . . third in my age group.' And they do themselves a huge disservice by doing this."

Follow these tips to put yourself in the right frame of mind to run your best race.

**Worry only about yourself.** Since you can't control who shows up or who will race well, stop wasting energy worrying about how other people will perform. One woman I know, named Sarah, recalls a race she entered with hopes of winning. During her warmup, she saw a tall, lean woman preparing for the race. The woman was dressed in the latest flashy running apparel. She looked fit. She looked fast. "I was even intimidated because of her tan, figuring that she'd been working out a lot!" Sarah jokes. As it turned out, the "threat" finished well back in the pack. But Sarah did finish second—to another woman wearing a plain old T-shirt.

The more relaxed and confident you are, the more likely you will be to perform up to your potential, to learn from your mistakes, and to have a more positive racing experience in general. Even if you're the type of person who comes down with insomnia, dry mouth, gastrointestinal distress, and just plain jitters during everything from job interviews to speeches, you can still learn to race well. Just as your training determines your level of physical preparedness heading into a race, it also molds your emotional state and your mental capabilities. During training, practice mental concentration. It will help you in a race.

**Face your fears in practice.** Moller looks for mental stumbling blocks in her runners and then specifically tailors workouts that play to those weaknesses. "An athlete should practice the situations of which she might be fearful," she says. "For example, some runners go to pieces when somebody passes them. That's something you can easily stage in a workout situation with your running partners." Other stumbling blocks might be fear of leading, or of not running in front of the pack, or of having a long distance to make up on a competitor. All of these situations can be re-created in workouts. One runner can start in front and then be passed, for example. Or runners can trade sharing the lead and following. Or they can stagger their starts to practice catching up with a runner who has a hefty lead.

**Listen to your body objectively.** The best racers learn to view "negative" sensations—heavy breathing, a slight burn in the legs—as information from their bodies and brains rather than as signs of impending doom. Fatigue, for example, is a given in racing. Of course you're going to feel tired. But quite often, if you can hang on through a rough segment of a run or race, you'll eventually feel fresher—in fact, chances are that you'll go through several such ups and downs in the course of a race.

If you are busy destroying your momentum with negative thinking ("That's it; I blew it. My race is over. Here they come, passing me . . .") you'll never feel that second wind. By becoming used to the sensation of fatigue and responding with assurance ("Okay, I knew this feeling would hit; just hang in there and it will pass. It's not so bad . . .") you can train yourself to run through it.

To do this, choose some track sessions or tempo runs and execute them mindfully, with the specific goal of developing a confident outlook. Aim to complete the workout with self-assurance and self-control. Focus at the start as if it were a race. If nervousness or doubt about the upcoming effort creeps into your mind, replace such thoughts by reminding yourself that running your best is all you can do. Tell yourself that you are calm and confident. Remember that nerves are often a function of worrying about external factors over which you have no control.

**Visualize yourself relaxed.** Visualization is a powerful tool that can help change your behavior. As you test yourself during hard

Women-only races have become increasingly popular over the last decade, as more women have discovered the joy of running. These female-friendly events make a point of welcoming runners of all abilities, and they often feature some special touches for their participants. The Idaho Women's Fitness Celebration, for example, has become known for its healthy postrace feast—granola, yogurt, and fruit—and for honoring all of its older runners with roses on the award stage. Growing by several thousand participants each year, the event is testimony to the success of women-only races.

Here are some of the premier women's events in the country.

● Idaho Women's Fitness Celebration: P.O. Box 1596, Boise, ID 83701; www.celebrateall.org

● Avon Running–Global Women's Circuit: 26th Floor, 1345 Avenue of the Americas, New York, NY 10105; www.avonrunning.com

● National Race for the Cure: 1320 Old Chain Bridge Road, Suite 330, McLean, VA 22101; www.natl-race-for-the-cure.org

workouts, picture yourself on the starting line with a positive attitude, knowing that you belong there with your worthy competitors. As the workout progresses and you grow tired, concentrate on gently pushing despite your fatigue. Become accustomed to the feeling of weary legs. Toward the end of a workout, visualize yourself coming on strong and successful, as if the workout were the finishing stretch of a race.

Pay attention to the emotional and physical responses that arise as you run the workout. Work with your training partners, trading off during hard efforts to practice running in the lead or from behind the pack. Practice responding calmly and positively in your training situation, and you will be prepared to do the same in your race.

## CHOICE

If you are running in hopes of achieving a personal record (PR), choose a race that will optimize your chances. Flat courses are generally better than hilly ones. Many people can run faster at low altitudes than at higher ones. Other factors can come into play, too. Find out about the average temperature and humidity level on race day, and choose a race that plays to your strengths in those areas. Some runners perform well in heat, for example, while others wilt. If you live at a high altitude, you might do better running in the mountains than in the humidity customarily found at sea level.

Consider the size of the field as well. Most runners find it easier to run a fast time in a race of at least several hundred people, where they know they'll have cheering crowds and company and competition, than in a smaller race, where they might find themselves alone out on the course.

## THE TAPER

A week or two before your race, start cutting back on your training. A 1-week taper is sufficient for shorter, less crucial races. For longer or more significant events, you might want to gradually back off of hard training for up to 2 weeks. Some runners don't taper at all for small local races that they run as workouts rather than as serious races. That's fine—just remember to adjust your expectations for the race accordingly.

Many runners have a tough time tapering. When you cut back on your training, you can't help but think that your fitness is slowly slipping away. It's not. In fact, during your rest, your body is getting stronger. It's repairing muscle damage, topping off your fuel tank, and boosting your energy. Tapering actually helps you maximize your fitness for race day.

This means, however, that cramming last-minute workouts into the week before the race won't help. Many runners fall prey to this temptation when they have missed previous workouts due to injury or illness. Remember that there are no shortcuts to fitness. Training hard too close to the race can only hurt by tiring you

## IN YOUR OWN WORDS

# Why Do You Race?

*I* race to challenge myself, to set goals, to meet people, and to unite with other athletes with the same interests.

**Liz**, 37, Boise, Idaho

*I* love the energy and enthusiasm I get from everyone around me. I become highly motivated.

**Gwen**, 40, Fort Worth, Texas

*I* enjoy pushing myself. I want to see just how good I can be, and races are a good measure of that.

**Alexis**, 26, Chicago

*I* like the feeling of accomplishment and the camaraderie of experiencing a common challenge.

**Betsy**, 33, Boise, Idaho

*By* having races as goals, I stick with my training schedule.

**Linda**, 49, Ketchum, Idaho

*I* like to try and beat my PR. It's great to have a goal to get in shape for.

**Lisa**, 33, Boise, Idaho

*It's* a great feeling to be around motivated people.

**Jennie**, 32, Boise, Idaho

*I* like to have something to look forward to in my training.

**Kelly**, 39, Eagle, Idaho

*I* race in order to dig deep within myself and see what I'm really made of.

**Maggie**, 46, Boise, Idaho

without adequate recovery time. If you are in doubt about your time frame, bear in mind that most runners are best served erring on the side of recovery before their race efforts.

Although there are general rules for tapering your training, every runner responds differently. You will have to experiment over the course of several races to find the formula that works best for you. Generally speaking, however, you'll want to follow this advice:

**Cut back on your mileage.** During the week leading up to a 5-K or 10-K race, you should cut your mileage in half. For a half-marathon, start halving your mileage about 10 days out. A marathon taper should last about 3 weeks, each week cutting the mileage by about one-quarter. For example, if you were averaging 40 miles a week, 3 weeks before the race you would run 30 miles, 2 weeks before you would run 20 miles, and the week before you would run 10 miles.

**But keep running.** Several studies have shown that a complete lack of physical activity in the days preceding a race leaves runners not energized but sluggish on race day. Assuming that the race is on a weekend, do a short, modified fartlek or track session on Tuesday to keep your speed and sense of pacing honed. A set of four 400-meter repeats at race pace or up to ten 200-meter repeats will do. Trade your Thursday tempo run for an easier run with several pickup strides thrown in. On Friday and Saturday, 20 to 30 minutes of easy running should suffice, with plenty of stretching and a few strides tossed in to keep you sharp. If you want to take a day off, research shows that 2 days before your race is actually a better time to do so than the day before.

**Resist temptation.** Some runners feel edgy from the excess energy that comes with cutting back their routines, while others feel sluggish from the change in pattern. Avoid the temptation to modify your taper based on these feelings. Your body is storing energy for the race, and it's expected that you will feel different. A hard run might make you feel better temporarily, but you'll be burning off the very energy that you are trying to store.

Women in particular also report feeling "fat" during their tapers, and many panic that they will gain weight before the race. Such feelings are typically more psychological than physical. (A minor weight gain can result from a return to proper hydration, which typically comes with a decrease in exercise.) Since your calorie expenditure has dropped, it's not a bad idea to cut back slightly on your food intake. But don't fast or skip meals or take any other drastic measures. It's crucial to eat enough to maintain your energy and health. You'll hurt your performance far more by sabotaging your energy than by gaining a pound or two before the race.

## TRAVEL TO RUN

Racing away from home is fun and exciting. It's a great way to see new places, challenge yourself against different competitors, and discover new courses. But when your race is out of town, a whole host of complications can crop up to threaten your performance. While attempting to concentrate on your running, you are in new and unfamiliar territory that can present distractions ranging from the merely tempting to the thoroughly aggravating. The key is to keep your routine as similar as possible to the one you follow at home. Here are some specific tips to keep you on track.

- Save the sightseeing and socializing for after the race. More than one Sunday race has been ruined by a Saturday of exploring a new city on foot. Beware of large prerace expos for the same reason. It's fine to look around for an hour or so, but spending the day walking around on cement floors can sap the energy from your legs.

- Review the race course before the event. By familiarizing yourself with the course, you can prepare for hills, get a rough idea of mile marks, and make a mental note of markers near the finish so you can decide ahead of time where to make your final push. The best review is done by foot; running allows you to notice the subtlest changes in terrain. If you arrive too late for this, however, or if it's too long a race to jog, at least drive the course in a car.

- Drink, drink, drink. Air travel can be dehydrating, and any type of travel can throw you off your normal, healthy patterns, including that of drinking enough. Carry a water bottle, preferably filled with a diluted sports drink, and drink regularly while you travel and in the days prior to the race.

● Don't be tempted by exotic restaurants until after the race. Search out a prerace meal like the ones you are used to

## Your First Race

**Y**our first race can be intimidating—all those fast runners, all those women with more experience. But don't be scared away: Today's events are designed to welcome runners of all abilities. You'll find plenty of participants just like you, new to the sport or new to an organized event. Think positively and plan on having fun, and your race will be a good one. Here's a 5-step plan to the perfect race.

**1. The night before:** Prepare everything you'll need for the next day, including your running outfit, bad-weather gear, shoes, race number, sunglasses, and water bottle. Now is not the time to test out new attire. To ensure that they won't chafe or cause blisters, be sure to wear shoes, shorts, and a bra that you've already run in a few times. Stuff some toilet paper into a pocket of your warmup clothing. Some women also like to pin a tampon inside their shorts for longer races, just in case.

**2. Race morning:** Wake up at least 2 hours before the race; that will give your body plenty of time to shake off any sleepiness. Eat a simple, light meal right away; that will allow enough time for the food to settle. Stick to foods with which you know your stomach is comfortable: a banana and half a bagel are a favorite for many runners. Drink plenty of water or diluted sports drink now. If you wait until just before the race, you might need a bathroom at the last minute.

**3. Travel to the race:** Plan to arrive at the race 45 minutes to an hour before the start. That way, you'll still have plenty of time to warm up if there are traffic delays or if you must park far away from the start.

**4. Warmup:** Tailor your warmup to the race and your own particular comfort level.

**5. The start:** Line up at the start of the race in a position appropriate for your pace. Generally, the fastest runners will start in the first few rows, with the rows behind them getting successively slower. Joggers and walkers should line up at the back of the pack. Resist the temptation to line up too close to the front. Although you may lose a few seconds or minutes waiting for the pack ahead of you to cross the starting line, you will ensure that you'll start out at a conservative pace—and that you won't get trampled by faster runners behind you.

eating at home—the simpler the better, to avoid any possibility of stomach upset. Play it safe with menu choices: Pasta is a good, conservative bet in most any place.

- Bring a selection of familiar prerace foods for the day before and the morning of the race. Otherwise, you'll be sorry if bagels, bananas, and energy bars are in short supply at the neighborhood convenience store.

- Inquire ahead of time about things that you'll need on the day of the race so you won't have to scramble that morning. Ask the hotel's front desk clerk where you can get a cup of coffee at 5:00 A.M. Find the shuttle-bus stop for transportation to where the race will start. Know where to go to pick up your race number.

- Get plenty of rest in the days before the race. Try to go to bed at the usual time. If you are in a different time zone and have trouble falling asleep early enough the night before the race, don't despair. Being well-rested in general is more important than the last night's sleep just before the race.

- Don't just ask for a wake-up call; set a backup alarm as well. You'll sleep better trusting that you'll be up in time for the race.

## COUNTDOWN TO THE START

A good warmup will prepare your body for an optimal performance. By the end of the warmup, your mind and muscles should feel loose and relaxed. You should not feel overly tired. Over time, you will likely develop a personal warmup strategy that you know brings out your best.

Your warmup will depend on the length of the race, the weather, and your own personal preferences. You can, however, use the following countdown as a general guide.

**45 minutes to race time:** Jog easily for 2 miles or about 15 minutes.

**30 minutes to race time:** Stretch all your muscle groups. Determine whether any areas feel particularly tight and do some self-massage if necessary. Find toilet facilities now if you need them; don't wait until the last minute, when lines can be very long.

**15 minutes to race time:** Change into your racing shoes.

**10 minutes to race time:** Jog a bit more, and do some strides of 100 meters or so at race pace or slightly faster. Stretch any areas that still feel tight.

**5 minutes to race time:** Head to the starting line and listen to any last-minute race instructions. Continue to move and stay loose, jogging very slowly or stretching lightly until the starter tells you to line up for the start.

For longer races—a half-marathon or more—the emphasis should be on conserving energy. These distances require less of a warmup, since the pace will be slower at the start. You probably don't need to do any fast strides, since you won't be running that rapidly during the race. For the marathon, you can jog lightly and stretch for a few minutes before the race, and then essentially warm up during your first mile by easing into the pace. Not only will you have saved precious energy, but this abbreviated warmup can also work in your favor by discouraging you from going out too fast.

Shorter races, such as the 5-K, require a much more concentrated burst of energy. For these races, you must be primed and ready to go at the sound of the gun. Allow 30 to 50 minutes to warm up for this type of race. Be sure to stretch thoroughly, and do several strides at race pace or slightly faster. Leave enough time after these pickups so that you are not winded at the start.

If the weather is exceptionally hot, consider cutting back on your warmup. This will help you conserve energy and avoid premature dehydration. In very hot, humid weather, you're far more likely to feel sluggish, so your primary concern should be staying cool until the race begins. In cold weather, on the other hand, be sure to allow for a full warmup, beginning with very easy jogging to ease your muscles into their working mode. Leave plenty of time to stretch, and to avoid tightening up again, keep moving until the race starts. Keep warm clothing layers on until the last possible minute.

Use your warmup to the best mental as well as physical advantage. Does the sight of other competitors before the race make you edgy? Then do your jogging and stretching on a lonely road away from the race site. Do you need to psych yourself up beforehand?

Use the time to quietly compose yourself and review your race strategy. Does focusing on the event make you more nervous? Some runners actually do better by socializing and joking around with friends until the gun goes off, saving their mental energy for the race itself. There is no right or wrong; different styles work for different runners.

Although it's good to have a set warmup routine, try not to reach the point of superstition or phobia. Many runners have set patterns that they follow before a race for good luck. They may have raced well one day after warming up in a certain pair of shoes or after eating a particular brand of bagel, so now they feel that they must always do so. But what happens if your shoes get lost on the way to the race or if you don't arrive in time for your regular warmup? What if the store is out of cinnamon-raisin? Does that mean your race is ruined? Beware of any rigidity in thinking. It can set you up for failure.

Chris McNamara, a professional runner from Boulder, Colorado, who won the USA Women's 10-Mile Championship in 1997 in horrendously humid conditions, cautions that runners should "always be prepared to be surprised." "It's good to have a routine, but don't be too rigorous," she says. "You must be flexible within that routine. If you really must have something, like a particular drink, then bring it with you. Don't leave it to chance."

And don't obsess if something doesn't go as planned before the race. Great races have been run by competitors who have had all kinds of crazy mishaps and distractions beforehand or even during the race. Perhaps the most important element of your warmup is a continual reminder to yourself that nothing will get in the way of your having a good race: not heat, not wind, not bad convenience-store coffee, not even lost racing shoes. It's far better to believe that you are the kind of woman who runs well no matter what the circumstances than to believe that you run well only under certain circumstances.

## BE A TORTOISE

Hands down, the most common way for a runner to "blow" a race is to start off too fast. When the gun goes off and other runners shoot out quickly, it takes great confidence to maintain your race plan and your pace. You must exercise ferocious self-control, or you run the risk of derailing the rest of your race because of a rash decision made in the first few minutes of excitement. Keep in mind that because you feel fresh and eager, your pace will feel deceptively slow. You may feel so good that you're sure you can go faster. Use caution: Chances are that you're running faster than your body clock is telling you.

Remind yourself to run your own race. Some competitors literally get carried away by staying with (or passing!) faster runners because it suddenly seems like the "right" pace to run. Most of these rabbits end up paying the price and slowing after a mile or two, when they find out that they've run beyond their ability. There's no way you can win by following somebody else's race strategy. It's far better to lose 10 to 15 seconds at the start of the race than it is to lose a minute or two— or five—at the end when you find yourself in severe oxygen debt.

A bad habit of going out too fast can be hard to break. Here are a few tips to help you overcome the urge.

**Put on mental blinders at the start of your next race.** Focus only on yourself, and don't be distracted by what other runners are doing. Tell yourself that the only mistake you can make is going out too fast; then force yourself to hold back, especially for the first 400 meters. After that, the initial adrenaline rush will be out of your system, and you can more accurately gauge how fast you are running and whether you should pick up the pace.

**Line up with a similar runner.** Look for a friend or training partner who runs at your pace but knows how to pace herself. If she's a seasoned racer, that's even better.

**Check your times.** Measure the first quarter- or half-mile marks on the course by bicycle or by car prior to the race. Calculate what time you should hit these marks based on your optimal race pace. Then check your times during the race. Although this takes a little work, it might be worth it. Most races will have the first mile marked, but at that point it's probably too late if you've gone out too fast.

## A STEADY PACE IS THE WAY TO GO

Over the years, a number of studies have shown that the fastest races are generally those run at an even pace. This means that you stand the greatest chance of running your best race when you can complete the second half of the race in the same time that (or faster than) you ran the first half. Runners who start off fast in the hopes of "putting time in the bank" typically slow down, losing more time than they gained in the first place.

The goal, then, is to shoot for the pace that will allow you to run evenly throughout the race. Tempo runs and track workouts can help you predict this pace. But times—seemingly so objective— can be misleading guidelines, since hills, weather, and running surfaces will all affect the speed of a particular race course. Ultimately, it can be more useful to rely on the way your body feels. Your workouts are the best gauge for giving you a sense of pacing and an understanding of the effort that you can maintain over a given distance. Although you can certainly look at your watch for guidance during the race, always pay attention to your body signals first and foremost. If the ideal pace that you predicted feels far too hard early on, back off. If you are halfway through the race and you feel like it's your day for a breakthrough, don't let the time on your watch scare you into slowing down.

Although your *pace* should remain consistent over the course of a race, your *effort* will not. The same pace will feel like a walk in the park at the start of a race compared with how it will feel at the end. Remember this as the miles tick by. "As you grow more tired, the same pace will feel harder and harder," says Willie Rios, of Boulder, Colorado, who specializes in coaching women distance runners. "That means that if you feel too comfortable toward the end of a race, chances are that you've lost concentration and slowed down." One way to ensure that you stay at your target pace is to choose regular intervals at which to check in with your body. Crank up your effort a notch if you've lost concentration and let your pace slip.

## HOW TO HANG TOUGH

Coaches and spectators often admonish runners to hang tough in a race. But just how do you do that? What goes on in the mind during a race is a highly individual thing. Every runner tends to develop her own secrets of success when the race grows difficult. Here are a few examples of how to practice race toughness.

**Concentrate on what's in front of you.** When you feel yourself struggling, it can be devastating to try to envision yourself maintaining your pace for several more miles. Instead, concentrate on maintaining your pace just for the next mile. Toward the end of the race, you may need to think even shorter-term: Make your goal to

Professional runners need to be experts at racing well. Their careers depend on their abilities to deliver consistent results. Here, the elites share their secrets.

● "Prioritize your races and focus on a select few. Mentally and physically, you can't treat them all with the same intensity. My coach and I will sit down and decide what the most important thing is in the coming year: nationals or a major race. There will be other races in the interim, but I won't emphasize them as much."

**—Shelly Steely**
four-time World Championship cross-country team member

● "Sometimes I'll go back and reread my training logbook before a race. This can help when you start to question your readiness. You realize that you trained, you did the work, and you're fit. You end up saying, 'Oh, all right, I'm ready to race.'"

**—Jane Welzel**
five-time Olympic Marathon Trials qualifier

● "I tell myself that I can't compare myself with others. The competition does help me to go beyond my own limits, but I remind myself that I am competing ultimately to go beyond my own self, not others. In racing, it's important to respect others and not to underestimate the competition—but you should respect yourself the same way!"

**—Nadia Prasad**
1995 French national 10,000-meter champion

hold your pace to the next block, or even to the next telephone pole. When you reach your target, pick another one, and repeat the process as needed.

This strategy works because, though you might not believe that you can hold on for the rest of the race, you do know that you can

● "It helps to break the race into segments, like each mile or every few kilometers in a 10-K. The first section you can think of as a warmup. In the middle section, you should be prepared to feel up and down, good and bad, just like in an interval workout, where one might be yucky but the next you feel better. Then— the last 1000 meters or mile—you are close to the end, so it shouldn't be too hard mentally, but physically you must keep it going. The key is knowing that you'll feel better and worse at different points. By anticipating that, you can keep running strong."

**—Chris McNamara**
1997 USA Women's 10-Mile Championship winner

● "Nearing the end of a race, I internalize as much as possible and eliminate distractions. That means, instead of saying, 'Oh, God, somebody's closing in on me,' I focus my mind inward, using it to relax my shoulders, my ankle flex, all the parts of my body. That way, when I'm starting to strain, it pulls me back inward, and I can put all my energy into making myself go as fast as I can. It's one thing to say, 'Go hard at the finish,' but this gives you a way to lose all the distractions and pull it all together to make it happen."

**—Libbie Hickman**
1997 USA Track and Field National champion
in the women's 5000-meter

hold on for one more block. String those blocks together, and you'll have finished the race.

**Count to 10.** This is similar to breaking the course into short segments, as it helps you to maintain your pace for a less intimidating chunk of time. Count your footsteps up to 10 over and over again in order to concentrate on the task at hand.

## TRAINING LOG

*T*he races of which I am most proud are not necessarily my fastest or the ones that I won. Triumph in racing can take many forms, as can disappointment. Indeed, it is a seventh-place finish in a small, local event that stands out as one of my favorite races. It was the first running of the Pearl Street Mile in my adopted hometown of Boulder, Colorado—and therein lies the catch. Since many world- and national-class athletes live here in order to train under optimal conditions, the elite field was stacked with hotshots as well as plenty of once-weres and wannabes.

My coach had encouraged me to enter the elite field instead of the all-comers' category. I had come off a yearlong break and had been training hard for all of 2 months in my new town with my new coach. Although I was excited to test myself, I expected the usual nervousness to afflict me at the start. Much to my surprise, it didn't.

While warming up, I saw all manner of tough competition, including a whole team of Japanese runners. When I started to feel intimidated, I shifted my focus to one of excitement: It was energizing to be a part of such a field. I thought back on the workouts I had done over the past 8 weeks in preparation for the event. I felt confident. Most important, when I stepped on the starting line, I felt that I belonged among these athletes.

When the race started, I stuck to my plan. I felt in my bones that I had perfectly targeted my pace, drilled into my very fiber from track workouts. For the entire race, I truly believed that I could win, no matter the caliber of the women

**Check in with your body.** Run down how you feel from head to toe. Consciously relax your eyes, jaws, neck, shoulders, arms, and feet. Correct your posture. Check your footfall. Instead of focusing on fatigue, make sure that you are running as efficiently as possible. If you need to, when you reach your toes, start over and check yourself again.

*I was running against. Noting the competition in this manner was different from anything else I had felt in a race before: It was less a matter of worrying about them than of feeling absolutely confident and certain that I was running my best race.*

*I didn't win, but I never gave up. After the turnaround at the halfway point came the tough part, as the course became slightly uphill. I ticked off the blocks on the home stretch, making every step count as I never had before. Because I had followed my own game plan at the start, I was able to give everything I had and maintain my pace. Passing several runners in the last half mile, I finished in 5:17, good for seventh place and a personal best at altitude.*

*Now, that time won't go down in the annals of running history, but for me it felt glorious. The feeling of accomplishment I had after that race resonated far more than other efforts, even victorious ones. I felt as if I finally knew what it meant to execute every step of a race properly, to truly know that I had done my best, not to wonder, What if . . . ? or to think, I could have . . . or, I should have. . . .*

*I haven't been able to replicate that feeling in every race since then, and I eventually realized that it was foolish to believe that I could. Instead, I think of that race as my benchmark, my touchstone of what I am capable of. Why did it all come together then? It comes down to that ineffable mystery dance of mind and body. My brief training log entry from the day before that race does, however, present a strong clue: "Feeling confident heading into race."*

**Talk to yourself.** If you can manage to convince yourself that you won't be able to hold on, then you can certainly convince yourself that you will. Remind yourself of the hard training you've done. Tell yourself you love (fill in the blank): heat, hills, wind, whatever it is that's plaguing you. You can even tell yourself that you love the feeling of being tired because you thrive on a challenge and know you can rise above it. Do whatever it takes, even if it seems silly. Some runners tell themselves that they are warriors who feel no pain; others pretend that they are soaring birds. Some just tell themselves that they're the best damn runner out on the course that day.

**Become the meaning of tough.** The bottom line is that to race well, you must be "capable of enduring strain, hardship, or severe labor." That, by the way, is the definition of the word *tough*. There is no fancy way around it. Some runners do best to dispense with the mental gymnastics and attack the beast head-on. When you are running at the limits of your potential, it will hurt. When you feel that discomfort, it's a reminder of the task that you have set for yourself. Don't give in, and you will reap the rewards of knowing that you've done your best.

# WHY YOU CAN'T LOSE

What if, despite your best efforts, you didn't reach your goal? Perhaps you didn't hit the PR you felt certain that you could, or perhaps you started off too fast and died, or perhaps you didn't finish in the top three as you'd hoped. Not meeting a goal can be disappointing. Depending on the amount of training you've done, it can even feel devastating. But it's not a failure.

Races are simply a measurement of where you stand on a given day. They are best treated as information. Granted, you might like the information better when you run well, but you learn more when your run doesn't go exactly as planned. Did you fade on the hills? You might need to work on strength. Did you get so nervous beforehand that your legs felt like gelatin? Some mental training is in order. Did you misgauge your speed? Track sessions can help develop your sense of pace.

Avoid the misguided temptation to blindly increase your training in response to a poor race. "It's very typical for people to set standards too high, then to get disappointed after they race," says longtime competitor Shelly Steely. "They might not have rested enough, or their goal was unrealistic. So then they try to do more in training, when in reality what they need is to do even less, or to approach their training differently." Steely knows what she's talking about. After competing at a world-class level in the early 1990s and finishing seventh in the 1992 Olympic 3000-meter, she found herself floundering and racing far below her potential. After pinpointing the problem—a hormonal imbalance—she spent years patiently adjusting her training to find a formula that worked for her. By 1997, despite a busy schedule that allowed her to train far less than most of her competitors, her results once again ranked her among the top road racers in the United States. In 1998, she won the USA Track and Field Grand Prix road running circuit.

Every race can teach you something, if you are willing to pay attention. This attitude not only makes the last race feel a little better, but it also makes the next one a little less frightening. By keeping a positive outlook, you can walk away from every race having won something.

# 9

# Conquer the Marathon

A GREEK SOLDIER IN 490 B.C. named Pheidippides ran 26 miles from Marathon to Athens to deliver word of a Greek victory over the invading Persians. After uttering the words, "Rejoice, we conquer," he collapsed and died. There's some doubt as to the truth of this story, but from it a legend, and the marathon, were born. Since the modern Olympic Games were revived in 1896, the 26.2-mile odyssey has been considered the ultimate test of machismo, a rite of passage for relatively few diehards. And those diehards have virtually all been male. It wasn't until 1984 that the women's marathon became an official Olympic event.

But leave it to women to reinvent the event. In the 1990s, women succeeded in creating a wonderful oxymoron: the kinder, gentler marathon. No longer a testosterone-fest of thin, driven men, the marathon has been cheerfully overrun by women of all ages and abilities—and reshaped in their image. In 1998, the Suzuki Rock 'n' Roll Marathon in San Diego was the largest inaugural marathon ever, with almost 20,000 entries. And it made history for another reason: For the first time, more than half the field of runners in a marathon was female.

Who are these new women marathoners swelling the ranks of the pack? Many are beginners who want to experience marathon magic; for many of them, a fast time is not important. Participants now combine running and walking in whatever combination it takes to get to the finish in one piece. Some women run to raise money for charity. Some decide to enter races with groups of friends for a social outing. Some women choose a race based on a travel destination and build a minivacation around the event. Some just want to test themselves in "the big one." All have one thing in common: a focus on having an enjoyable marathon experience. In the process, these women have proved that a marathon can be completed in relative comfort.

This is not to that say all the women are at the back of the pack. Indeed, women have created a renaissance at the other end of the spectrum as well. The historic Boston Marathon, with its mandatory qualifying standards, draws the country's upper echelon of marathoners. In 1993, 1,854 women entered the race, accounting for 21 percent of all its runners. By 1998—just 5 years later—the number of women entrants had almost doubled, with 3,549 females accounting for 31 percent of the marathon's runners.

That's phenomenal progress considering that just a generation ago, the Amateur Athletic Union prohibited women from running the distance. The first woman to run the Boston Marathon, Roberta Gibb, did so unofficially in 1966, after officials refused to give her an entry form. She ran much of the way disguised in a hooded sweatshirt, finishing in a phenomenal 3 hours, 20 minutes. The next year, women were still banned, but Kathrine Switzer made history as the first woman to run officially, registering only as K. V. Switzer. Things got physical when a race organizer attempted to remove Switzer's race number after 4 miles, but she still finished the race. The famous incident, captured in photographs and run on the front pages of newspapers around the world the next day, helped to open the door for female runners. "Running gave me a sense of achievement and confidence," Switzer says. "I always felt like I was a hero in my own life. It makes sense that so many other women have discovered the endless fascination of pushing beyond their limits."

In a way, the marathon has become two events. For those who simply want to finish, it has become the sports world's biggest block party. For those who wish to race a certain time, it remains running's greatest challenge. Both approaches, however, require challenging preparation. Here you'll find training schedules and tips for finishing a marathon comfortably and for finishing one fast. The workout programs were developed in conjunction with Maureen Roben, cofounder and codirector of Women's Running Camps in Denver and a five-time Olympic Trials Marathon qualifier.

## WHEN YOUR GOAL IS TO FINISH

"I'm going to do a marathon." More recreational women runners are uttering those words every year, surprising family, friends, coworkers, and even themselves. Heather, 27, is typical. After years of inactivity, she joined a running group, completing 1 mile in her first workout. Two months later, she'd worked up to 13 miles

• Purchase a second pair of training shoes. Running additional miles means more stress on your shoes and your legs. Alternating runs between two pairs of shoes—preferably different models—can extend the life of each pair by allowing the spongy midsole to recover. It also lowers your injury risk from the repetitive motion of all those miles in one type of shoe.

• Train yourself to eat and drink on the run. Taking in calories and fluid while you run can extend your energy, but your system will need to adapt to liquid sloshing in your stomach and sugar coursing through your blood. A good time to practice is on your long runs. Put a packet of energy gel in a pocket, or pin one to your shorts. You can carry water or a sports drink in a bottle or in one of the specially crafted hydration devices on the market. Or drive your long-run route before you run and stash bottles every 3 miles or so. Ideally, you want to take in 100 to 300 calories during every hour of your training runs and race.

• If you're racing for time, you'll want to practice grabbing a cup and drinking while you're running. Don't laugh: It can be surprisingly tricky. Sometimes you're lucky to get a sip while the rest goes up your nose and down your chest. Set a table in your driveway and put out paper cups containing a sports drink. Practice

and was well on her way to her first marathon. "I'd always toyed with the idea of running a marathon, but that was all," Heather says. "It sounded—and still does—like such an insurmountable challenge. I thought that people who ran marathons were athletes, nimble race horses with a different genetic code.

"I still don't consider myself an athlete per se. When I joined the running group, it rekindled thoughts that maybe I could do this. I was hooked by the progression. I like how supportive the group is and the challenge. Each week, in the deep recesses of my brain, I fear that this is the week I will figure out I'm not a marathon runner. It hasn't happened yet."

For women like Heather, the marathon is not a cut-and-dried, 1-day effort of 26.2 miles. It is a challenge that illuminates the depths of your fortitude. As with so many things, what you get out

running by and grabbing a cup. To avoid spilling, pinch the top of the cup closed as soon as you grab it; then drink from the resulting "V" in the cup.

● Get creative with training partners. Even runners who like to go it alone find that they enjoy company on the long runs leading up to a marathon. Three hours or more is a long time to be on the road alone. If none of your friends is on the same training plan, schedule your run so that a friend can run part of it with you. Some runners even schedule several friends to take turns joining in on loops of the same run.

● Test out the shoes and clothes you'll be racing in. Whatever you wear in the race should be tested during the long runs leading up to your race. A bra that seems comfortable on a short run might begin to chafe terribly after an hour, and you don't want to wait until race day to find out about it. Never use anything—clothes, food, and so on—on marathon day that you have not tested out during a longer run.

● Eat right, take a good multivitamin, and get plenty of sleep. Marathon training asks a lot of your body. Several studies have shown that long runs can temporarily suppress immunity, making marathoners more susceptible to colds and flu. Pamper yourself while you are training so that when you arrive at the big event, you'll be in optimal health.

of a marathon depends on what you put into it. In this case, the more careful and complete your preparation, the more enjoyable your experience will be. Here are some tips to keep in mind while you train.

**Focus on your long runs.** The most important part of any marathon training program is the long run. The purpose of long runs is to strengthen your legs and body and to develop the fitness of your cardiovascular system so that they can withstand the rigors of the marathon distance. Be sure to get the majority of these workouts in; if you have to skip a day, forgo one of the shorter runs during the week.

You'll notice that the long runs in this program increase steadily until you top 2 hours in length; then you have "shorter" long runs interspersed. The reason for this is that runs of this duration can be very stressful on your body. This program increases your workload while giving you a break every now and then to avoid burnout and injury.

Keep these additional points in mind for successful long runs.

- Walk early and often in order to go the distance. Roben refers to the length of these workouts not by the amount of running but by "total time on your feet." It's assumed that you'll spend some time walking. Walk for 1 minute after every mile or after every 10 minutes of running.

- Find a safe, pleasant route. Look for a soft surface away from traffic. A dirt road or a grassy area in a large park is ideal. If you are not sure where to find such a location, ask at your local running store or contact the local running club.

- Consume a sports drink. You'll be exerting yourself for several hours in these workouts, so be sure to stay hydrated. A sports drink, rather than plain water, can replenish much-needed carbohydrates and electrolytes along the way. Stash a bottle or two along your route before you run.

**Pay attention to time, not miles.** As in the beginning and intermediate programs, this training program will have you running by length of time as opposed to distance. Running by the clock is simple and more convenient for most women because they don't necessarily have measured routes nearby. It is also less intimidating for first-time marathoners, who may find that a 20-mile training run sounds rather impossible. Obviously, different women will run these workouts at different paces, which means that some will cover more miles than others. Don't worry about your mileage in this program.

Some beginners feel that they must cover a full 26.2 miles on a training day before the race so that they know they can go the distance. But this can do more harm than good. The longest run in this program is 3½ hours, enough for a woman running 10-minute miles to cover 21 miles. That's the most any runner need cover before tackling a marathon. But most important, even if you are going slower than 10 minutes per mile, *you needn't run any farther*. Three-and-a-half hours should be considered the upper limit for any training run, no matter what mileage you cover. Anything longer and you risk getting injured or sick before the race. Trust that if you've gotten through a several-hour training run, the cumulative effects of your training, the excitement of race day, and the benefit of being rested will get you the rest of the way when it counts.

**Be flexible.** Rigidity is a good way to get injured or sick. Adapt the schedule to your own needs and commitments. If the weather is bad or if you must work late on a Wednesday, run on Thursday. If you must switch days, space your runs so that you're not working out 3 or 4 days in a row, then skipping 3. The schedule puts long runs on the weekends because that's when most people have the time. Note that off days surround the long run; try to maintain that pattern if you flip days around. If you must miss a day, try to skip one of the shorter runs during the week instead of the long run.

**Build in some rest.** Note that Weeks 8, 11, and 14 in the schedule are rest weeks. You won't stop running, but you will decrease your training time considerably by reducing your long runs. This gives your body a chance to recover from your training, and it builds in a "safety valve" to avoid injury and exhaustion. Again, feel free to adapt this to your own schedule. If you know that you have an exceptionally hard week coming up at work or that you will be gone on vacation, that might be a good time for your rest week. Just swap the week you'll miss with the one before or after.

**Find a partner or running group.** Many women love to run alone. The marathon is one undertaking you do not want to attempt in isolation. You can still do plenty of training by yourself,

# Marathon Checklist

**A** lot can happen during a run of 26.2 miles. The more prepared you are, the fewer things you leave to chance. Use this checklist to make sure your marathon goes as smoothly as possible.

### The day before the race:

● Pick up your race number and information. These are usually available at the race expo, which is a prerace event that features running-product retailers and organizations. Consult your entry form for information.

● Prepare a bag with clothes, shoes, your race number, and anything else you will want the morning of the race. This might include petroleum jelly for toes, underarms, and around your bra line; energy bars and gel; a water bottle; sunscreen; a baseball cap; and additional warm clothes.

● Pin your race number to the top you'll be wearing during the race. Prepare a pouch with whatever you need to carry for the race, such as toilet paper and energy gel packets, or pin those items to your shorts.

● Gather some "disposable" warm clothes to wear at the start. An old T-shirt and a pair of socks for your hands can keep you warm at the starting line, and you can discard these before the race begins or after a few miles when you've warmed up. If it's raining, a large garbage bag with a hole poked in it for your head will keep you dry.

● Figure out race-day logistics. Where are you going to park? Where will you meet friends after the race? How will you get back to the start? Remember that many roads are closed the morning of the race, so consult your race information packet and plan accordingly.

● Eat a dinner that's high in carbohydrates and not so high in fiber. Do not eat any foods you are not used to.

but running partners and groups make long runs far more bearable. To find partners, check your local newspaper, road runner's club, athletic clubs, running stores, and colleges.

**Choose your race carefully.** Completing a marathon can make an ordinary runner feel like a hero. Courses are lined with bands

● Drink plenty of liquids to ensure that you start off the morning hydrated.

● Try to relax. And by the way, a few sips of beer won't hurt you. It might even help you sleep.

**The morning of the race:**

● Don't panic if you didn't sleep well. (Almost nobody does.) The night before the race matters much less than your sleep habits during the week leading up to the race.

● Wake up at least 2 hours before the race. Eat a light meal, such as a banana and a bagel. Don't eat anything unfamiliar. Avoid foods that are high in fiber, or you'll be making pit stops during the race.

● Drink some water or sports drink, but stop drinking a half-hour before the race. That will give you time to go to the bathroom before the start.

● Apply a thin layer of petroleum jelly anywhere you have chafing problems. Typical areas are the underarms, inner thighs, under the bra band, and toes. Go easy on the toes; too much can make them slippery, which can contribute to blistering.

● Jog slowly for a few minutes and then stretch before the start to loosen up. Recreational runners needn't do long warmups; they can use the first mile to ease into their paces. Serious racers should still limit their warmups. A mile of jogging and a few strides and stretches are enough for most women. Any more than that is a waste of energy.

● Position yourself on the starting line according to your predicted pace. Large races will post signs as guides along the starting area, marked "6-minute mile," "7-minute mile," and so on.

and entertainment. Cities turn out to cheer participants for miles on end. Food, drink, music, and a coveted finisher's medal await runners at the finish, along with a supreme feeling of accomplishment. But frankly, all races are not created equal. When choosing a first-time marathon where the emphasis is on fun, research your choices. Sometimes the best race will not be the one in your backyard. Consider the following:

- Size. In general, the larger the event, the more race-related activities and entertainment it will include. Also, more runners means more company out on the course. (Twenty-six miles can get awfully lonely when there are only 500 other runners spaced out over a long distance.)

- The course. City courses tend to have more crowd support. Don't underestimate the power of thousands of screaming fans when the going gets tough. Rural courses are much quieter but often very beautiful. Think about which of the two better fits your personality.

- Hills and altitude. Both can make the race much tougher to complete. These are often described on the race's entry form, or you can call the race information number to inquire.

- Average race temperature. The hotter and more humid the race conditions, the harder the marathon will feel. Ideally, you want to run a marathon with low humidity and temperatures in the mid-60s.

Check out *Runner's World* magazine or www.runnersworld.com for information on races throughout the country.

**Give yourself plenty of time to train.** Depending on your starting point, 5 to 6 months is a reasonable amount of time to prepare for a marathon. The program offered here assumes that you can run comfortably for 30 minutes four times a week. Work up to that point first, if necessary, and then choose a race no sooner than 5 months out.

By leaving a few extra weeks in the plan, you'll allow for setbacks. An old saying goes, "The one guarantee in marathons is that nothing is guaranteed." That goes for the training as well as for the

## Beginner Marathon Training Schedule

| | MON | TUES | WED | THURS | FRI | SAT | SUN |
|---|---|---|---|---|---|---|---|
| Week 1 | Off | 30 min | 30 min | Off | 30 min | Off | 40 min |
| Week 2 | Off | 30 min | 35 min | Off | 30 min | Off | 50 min |
| Week 3 | Off | 30 min | 35 min | Off | 30 min | Off | 1 hr |
| Week 4 | Off | 30 min | 35 min | Off | 30 min | Off | 1 hr, 15 min |
| Week 5 | Off | 20 min | 40 min | Off | 30 min | Off | 1 hr, 30 min |
| Week 6 | Off | 20 min | 40 min | Off | 30 min | Off | 1 hr, 45 min |
| Week 7 | Off | 20 min | 40 min | Off | 30 min | Off | 2 hrs |
| Week 8 | Off | 20 min | Off | Off | 20 min | Off | 1 hr |
| Week 9 | Off | 20 min | 40 min | Off | 30 min | Off | 2 hrs, 15 min |
| Week 10 | Off | 20 min | 45 min | Off | 30 min | Off | 2 hrs, 30 min |
| Week 11 | Off | 20 min | 45 min | Off | 30 min | Off | 1 hr |
| Week 12 | Off | 20 min | 45 min | Off | 30 min | Off | 2 hrs, 45 min |
| Week 13 | Off | 20 min | 45 min | Off | 30 min | Off | 3 hrs |
| Week 14 | Off | 30 min | 45 min | Off | 30 min | Off | 1 hr |
| Week 15 | Off | 30 min | 45 min | Off | 30 min | Off | 3 hrs, 15 min |
| Week 16 | Off | 30 min | 45 min | Off | 30 min | Off | 3 hrs, 30 min |
| Week 17 | Off | 30 min | 45 min | Off | 30 min | Off | 1 hr |
| Week 18 | Off | 20 min | 30 min | Off | 30 min | Off | 45 min |
| Week 19 | Off | 20 min | 20 min | Off | 20 min | Off | Race |

racing. But you can minimize the impact of setbacks by giving yourself plenty of time to reach marathon fitness. That way, a week off due to a cold, an unexpected business trip, or a family emergency won't throw your schedule out of whack.

If you do miss some workouts, do not attempt to "cram" and run extra to make up the miles. If you miss a long run, do not jump up to the next level. Rather, pick up where you left off. If you miss time due to an illness, you may need to spend a week easing back into your schedule with some shorter runs. Then pick up where you left off. If you have planned some flextime into your training schedule, you'll still be on target. If you miss several weeks or a month of training, however, consider rescheduling your race.

**Listen to your body, then be nice to it.** Staying healthy is perhaps the toughest part of marathon training. You must train enough to achieve proper conditioning. You must not train so much that the stress leads to exhaustion, injury, or illness. It's a fine line. Beginning runners in particular risk overdoing it because they are not as familiar with signs of overtraining. Abnormal aches and pains, a sore throat, difficulty sleeping, a higher-than-usual resting heart rate: These are all warning flags. If in doubt, skip 1 day's run rather than grind through a workout that leaves you sick, exhausted, and demoralized.

This point bears repeating. Women are notorious for denying their own needs even when symptoms of stress are obvious. They focus on family, work, and even friends before themselves. If you want to make it to the starting line, you must make a commitment to taking care of yourself well through the training process. That means eating well, getting enough rest, and even taking time for a hot bath or massage when the going gets very tough. Not a bad lesson to learn.

## WHEN YOUR GOAL IS TO RACE

Racing a marathon is unlike racing any other distance. Because of the length of the race, a slight miscalculation in pace can be magnified tenfold at the end. Ailments and discomforts can crop up after miles of smooth sailing. Everything from a slight breeze to a wrinkle in your socks can seem monstrous after the 20-mile mark. "In the marathon, even when the race is going as planned, you will get to the point where you question your existence," says Willie Rios, of Boulder, Colorado, who specializes in coaching women distance runners. "What you do then is up to you—and the training you've done."

When you decide to see how fast you can run a marathon, you enter a new realm. Put bluntly, you open yourself up to the big bonk. Plenty of runners can tell stories of trotting along happily on pace only to tie up around 20 miles, losing 2, 3, or even 5 minutes per mile. That's why the greatest challenge of racing the marathon is pacing. It requires great patience to go more slowly than feels comfortable at first. It then requires great fortitude to maintain that same pace at the end of the race. And, perhaps most of all, it requires tremendous self-knowledge to figure out what that target pace should be.

"The key to running the marathon is accurately determining the shape you are actually in and running it at an even pace," says Jane Welzel, of Fort Collins, Colorado, a five-time Olympic Marathon Trials qualifier and a masters runner standout with more than 50 marathons under her belt. She explains that determining

# smart
## tips

**Follow these tips to have fun and run a great race.**

● **Start conservatively.** When you think you're at the right pace, slow it down one more notch. Between having rested for weeks and the excitement of the start, you'll be fueled with so much energy that you're likely to almost fly through your first mile. The biggest mistake you can make in a marathon is to start off too fast. This event is an exercise in patience. Look at it this way: Starting 10, 20, or even 30 seconds slower per mile than planned is a heck of a lot better than slowing by several minutes a mile at the end.

● **Drink early and often.** Don't wait until you feel thirsty. Begin at the first available water stop, even if it means drinking just a sip or two. One of the most common mistakes marathoners make is consuming too little liquid and too few calories.

● **Maintain your form.** Everyone's body has a natural tendency to tire in a certain manner. Some women find that their shoulders hunch up; others bend forward at the waist; others start taking tiny strides. The more you allow yourself to deviate from proper form, the harder you are making your body work to move forward. Try using the mile markers as reminders to do a form check. Take this time to relax every part of your body and regain proper running form.

your target pace takes both practice and intuition. "On race day, everything goes out the window. It could be hot, cold, or windy, or you might just not be 'on.' So everything at that point must be based on how you feel. And you learn to trust that by practicing. In training, I pay attention to how my body feels, learning what it feels like, for example, for my body to know that I can do such-and-such a pace for this distance. It might not be as fast as I thought or wanted, but that's not the point."

The workout schedule offered here assumes that you are an intermediate-level runner who has been training three to five times a week for at least a year and who has some experience with in-

## smart
### tips

After the marathon, be sure to follow these tips for a quick and full recovery.

● Drink plenty of fluids and eat immediately. The sooner you refuel, the better off your immune system and your muscles will be. If you don't feel hungry after the race due to the intensity of your effort, seek out a food that goes down easily, such as a fruit smoothie or milkshake. This is one time that you might want to ignore your body's signals and eat more than you feel like eating.

● Get to your warm clothes, or use the race blankets handed out by volunteers.

● To ease sore muscles, jump into the pool if you have access to one. An ocean or lake will also do. Although a hot tub or a toasty bath might sound good, a cold bath—even one with ice in it—will be better for your legs.

● Don't plan on running for a few weeks. You've earned a break; now let your body recover.

terval and tempo workouts. If you are not, this program will likely be too difficult. It is very challenging to run fast-paced workouts while you are increasing your distance. If you are not ready for this program but still wish to challenge yourself, try using the training schedule from the first half of the chapter, each week replacing one of the easy runs with a tempo or interval workout from this schedule.

**Concentrate on quality, not quantity.** Many women think that if they're going to race a marathon, they must log 60, 70, or 80 miles a week. That thinking is not only untrue but also dangerous. Too many miles can make you sick or injured—or both. "The whole goal in training—especially marathon training—is to get the most out of the least," Roben says. "People become so crazed with big mileage totals, when the trick really should be how *little* you can do—especially when you have a real life!"

Excellent preparation can be accomplished with 5 days of training a week; 6 is the maximum most women should do. A day or two of rest will allow your body to more fully recover and to come back with strength for the next series of workouts. "I tell my compulsive types, who absolutely must do something every day, to go for a walk or a swim," Roben says. "But make sure that those alternate activities are something gentle. It defeats the purpose to go and Spin your brains out."

**Focus on your long runs.** Literally, that is. If you want to race, unlike the runner who just wants to complete the distance, you should *not* treat long runs as "time on your feet." "The long run is something you should really put mental energy into," Welzel says. "Even though they're not all at race pace, this is the place you really have a chance to learn your body and how it will respond in a long race."

The training program offered here combines two approaches to long runs—slow and fast—for a number of beneficial results. You'll note that once the long run reaches 14 miles, the weekends alternate, one weekend with a run increasing by 2 miles, the next weekend with a run of 10 to 12 miles. Although the primary reason for this is to avoid overtraining and injury, it also allows you to benefit from two different workout focuses.

*T*he marathon entered my running vocabulary only because a great number of my friends were planning to travel to the 100th running of the Boston Marathon in 1996. It was to be a huge bash, the most significant anniversary of the grandest footrace in the land—in short, a party not to be missed. There was one problem. Unlike most other marathons in the country, an entry form and a check aren't enough to get in. Boston has qualifying time standards based on age and sex; that meant I had to run 3:40 in another race first. Fair enough. I started training.

But something funny happened along the way. I found that I relished the weekend's long run. The harder the better. I felt great, held up well under the extra training, and grew stronger and faster. I had found my niche. A friend mentioned casually—jokingly—that a 2-hour, 50-minute marathon would get me into the Olympic Trials. And thus a dream I had laid aside ages ago quietly re-entered my heart. Don't get me wrong. I never believed that I could qualify for the team. But maybe, just maybe, I could qualify for the Trials race, also to be held in the spring of 1996.

My coach at the time warned against disappointment. Not enough time to shift gears in training, he said. I was running only 40 miles a week. Sure, I was doing great, but why not shoot for 3 hours, a goal I knew I could reach? Uh-huh, I nodded. Sensible. But when I lined up for the start of the Twin Cities Marathon in the fall of 1995, I knew that I was running with one purpose: to qualify for the Olympic Marathon Trials. I never wanted to be stuck wondering, What if?

For 20 miles, I ran perfectly on pace for my 2:50. Then, simply and inexorably, I ran out of gas. I finished in 2:55—and burst into tears. Faster than I'd ever dreamed, yet not fast enough. My coach, waiting at the finish, could not understand my sobs. Joy or sorrow, he asked, trying to help his exhausted, weeping athlete.

Joy or sorrow? Both. As pure a contradiction and as complete a spectrum of emotion as I have ever felt in my life. Welcome to the marathon.

The long runs of 14 miles and more should be run at whatever pace is comfortable for completion. Run as slowly as you wish; these workouts will condition your body to handle long distances.

The 10- to 12-milers on the alternating weeks should be faster, about 30 to 50 seconds per mile slower than your goal marathon race pace. The purpose of these workouts is to get your body used to pushing for an extended period and to become comfortable at an effort near your race pace.

The longest run in this program tops out at 20 to 22 miles. Although some competitive runners like to know beforehand that they can go the full marathon distance, it's best to save your legs for the rest of your training and the race.

**Determine your race pace based on training.** That might sound simple and obvious, but a common pitfall for marathoners is to choose a target time before beginning to train and then to stick to it no matter what. Such unrealistic thinking can lead to marathon disaster, when you go out at a pace far more challenging than you can handle.

A wiser approach is to begin training and see how your body responds. About midway through training (around the 8-week mark) you'll be ready to test the waters. Roben recommends using one of your 10- or 12-mile runs as a time trial, or jumping into a local half-marathon. The pace that you are able to run will be a good approximation of what you'll be able to handle for the marathon 2 months farther down the road.

**Train at race pace.** Many runners neglect this most basic aspect of training. "I've seen so many women who do track workouts at 6-minute pace and long runs at 8-minute pace, and then they go to the race and say, 'I'm going to run 6:30 pace'—and they have no idea what that feels like!" Welzel says. "You should be able to nail that race pace, any day, any time, whether you're tired or fresh. You need to be comfortable at that pace. You're going to ask your body to do it for 26 miles."

So incorporate race pace training into your workouts. Throw a mile or two of race pace into the middle or end of one of your long runs when you are on a measured course. Or begin one of your

## Advanced Marathon Training Schedule

| | MON | TUES | WED | THURS | FRI | SAT | SUN |
|---|---|---|---|---|---|---|---|
| **Week 1** | 4 mi easy | 1 hr with fartlek | Off | 2-mi warmup, 2-mi tempo, 2-mi cooldown | 3 mi easy | Off, or a few miles easy | 8 mi |
| **Week 2** | 4 mi easy | Track: 4 × 800 m | Off | 2-mi warmup, 2-mi tempo, 2-mi cooldown | 4 mi easy | Off, or a few miles easy | 9 mi |
| **Week 3** | 4 mi easy | 1 hr with fartlek | Off | 2-mi warmup, 3-mi tempo, 2-mi cooldown | 4 mi easy | Off, or a few miles easy | 10 mi |
| **Week 4** | 4 mi easy | Track: 4 × 1000 m | Off | 3-mi warmup, 3-mi tempo, 2-mi cooldown | 4 mi easy | Off, or a few miles easy | 12 mi |
| **Week 5** | 4 mi easy | 1 hr with fartlek | Off | 3-mi warmup, 3-mi tempo, 3-mi cooldown | 5 mi easy | Off, or a few miles easy | 14 mi |
| **Week 6** | 4 mi easy | Track: 5 × 800 m | Off | 3-mi warmup, 4-mi tempo, 3-mi cooldown | 5 mi easy | Off, or a few miles easy | 10 mi |
| **Week 7** | 4 mi easy | 1 hr with fartlek | Off | 3-mi warmup, 3-mi tempo, 3-mi cooldown | 5 mi easy | Off, or a few miles easy | 16 mi |
| **Week 8** | 4 mi easy | Track: 5 × 1000 m | Off | 3-mi warmup, 4-mi tempo, 3-mi cooldown | 5 mi easy | Off, or a few miles easy | 10-12 mi |
| **Week 9** | 4 mi easy | 1 hr with fartlek | Off | 3-mi warmup, 3-mi tempo, 3-mi cooldown | 6 mi easy | Off, or a few miles easy | 18 mi |

easy runs at the track, timing your first mile and hitting race pace. Go run the rest of the distance, then come back and time the last mile, again hitting race pace.

Roben has each of her runners go to the track and time 2 miles a few weeks before the race. The runner looks at her watch every 400 meters and comes as close as possible to hitting even splits for race pace. You'll find this workout in Week 15 of the training schedule.

**Do some training faster than race pace.** Your track sessions, fartlek, and tempo runs should be run faster than your marathon pace but no faster than 5-K pace. You don't need to develop sprint speed for the marathon, but you do want to develop enough speed

|  | MON | TUES | WED | THURS | FRI | SAT | SUN |
|---|---|---|---|---|---|---|---|
| **Week 10** | 4 mi easy | Track: 6 × 800 | Off | 2-mi warmup, 5-mi tempo, 2-mi cooldown | 6 mi easy | Off, or a few miles easy | 10-12 mi |
| **Week 11** | 4 mi easy | 1 hr with fartlek | Off | 3-mi warmup, 3-mi tempo, 3-mi cooldown | 6 mi easy | Off, or a few miles easy | 20 mi |
| **Week 12** | 4 mi easy | Track: 5 × 1000 m | Off | 2-mi warmup, 5-mi tempo, 2-mi cooldown | 6 mi easy | Off, or a few miles easy | 10-12 mi |
| **Week 13** | 4 mi easy | 1 hr with fartlek | Off | 3-mi warmup, 3-mi tempo, 3-mi cooldown | 4 mi easy | Off, or a few miles easy | 20-22 mi |
| **Week 14** | 3 mi easy | Track: 8 × 400 | Off | 2-mi warmup, 2-mi tempo, 2-mi cooldown | 4 mi easy | Off, or a few miles easy | 10-12 mi easy |
| **Week 15** | 3 mi easy | Track: 2 mi at race pace | Off | 5 mi with 10 × 100 strides | 4 mi easy | Off, or a few miles easy | 7 mi |
| **Week 16** | 3 mi easy | Track: 4 × 400 race pace, with 10 × 100 strides | Off | 4 mi with 10 × 100 strides | Off, or a few miles easy | 2 mi easy, with a few strides | Race |

NOTE: *If you are feeling especially tired in your training, you can turn a week into a "rest" week. Choose a week with a long run of only 10 to 12 miles so you don't miss the longer workouts. Then run only easy distance for the rest of the week's workouts.*

that your marathon race pace feels easy. Follow the guidelines below. (For more information on track, fartlek, and tempo runs, see chapters 6 and 7.)

- Track workouts. Warm up for 1 to 2 miles. Loosen up with eight high-intensity 100-meter strides. Then complete 800-meter and 1000-meter repeats at your 5-K pace. Jog 3 to 4 minutes between each repeat. Finish with a cooldown of 1 to 2 miles.

- Fartlek. Fartlek incorporates faster and slower speeds into one run that is conducted without stopping. Warm up with 10 to 15 minutes of easy running. Then alternate 3- to 6-minute periods of faster running with slower jogging intervals of 2 to 3 minutes. Shoot for a total of 18 to 24 minutes of up-tempo work, and run near or slightly slower than your 10-K race pace. For example, run six periods of 3 minutes, or four periods of 6 minutes. Cool down with 10 to 15 minutes of easy running.

● Tempo runs. Warm up for a few miles, as indicated in the schedule. When starting out with the 2-mile tempo runs, shoot for your 10-K pace. This pace will slow as the distance of the tempo run increases. Attempt to maintain even pacing throughout the run. Cool down as indicated in the schedule.

**Be flexible and smart.** Perhaps more than any other kind of training, marathon training pushes the fine line between working hard and overdoing it. Studies have shown that runners are more susceptible to colds and flu after long runs and while undertaking hard training. It's more important than ever to listen to your body when you're in the middle of your marathon training. Do not become a slave to your running schedule. If you feel run-down, take the day off. Likewise, if the weather is terrible and you have a hard workout planned, run easy that day and do the hard workout the next day. Be smart. Nothing is sacred about doing a certain workout on a particular day of the week.

**Enter the race well-rested.** During the last 3 weeks of training, you'll gradually wind down. The overall quantity of miles will drop, while a few faster efforts will keep your legs "sharp." Your body needs rest during these 3 weeks. Don't blow it! Some women get restless or sluggish when they cut back on training. Some don't trust their fitness and feel that they must run more. Some are afraid of putting on weight because of the lighter workload. All of these things are natural to feel, but none of them should be answered with a long run. Your body is storing energy. Allow it to do so.

# 10

# Solo or Social

FOR SOME WOMEN, running provides precious, sacred time alone, during which they can hear the sound of their breath and feet, have the freedom to think about whatever pops up, and relish the birds, the wind, and whatever else nature chooses to sprinkle across their paths.

For others, running becomes the heart and soul of their social lives, where great, looping conversation is punctuated with laughter so fierce that it ceases forward motion, where motivation to run comes from the promise of coffee and croissants miles down the road.

Most women choose a mix, their runs suiting their psyches on any given day. Some runs may be social and easy, where the company matters more than the workout. Others are hard training efforts, best done alone or with a familiar training partner. There is no better or worse; it's a matter of personal preference. In the end, the most important thing is to get what you need.

## RUNNING ALONE

Running is ultimately a solo sport. No one else will get your legs moving for you. No amount of support from a friend can keep you going when you've just plain conked out. Ultimately, running comes down to you and you alone. Perhaps that's why the sport tends to attract its share of loners. Nonrunners have been heard to ask, "How can you stand being out there alone for so long?" Plenty of runners think that solitude is the very crux of the sport. That time alone is as much the point of running for them as are a healthy heart and strong legs.

Indeed, not every woman wants to be alone with her thoughts for long periods of time. But for those who do, this time can be a wellspring of meditation, stress relief, and mental cooling off. Because the relaxed state that prevails during a run is con-

---

### IN YOUR OWN WORDS

## Do You Prefer to Run Alone or with Others?

*I prefer to run by myself because running is a way for me to do something for myself.*

**Kristyn**, 20, Caldwell, Idaho

*I prefer the company of good friends. It keeps me going and motivates me, especially when I am having a bad or off day.*

**Carolyn**, 42, Weiser, Idaho

*Alone, because I use it as cheap therapy!*

**Ann**, 36, Cleveland, Ohio

*Both—I love company, and I love some runs for solitude.*

**Patti**, 35, Boise, Idaho

*When I run alone, I don't have to worry about setting a comfortable pace for the other person. I can just run hard and fast or slow and easy depending on how I feel.*

**Gwen**, 40, Fort Worth, Texas

*I need both. My running partners help keep me going when I'm having trouble and give meaning to our triumphs. They are great, too, and understand when I need to be alone. Actually, I still run with my dog, so I'm not truly alone. She is so happy when we're out together, and I can't help but perk up if I'm down.*

**Betsy**, 33, Boise, Idaho

---

ducive to free-flowing thought and creativity, many women also consider it a time for problem solving. More than one work crisis has been solved during a lunch-hour run and its ensuing brainstorm.

Solo runs lend themselves well to all types of training. Because you set the pace, you can ensure that your recovery runs remain easy and that your harder efforts are tailored to your needs alone. When you run alone, you don't have to worry about being drawn into a run that's too long or too fast, or the opposite. And scheduling couldn't be easier: You can go when you have the time, and you aren't beholden to another runner's time demands.

For women, the main drawback of running alone is safety. Although safety during a run is largely a function of location, some women prefer never to be out alone. Others feel fine running alone at night in their neighborhoods. Ultimately, you must determine your own comfort level and act accordingly. (For information on running safety, see chapter 17.)

Other runners find that motivation is harder to come by when they play the part of the Lone Ranger. When it's just you heading to the door for a run, distractions and excuses can be more likely to trip you up on your way out. But for the most part, those who like to run solo tend to be highly motivated and won't let anything get in the way of their time alone.

## TRAINING WITH PARTNERS

A training partner can help provide the impetus to run when nothing else does. Just knowing that somebody is waiting at the park, or that the group is about to leave, can motivate you on days of lackluster energy. Many women also find that conversing during runs makes the time go by more quickly and enjoyably. Some groups initially gather for the running benefits but eventually come to value the socializing every bit as much.

The key to running with others is to find the right "others" to train with. Just because someone is your best friend doesn't mean that she's cut out to be your training partner. She might be too fast, too slow, too chatty, too quiet, too negative—too almost anything once it's just the two of you out on the road for 30 minutes or more at a stretch. If a nonrunning friend tends to carry over well into your new sport, it's a stroke of luck.

Ideally, running partners should be at similar points in their training. If you are a beginner, running with someone who can understand your struggles and share your triumphs may be comforting. If you're more advanced, you may appreciate a partner who can challenge you and provide feedback. Although it is possible for partners of mismatched abilities to work out together, it's trickier. (The faster runner can do an easy recovery workout, for example, when the other is scheduled for a harder effort.) On the other hand, some women prefer more a experienced partner, someone who can serve as a mentor.

The best running partner is also someone who shares or at least acknowledges your goals and enthusiasm. This goes for beginners and expert runners alike. "The people you train with determine your next level," says Ann Boyd, an elite runner and coach in Ann Arbor, Michigan. "And if the people you train with are bumming you out, then you have to do something to change your situation."

One of the pitfalls of running with others is that you are subjected to their mind-set, for better or worse. And just as some people can be inspirational and positive, others can be, well, downers. Negativity can take many forms, from subtle discouragement or lack of faith to downright disapproval. It can come from unlikely sources—a close friend who is threatened by her old friend's weight loss, or a husband who suddenly realizes that his wife can beat him soundly in a 5-K. All such disapproval has the same debilitating effect: It undermines your confidence.

"You have to have a belief in yourself that you can achieve what you set out to do," Boyd says. Having someone tell you that you can't, or that you shouldn't even be making the attempt, is a sure roadblock on the path to progress. If you find that you are getting a chilly response from training partners, don't be afraid to find new ones. As Boyd puts it, "Surround yourself with people who have the same aspirations, or who at least allow you to have those aspirations."

# RUNNING CLUBS

The best way for novice and intermediate runners to hook up with training partners is to join a local running club. These can range from structured institutions with dues to informal groups that meet regularly for workouts. Running clubs are a terrific way to meet other people with similar interests. Members typically represent a broad spectrum, from young to old, speedy to slow. You're almost guaranteed to find a partner at the level you need.

"The prevailing attitude at these clubs tends to be wonderfully welcoming," says Henley Gabeau, executive director of the Road Runners Club of America. "Especially for women who are tentative when they are beginning the sport, a club can provide great support."

You can tailor your involvement in such a group to suit your running needs. Clubs tend to hold organized runs once or twice during the week, but smaller groups often splinter off to meet at other times as well. Some hold track sessions and other harder workouts in addition to traditional easy distance runs. In all cases, you are free to run at your own pace and you can usually find somebody else of comparable ability to run with. Clubs can offer the benefit of training with a common goal in mind, too. Often, a running club will target a local race or a major event to travel to, then build a workout program for it and progress toward that goal over several months. The club may also offer coaching assistance, advice, and even customized workout schedules.

**smart tips**

To find a running club in your area, contact the Road Runners Club of America, 1150 South Washington Street, Suite 250, Alexandria, VA 22314. The club also has a Web site, www.rrca.org, which lists all the member clubs in the country. Executive director Henley Gabeau recommends that you also consult this resource if you are moving or if you want to find a group to run with while traveling.

# COACHES

It used to be that only school-age athletes and professionals used coaches. With the latest running boom, that's changed. Today, runners of all levels choose to benefit from external instruction and

## smart tips

Here's how to find a coach near you.

● Contact local running clubs, schools, and running specialty stores to get names of coaches in your area.

● Call or meet with the coach to discuss his or her running experience and approach to training and coaching.

● Ask to see a sample workout schedule for someone of similar ability.

● Attend a workout if that particular coach teaches groups. See if you feel comfortable in the environment. Talk to other runners and ask about pros and cons of the group.

● Coaching fees can vary greatly, from $25 to $30 per month on the low end to upwards of $250 a month for top-of-the-line assistance. (Fees don't necessarily reflect a coach's expertise, and plenty of good coaches don't charge an exorbitant amount.) Some coaches will ask you to sign on for 6 months or a year, much like a health-club deal. If a trainer asks for a long-term commitment, ask to sign up on a trial basis at first or to pay for only a limited period of time.

● If you are considering being trained over the Internet, ask the coach for names of other clients whom you can contact for references. (Internet coaches are better suited to advanced runners. Novice runners generally are better off sticking with a local coach who can observe their workouts and offer more feedback.)

guidance. If you are beginning a running program, if you hope to increase your fitness to a new level, and certainly if you hope to maximize your potential, you can benefit from coaching.

Every coach will have a unique philosophy and training method. The key to a good runner-coach relationship is to find a fit that feels comfortable for you. That applies not only to workout preferences but to ideology as well. If you don't respond well to old-school tactics, don't sign on with a coach who barks out orders. If you want to push your limits, don't hire a coach who is essentially running a social group. The best coaches don't use a "one-workout-fits-all" approach; they tailor workouts and schedules to their individual runners.

The more serious you are about your running, the more important it is that you have utter faith in your coach. The wrong training program can leave you plagued with self-doubt: Have I run hard enough? Too hard? Long enough? Too long? Your coach should be willing and able to answer questions about the rationale behind your workouts. He or she should also be able to set out both long- and short-term programs for you.

Recognize that it is possible to outgrow a coach. While some runner-coach bonds last virtually a lifetime, others naturally reach a point of diminishing returns. This can be due to many things, from changing levels of maturity to changing bodies and fitness needs. A good coach will not impede your growth but, hopefully, will offer constructive advice when you are contemplating changing course.

## PERSONAL TRAINERS

Personal trainers are best for women who are beginning a running program and for women who wish to incorporate running into an overall fitness program. They can also provide guidance for overweight or older women or for those with other challenges who need close monitoring of their fitness programs. Trainers can be useful in providing a workout schedule that combines running and other aerobic exercise with strength and flexibility work.

If you are an expert runner, you might also consult a trainer at certain points in your schedule. He or she can be particularly helpful for tips on strength and stability exercises. (Make sure you tell the trainer that you want a program to complement your running, focusing on endurance rather than power.) Although personal trainers are well-versed in general fitness, they are usually not experts in running. Because of this, they are less likely to recognize signs of injury or overtraining in serious runners.

Most gyms and health clubs now have trainers on staff. Interview a trainer much as you would a coach, to find one with a training approach and philosophy with which you feel comfortable. Some trainers will offer a free consultation before you sign on.

## CAMPS

Like coaches, running camps are no longer only for the speedy. A wide variety of camps now exist, with most adult camps wel-

## Running with Dogs

**D**ogs never whine or complain, miss a workout, or make snide remarks about your pace. Dogs make great running companions, especially for women, since they add an element of safety. If you decide to run with your dog, first make sure that Fido is up to the task. "The same things that hold true for people hold true for dogs," says Leslie Sinclair, D.V.M., director of veterinary issues for companion animals for the Humane Society of the United States. "Just as you wouldn't start right off on a hard workout program, you can't do that to your dog."

Dr. Sinclair recommends the following steps for canine safety on the run.

● Have your dog examined by a veterinarian. In addition to performing a regular checkup, the doctor should look for any orthopedic maladies, such as arthritis or hip dysplasia, and for heart and breathing abnormalities.

● Start off slowly, allowing your dog to become conditioned much as you would need to if you were starting your running program.

● If your dog is a puppy, avoid intense exercise. Some breeds can have problems with developing joints, so talk to your vet about your dog's breed's growth period.

coming runners at every point on the spectrum of ability. Camps are a great way to learn more about running and to make new friends. They typically mix organized runs with instructional sessions on running form, nutrition, stretching, training, and more, as well as recreation and relaxation. The inspiration gleaned from a few days of soaking in a healthy pastime with like-minded runners can last for months after you head home.

Camps are available around the country, so you can probably find one in your backyard, should you desire. Or you can travel to the mountains or to a lake for a more comprehensive getaway. When you are choosing a camp, if it's important to you to find runners of similar ability, inquire about the level of expertise of the other run-

● Pay attention to the characteristics of the breed. Some dogs, such as hunting dogs, were bred for endurance; others, such as pugs, are clearly not athletic.

● Remember that your dog can't say, "I'm tired," and he will likely run to the point of exhaustion to keep up with you. "Just because they will keep going doesn't mean they should keep going," says Dr. Sinclair. Monitor your partner closely, looking for excessive panting. If the dog has lost energy and lags behind, it's a sign to stop.

● Offer your dog water often during the run. Some water bottles have a cup attached that works well for this purpose, or you can train your dog to drink from a squirt bottle.

● Keep an eye on your dog's paws. Make sure that they don't have broken toenails or cuts before you start. On hot days, choose grass over pavement, or run in the morning or evening when it's cooler. In the winter, make sure that ice and snow don't build up between your dog's toes.

● Brush up on obedience training. Since your dog will be running and there will be other dogs and people around, you won't have as much control as usual. Make sure that your dog responds to voice commands.

ners attending. Facilities tend to vary greatly—as do prices—so if you prefer hotel luxury to dormitory economy, pick a camp accordingly. Ask yourself whether you'd prefer a single-sex environment or one with men. If you go the coed route, ask the coach about the atmosphere, which can range from sedate to a singles scene.

To locate a camp, check out *Runner's World* magazine's periodic listing at www.runnersworld.com. The Road Runners Club of America also periodically posts a list of camps at www.rrca.org.

## TRAINING LOG

*I* grew up as one of the guys. In high school, since there was no girls' cross-country team, I ran with the boys. In the 1970s, that had all the makings of a nasty, ostracizing experience, but I was lucky. My older brother, who was also on the team, and his friends essentially adopted me. They made sure that I was always okay. The result: I felt more at home among the relaxed competition and teasing banter of the boys than I ever did when the school finally got around to creating a girls' team. To me, the girls seemed silly, gossipy, and most of all, uptight and catty when it came to competition.

Yup, I was biased. A blatant case of reverse discrimination. And as soon as I entered college, my bad attitude cleared up and I developed close female training partners. To this day, though, I enjoy training with the guys—now perhaps as much for the memories as for anything else. And of course I've found along the way that not all men are such easygoing training partners as the bunch in high school.

There are the guys who insist on picking up the pace on easy runs in order to prove that a woman couldn't possibly keep up with them. (You are faced with the choice of ruining your "easy" run or allowing them their smug satisfaction when they prove their point.) There was the running club guy who spouted off about how impressive elite women runners are: They can actually run faster than he can! (Heavens, what a measuring stick, I thought.) There was the first date, when I mentioned that I'd be doing my 15-miler the next day and the guy invited himself along, then got upset when I dropped him. I

# RUNNING WITH MEN

Running is one of the few sports in which women and men compete on a truly level playing field. They work out in the same manner and usually run in the same races. So, unlike in other sports, male and female participants can easily wind up out on the road together as training partners. Luckily for women, bad encounters when running with men are the exception rather than the rule. There was a time—a few decades back—when the run-

had told him exactly how fast I planned to run, after all, and he had said, "Perfect." At about 10 miles, as he was dying a slow death and I was faced with the prospect of slowing to a crawl, I instead continued on without him (and never saw him again).

But my favorite "running with the guys" story comes from a trade-show business trip. A major running shoe manufacturer planned an all-comers run early in the morning. All paces were invited, but when I showed up, the organizer said that it was pretty much novices only and that it would be more of a social outing. I told him that I needed to get in a harder workout that day, and he recommended that I trot over to a hotel several blocks away, from which the hardcore guys would be departing. As I jogged up, a group of about seven men was just leaving, and I asked if I could join them. "Sure, whatever," one muttered.

We proceeded along and they talked their guy talk, basically ignoring me, which was just fine with me. I was just there for the workout anyway. After a few miles the pace quickened, then more so, and more so. Soon we were clipping along a hilly park at a rate that had dropped one guy, then two. The chatter had stopped. At the turnaround it was clear that two more guys were about to fall off the back of the pack. "Hey, she's gonna kick your butt," called out one of the guys in front. With a mile to go, with two men and myself remaining in the lead pack, I was acknowledged for the first time: "Hey, who are you, anyway?" one asked. Sweet triumph, I thought. I'd become one of the guys again.

ning world was a bastion of testosterone and women worried about being on the receiving end of snide remarks or other bad behavior from men. But even in the early days of running, most men were supportive of women's efforts.

Gabeau remembers first joining a running club in the mid-1970s, when she was one of only five women in a group of some 75 men. "It was such an inclusive bunch, representing everything from carpenters to judges. They welcomed women with no more question than anyone else," she remembers.

Today, most running groups feature a comfortable mix of both sexes (they're far closer to 50-50 than they were in the 1970s), and group runs tend to break down on the basis of pace, not chromosomes. "Women today are far less hesitant to run with men," Gabeau says. "They are not intimidated, and many of the younger ones would rather be in an environment with both sexes. Then the run becomes a social thing, even a way to meet the opposite sex."

Still, when it comes to choosing training partners, some women—older women and novices in particular—might prefer the comfortable company of other females. They feel less self-conscious conversing about their training or about body or scheduling issues with others who can relate to their particular challenges. If you feel this way, you shouldn't rule out running clubs or groups, though: You can still enjoy the social aspects and break into your own group of women for the run.

When the male training partner in question is a husband or boyfriend, the equation becomes loaded with more complex emotional issues. Of course, if both of you are runners, consider yourself lucky. Couples who share sports and fitness pursuits tend to stick with them longer and be healthier for it. They also have fewer misunderstandings and problems of jealousy when it comes to spending time on their chosen activity.

Some partners, particularly if they are of similar abilities, can train together with no problem, enjoying their runs as quality time together. But running relationships are not always rosy. Some couples find running together to be a source of tension, especially when they are at mismatched levels of expertise. If the man in your life tends to be impatient or even derisive about your slower pace, you're probably better off training separately. Same goes if you're a speedier woman with a mate who tends to become threatened and angry when he's passed by his beloved.

If you find yourself in either of these situations but you like the idea of sharing your workout time, there are solutions. Try leaving the house for your workout or driving to your running spot as a duo. You can warm up and stretch together, then head off for your runs separately. This works well if you are planning to run for a similar amount of time. If you actually enjoy running together but the difference in your paces makes it difficult, try planning workouts once a week that will work for both of you. For example, if he's faster, you can schedule your weekly high-intensity run for a day that he is doing an easy run.

Don't let "running fights" permeate the relationship. Some couples just aren't cut out for training together. It's better to train alone or with others than to let the stress harm either your relationship or your running. Consider it your time apart, and enjoy comparing notes when you return from your separate workouts.

# 11

# The Balancing Act

THERE'S A NAME FOR WOMEN who try to pursue a career, family, exercise, spirituality, and social life. They're called superwomen. But by that measure, what woman isn't a superwoman? Today, increasing and myriad demands on time mean that every day is a balancing act of priorities. Although on some days you might juggle it all with aplomb, at other times your tugging requirements cause life's fabric to fray at the edges.

Running presents both a solution to the problem and a contribution to it. Finding the time to run adds another line to the to-do list in an already overbooked day. Yet for so many women, running is their salvation, their key to health and sanity. That is the justification for taking the time to run.

## WHY YOU SHOULD TAKE THE TIME

"Exercise is not a selfish thing," says Susan Kalish, executive director of the American Running Association. "You become a better person, and that ultimately helps your family, your work, and everything else. Exercise keeps you young. It helps keep you who you want to be over the years." Kalish, a mother of two, says that she's known for years that running makes her a healthier, more confident and optimistic person. "I'd rather give my family an energetic mom who's going to be around a long time than not take the time to run," she says.

In fact, research has shown that a program of regular running or walking reduces anxiety, stress, and depression and increases feelings of well-being and self-esteem. Those things in turn translate into a healthy lifestyle that fosters more energy, better relationships, and even a better outlook on life. Getting fit makes you a positive role model for children. It creates a foundation of self-respect that permeates your other relationships. And it inspires confidence in all of life's exploits. "When you are a strong person, you will be treated as a strong person," Kalish says. "And when you go into an environment saying that the sky's the limit, then people will believe that you are capable of that, too."

## WHEN PARTNERS OBJECT

Some boyfriends and husbands don't find all of the benefits of running particularly appealing. Reactions in partners can range from the rather silly (he's embarrassed because it turns out that you're faster than he is) to the frightening (he's threatened by your newfound confidence and discourages you from continuing).

If your partner is less than supportive of your running, try to determine the reason. If he's a nonrunner, he might be jealous of your time away from him or of your improving fitness. In this case, simply encourage him to take up the sport. Otherwise, as you grow more serious about your running, the gap between you and your honey in terms of fitness, lifestyle, and time commitment will only grow wider.

If he already is a runner and still disapproves, he might be uncomfortable with the idea that you can keep up with him—or beat him—on the road. Yes, some men still believe that they should be able to beat any woman at any athletic pursuit. If you happen to be with one such man, you can sidestep this affront to his masculinity by always running separately. But perhaps better for the long term (and for womankind in general) is to let him come to grips with it on his own terms. And be sure to inform him that the best women runners can beat virtually *any* man, so he's not in bad company.

Women whose partners never come to accept their running might have a problem that's much larger than disagreement over a workout. Although a husband might complain about the amount of time spent running, the real issue could be one of control. If a healthy pursuit such as running develops into a serious sore spot with a partner, it's probably appropriate to investigate the nature of the conflict with a professional therapist. More than one woman has started running and found that she finally has the strength to run right out of an abusive relationship.

## MAKE THE COMMITMENT

Even if you are already convinced that your health—and your running—is a priority, scheduling your runs on a busy day can still be a struggle. You may often ask, How do I find the time? The first step toward your answer is simple: Change the question. Instead, ask, How do I *make* the time?

---

### IN YOUR OWN WORDS

## How to Find the Time

*I make the time; it's as important to me as brushing my teeth daily. I schedule my runs in my day planner as I would an appointment.*

**Ann**, 46, Denver

*I run before everyone wakes up, from 5:45 to 7:00 A.M. Then my husband and I trade for my long runs on the weekends. I run for 3 to 4 hours while he watches the kids, and he golfs when I get home. (Okay, I run for maybe 3 hours, then stop for bagels and a latte and chat with friends after the run.)*

**Gyll**, 29, Fort Collins, Colorado

*I run right after work for about an hour. If I don't run right when I get home, I won't at all.*

**Deborah**, 30, Manchester, New Hampshire

*Plan ahead. I try to schedule my runs, have them mapped out in my journal. It's like an appointment to be fulfilled.*

**Mary**, 46, Gainesville, Georgia

*I meet with a group of people, which helps ensure that I go.*

**Karen**, 36, Elko, Nevada

---

To successfully commit to any workout program, you must schedule exercise as a priority on par with work, family, and other commitments. If you leave "finding" a half-hour or an hour a day up to chance, odds are that you won't find that block of time. On the other hand, if you wouldn't skip a run any more than you'd skip a day at work, you'll almost always make the time.

Here's a look at some of the best tricks of the trade to help you overcome scheduling debacles.

**Do it first.** Many women run as early as 4:00 or 5:00 A.M., when interruptions and excuses are least likely. If you have trouble overcoming the temptation to sleep another hour, set your shoes and clothes by your bedside so they serve as a reminder of your commitment come morning. Leave your shades open so the sunlight will encourage you to get out of bed. And start going to bed earlier.

**Do it immediately after work.** A run can help shake out job stress and serve as a relaxing end to the day. But beware of motivation sappers, such as the couch and the television. Instead of stopping at home first, go straight from work to your running location. That way, you're not as likely to be sidetracked by other things. If you run from home, switch into your running clothes and head directly out the door. Don't listen to phone messages or check e-mail until you get back from your run.

**Use creative scheduling at work.** Arrive earlier in the day or work later at night in order to take a midday break.

**Make your runs more than just exercise.** Instead of meeting friends for lunch or dinner, suggest a group run. If there's a non-runner in the group, suggest that she ride her bike. If you know other runners at work, suggest that you all head out to the trail to problem-solve.

# CHILD-CARE ISSUES

If you have an infant or toddler, you may have plenty of time on your hands—time stuck in the house making sure that Junior doesn't get into any mischief. Several of the following options will help you combine your workout time with family time, which works especially well for multitaskers with busy schedules.

***Strollers.*** These days, it's easy to run with a baby (or even two) in a stroller. Choose a stroller that is specifically designed for running so that it can handle wear and tear from the road. These can be found in running shops, sporting goods stores, and running catalogs.

***Treadmills.*** Investing in a treadmill is an instant child-care solution that will last for years. You can run at home and maintain a close watch over your child. (A bonus: You'll be happy to have the machine on hand when the weather turns ugly.)

***Pool running.*** You can take your child along while you run in the deep end of a public pool. Pool running is accomplished with the help of a special flotation belt that is available at sporting goods stores or that can be borrowed or rented at most public pools. A baby can sleep in a stroller while you keep an eye on him; an older child can play in the kiddie pool under a friend's watchful eye.

***Babysitting co-ops.*** Find or start a group of women runners who have young children. Each woman can take turns watching the little ones on one day while the others run. The number of days you run each week will depend on the size of the group.

***Tracks and parks.*** When children are old enough to play on their own, you can bring them with you to a track, park, or other area of limited size. While they play, you can run around the perimeter, keeping an eye on them.

***Family fitness.*** Have young ones ride a bike alongside you as you run.

## ON THE ROAD

No matter how disciplined a runner you are, it's tough not to hit a roadblock that sabotages your training schedule when you travel. An out-of-whack body clock, a crammed itinerary, dining out, and late-night entertainment all encroach on your best intentions.

If travel is rare in your life, don't worry about missing a few runs while on vacation. Sometimes a break from the routine can be welcome and refreshing. If, however, you are going to a location that's conducive to running, you'll probably want to pack your shoes. Instead of looking at running as a chore while you're away, view it as another way to see the city or countryside you are visiting. It can be thrilling to wake up early in a new place and explore it by foot while others are still sleeping. You can get your bearings, scope out places you want to check out later in the day, and find hidden gems that you wouldn't discover in a rental car.

Business travel is a trickier matter. If you have a career that requires you to be on the road often, you will want to find ways to continue running without constant interruption. JoAnn Behm Scott, of Carlsbad, California, who managed to compete at a nationally ranked level as a masters runner while juggling a career as a flight attendant, understands the travel challenge better than most. "Sometimes you just have to train tired," Scott says. "You might not hit the times you want to, but you adjust your expectations and go out and do it." Her pointers on running while on the road include the following:

**Be disciplined but rational.** Don't lose sight of safety concerns. If you are in a strange city without obvious running routes, work out on the hotel's treadmill. If your hotel doesn't have its own treadmill, ask the staff at the front desk about exercise options. Chances are that they have a deal with a neighboring gym.

**Drink, drink, drink.** Travel can be dehydrating. Limit your intake of coffee, tea, and soda, and drink plenty of water, juice, and sports drinks.

**Try to eat right.** Buy fruit to keep in your hotel room. Bring energy bars along to fend off hunger in business settings. By eating healthy foods during the day, you'll be less likely to feel starved and splurge on fatty foods and dessert at night.

**Respect jet lag, but don't let it get the best of you.** If you're in London but your legs still think they are in San Diego, factor that into your workouts. Adjust your mileage and pace accordingly so that you don't train too hard.

**Get plenty of rest, and limit your late-night entertainment.** Scott thought up this effective line to fend off coworkers who implored her to come with them for nights on the town: "I'll go have a glass of wine with you tonight if you get up and run with me in the morning!"

## A CHANGING ROLE

To strike a balance, you must find a place for running not only during your day or week but also within your life. The role of running in your life inevitably changes over time. Your fitness goals may fall by the wayside when life intervenes in the form of work, children, marriage, or anything else that puts demands on your time and energy.

If you have become more serious about your running, and especially if you are competitive, it can be hard to accept these changes. "You have to roll with the punches," says Kalish. "You do what you can do, and you set priorities, but then you must be willing to give yourself a break." For Kalish, it was children who rearranged her priorities. "Work didn't do it; marriage didn't do it; but boy, kids did it!" she says. She had been competing seriously before the birth of her first child and thought she'd quickly pick up where she left off. "If you'd asked me before, I'd never have said that I would let that affect my training. But then, 4 months after giving birth, I realized that my expectations had to change."

It was years before Kalish was able to resolve the anger and frustration of not being able to resume her running career at the same high level. "I finally realized that I was at a different segment of my life but that I could still have fun with running. My focus now is on building a fit family.

"You just never know which category you'll fall into, whether it will be a piece of cake to run with kids or a job, or whether it will be impossible. And it can change from one experience to the next for the same woman. If you live long enough, you eventually will find balance," Kalish says.

Many women echo her frustration when they are forced to back off their training. They miss the feeling of being at peak fitness and the confidence that comes from pushing limits. They don't like the way their less-fit bodies feel—or look. At times like these, it's helpful to focus on positives. Running can still be a stress reliever, a social outlet, a healthful pastime, and a way to get outdoors. For all these reasons, any running is still better than no running. Sometimes it can take months or years to adjust, but all those good aspects are still there when the competitive aspects of the sport are stripped away.

When things aren't going as planned, perspective can be a hard thing to come by. But running itself teaches the importance of patience, endurance, and a long-term outlook. "Occasionally, I have let running control my life," says Betsy Roberts, of Boise, Idaho, who has been a runner for almost 20 years. "At those times, it ceases to be fun and it becomes the source of my stress rather than the release. But now I realize that even *that* has helped me to grow. I've learned to recognize when it is happening—not to take the bait of every challenge—and to have fun with my running. That's the key, since I know that it is a thread that will weave its way through my entire life."

## WHEN ENOUGH IS NOT ENOUGH

While most women struggle to make enough time for exercise, a smaller number struggle to find time away from exercise. For these women, running can become a focus to the exclusion of other things, even family and work. "I call it the magnificent obsession," says David Martin, Ph.D., exercise physiologist and sports science chairman of USA Track and Field, this country's governing body for track and field athletics.

You don't have to perform at an elite level to fall prey to this obsession. Runners at all levels of competition can lose perspective. Dr. Martin says that although researchers are only beginning to understand who might be prone to such behavior, many agree that the trigger is success. "When a woman runs a marathon and she didn't think that she could do it, or she wins an age-group award, that is powerful validation," he says. "This gratification is very appealing." The seduction can take on many forms, as other people compliment you on your accomplishments, and as you feel better about your body, your performance, and your capabilities.

"The obsession comes when normal behavior goes awry," Dr. Martin explains. "The more success you have, the more you try to do. That's followed with more success, so you try even more. You

## TRAINING LOG

*$O$ne of the toughest but most gratifying times of my life was when I was working as the editor in chief of a national magazine and at the same time attempting to see how fast a runner I could become. I was training twice a day, and I allowed nothing to interfere with my running. That meant sacrificing dinners, movies, parties, dates, and vacations. Everything. I had told myself that I would never skip a workout because of anything except illness and injury, and I never did. Once, when I was due to depart on a 7:00 A.M. flight for business, I dragged myself out to the track at 4:00 A.M. It was still pitch-dark and my body was still asleep, but I ran my workout.*

*Now, there are two points to be made here. The first is that—ah, the clarity of hindsight—I was out of balance. I never did qualify for the Olympic Trials that year as I had hoped. Instead, I caught the flu a week before the race. I was easily fit enough, but I was burned out. Toast. Okay, so that's how I learned the lesson that there's such a thing as too much discipline.*

*But do I have any regrets about what I gave up that year? Not one. My mistake was in the way I went about going for it—due to lack of information, lack of recognizing when enough was enough. My mistake was not in "going for it."*

*I kept my bargain with myself, and I know in my heart that I couldn't have given an ounce more than I did. In doing so, I learned that I was capable of far more than I ever thought possible. If I hadn't tried, I always would have wondered.*

*It was also the right time in my life. I had no children; I wasn't in a relationship. I had the freedom of selfishness.*

*Balance can mean different things at different times. Plenty of folks observing that year of mine—not one movie, not one!—would have said that I was out of balance. But I knew that I was grabbing that year for all it was worth. Opportunities like that don't present themselves often in life. Balance? I can now balance out that year of intensity with the years to come, in which my running is the recreation that punctuates the richness and fullness of the rest of my life.*

literally drive yourself to your limits—and unfortunately, you know your limits only when you have surpassed them."

Some coaches believe that women are more prone to running obsession than men, but there is no evidence to support this idea. Dr. Martin believes that the perception might result from women manifesting such behavior differently from men. For example, women might feel pressure from a need to prove themselves, or from years of being expected to "do it all," or from women's traditional role of looking out for everyone except themselves. These factors can mean that women are less likely to question a coach on what is expected of them in a workout and more likely to question themselves.

Some women report using running to fill a void or as a numbing device. By concentrating on running, they can ignore other problems in their lives. By feeling so tired from workouts, they don't have the energy to feel much else. If your running has gotten to this point, it is no longer a positive part of the equation. You need to step back and ascertain whether you are using running as an unhealthy form of medication. If you feel powerless to control your behavior, seek counseling from a therapist or sports psychiatrist who specializes in such problems.

As ever, balance is the key. "It's not bad to pursue excellence," Dr. Martin says. "Some people say that you should never be obsessed, but that's how you get to be good. I'm sure Beethoven was obsessed. But it's a fine line between obsession and having no other meaning to your life."

# 12

# Staying Motivated and Beyond: Mental Aspects of Running

THE LONGER YOU ENGAGE IN A RUNNING PROGRAM, the easier it becomes to stick with it. In fact, after a few years of the sport, many runners report feeling "not quite right" after a stretch of inactivity—a feeling that is as much mental as physical. When you reach that stage, motivation is hardly a problem: A run is often the highlight of your day.

But until that point arrives, most runners will wake up to days on which bed seems more inviting than the dark, heat, cold, wind, or whatever else awaits them outdoors. On these days, figuring out how to stay motivated is crucial.

Motivation can droop for any number of reasons: Boredom, lack of results, stress, and a shortage of time are primary among them. Some people are natural experts at finding motivation even in the face of such adversity. But if you're more inclined to fold than to fight, you can still develop motivation, just as you'd develop your muscles.

When you find yourself dreading a run instead of looking forward to it, you should first determine whether your feelings are truly due to laziness or boredom or whether they are instead a sign of exhaustion or an oncoming bout of illness. If they are the latter, you'd be smart to listen to your body and modify or skip the workout.

But if you are otherwise healthy, beware the classic signs of lack of motivation: finding excuses not to run, stalling with other projects, or experiencing feelings of boredom or listlessness. When you find yourself in that lazy frame of mind, try some of the tips outlined in the rest of this chapter. And even if you succumb to the couch one day, don't put yourself down. Instead, just make sure not to let one poor day stretch into a pattern of inactivity. Every day is a fresh start; don't measure yourself by yesterday's troubles. Finally, remember that just about whatever you're suffering from, you'll feel much better after you go for a run.

**When boredom strikes, fight back.** If you're fighting boredom, it's probably a sign that you could use some variety and new challenges in your running. Do you always run in the same place? At the same speed? For the same distance? No wonder your motivation is flagging.

For some reason, many runners become creatures of habit; they do the same three or four loops over and over again. When you find that you've dug yourself a rut, shake yourself out of it. There are no rules in running, so go have some fun: Leave your watch at home and run just by feel. Drive to a new trail for a change of scenery. Plan a run with friends to a café in the next town (drop a car there before you start). When you have time, set out on an adventure, taking every turn your heart desires. Chances are, you'll discover a renewed sense of wonder along with a new running route.

**Take the first few steps.** You can often overcome lack of motivation by focusing only on getting started rather than working up the gumption to take on an entire workout. It's been said that the first step out the door is the hardest, and any runner will attest to that truth. When laziness strikes, make a deal with yourself that you'll at least give the run a try. Change clothes, head out the door, and start moving. In most cases, the fresh air and circulation will have an energizing effect, stimulating you enough to get through the run. If, after 10 minutes or so, you are still truly trudging, try walking or just call it a day. Chances are that you are overtired and your body is trying to tell you that you need rest more than exercise.

It might help to remember that even the best runners in the world have days when their minds and bodies would rather head out for ice cream than for a workout. Jackie Joyner-Kersee, considered the greatest female athlete in history, admits that she played the just-get-out-the-door game, too, when she was competing. "I'd tell myself just to start," she says. "Then, even if I couldn't get through it all, at least I'd done something."

**Make running a priority.** People don't marvel when you show up for work every day; it's expected. Try giving your run the same type of priority in your schedule. If this seems daunting, try it out for just 2 weeks—enough time to set a new pattern. Think of it as an investment in yourself.

**Be social.** Set a date to run with a partner. It's harder to skip a run when you know that a friend is relying on you.

**Do dwell on the past.** Think back to previous runs and how good you felt during and afterward. Chances are that if you're feeling unmotivated, your energy could use a jump-start, and running will be just the thing.

**Prepare the attire for your run.** Place your running shoes and clothes by your bedside if you run in the morning. If you run right after work, set them out next to your desk. The physical presence of your running attire will help motivate you to run.

**Have a goal.** Without a goal to strive for, working out can seem aimless and pointless. Some runners find it hard to train at all if they don't have a race, social event, or other goal to shoot for. Anyone can have a goal; it needn't be a fast time in a race. Beginners can aim for running 30 minutes without stopping or just for exercising 5 days a week for a month.

**Maintain a positive attitude.** All runners have days when their legs feel as if they just won't move. They feel sluggish and "flat," and no matter how hard they try, they can't find a comfortable groove. Some women react with tension when their bodies don't do what's expected. As expectations become loaded and muscles grow tight, running becomes even harder. Motivation can suffer as a result. The cycle, which can go on for days or weeks, can lead to frustration, anger, and even depression. Professional runners know that there will always be *those days*. No matter what your running level, you'd do well to keep their wisdom in mind.

Willie Rios, of Boulder, Colorado, who specializes in coaching women distance runners, drills the importance of staying positive into each of his runners' heads. Rios likes to recount one example of a runner who was having a frustrating workout. "She was getting angry because her times were so much slower than they had been," he says. "By changing the focus of the workout—in this case, to thinking about the triumph of just completing it on a day where it would have been easy to walk away—she had an opportunity to learn something about herself and to experience a success rather than a defeat."

Within every run, there are successes and defeats. As an advanced runner, you learn that you can make a conscious decision to focus on either the negative or the positive. Sure, you can always find defeats: not going as fast as you had hoped, not feeling light on your feet, not having time to run as far as you expected. But you can always find successes just as easily. Some days, it's going farther or pushing harder than ever before. Some days, the success is just getting out the door. Some days—on the really rough days—a success can be as simple as staying in good spirits and reminding yourself that tomorrow is a fresh opportunity to feel

## Why Do You Run?

**W**hen women are asked why they run, they usually list the mental and emotional benefits as often as they list fitness reasons. At a Women's Running Camp in Colorado, 30 women from around the country discussed what running meant to them. Ranging in age from twentysomething to fifty-plus, these women had been running anywhere from 2 months to more than 30 years. When asked why they ran, many of them listed more than one reason. Here's the breakdown of some of their responses.

Health and fitness: 11

Stress relief: 11

"The way it makes me feel": 6

Time alone: 5

Socializing: 4

Weight loss: 4

"It's 'my' thing": 4

Challenge/competition: 4

"It's in my blood": 1

better. It's a lesson that, once learned on the run, proves invaluable when applied to other aspects of life.

Rios has been known to admonish women who downplay their accomplishments or find fault after every workout. "When you beat yourself up like that, you invite every abusive person from your past back into your life. You reinforce any negative message ever heard from a boss, boyfriend, or husband," he says. "You don't want other people to treat you like that. Why would you do it to yourself?"

**After every run, find at least one success.** Perhaps you allowed yourself to relax and enjoy the clouds. Or perhaps you felt tired but didn't let that stop you. The more ways you can find success, the happier you will be with your running.

**Write or recite positive affirmations.** Negativity often stems from a difference between your perception of where you are and your perception of where you want to be. Instead of dwelling on negative self-talk, replace it with positive affirmation. For example, when you find yourself thinking, I can't believe I ran that slowly, try telling yourself instead, I am lucky to be blessed with strong, healthy legs.

**Build a positive support team.** It is important to surround yourself with people who want you to succeed. (That goes for every aspect of your life.) Professional runners are experts at creating support systems that encourage their best performance. Detach yourself from running partners, "friends," and coaches who downplay your achievements, question your goals, deride your weight, or make you feel generally miserable about yourself. Find others who boost your confidence and encourage your efforts.

**Keep running in perspective.** Just as women go through different phases in work and home life, they can expect to go through different phases in their running. Recognizing this can go a long way toward alleviating frustration and allowing only positive forces to flow from the sport.

If you have become used to the daily affirmation of an energizing run, an interruption in the routine can prove devastating. A new job, a return to school, a baby—any number of things can shift priorities and make running seem more of a chore than a rejuvenation. An ensuing cycle of failed expectations can foster self-doubt and negativity.

Susan Kalish, executive director of the American Running Association, went through such a period after the birth of her first child. "I felt gross and fat and embarrassed," she remembers. "I didn't return to fitness anywhere near as fast as I thought I would, and I felt like my running, which had been my good friend, was humiliating me."

After the birth of her second child, Kalish decided to take a different approach, removing any expectation of a timeline in which to return to her former level of running. The approach worked, and she once again reaped the positive benefits she had remembered. "I had thought running was letting me down, but it was just changing," she says.

It is particularly important for women, who are busy with so many responsibilities to others, to keep running in perspective. Remember that running should not become just another source of pressure or expectation. Think of your run as your own personal time to meditate, relax, enjoy, and think. You'll be guaranteed to find motivation for this time of the day.

## THE MANY BENEFITS OF MENTAL FITNESS

Staying motivated is an aspect of running that you must work at and develop. But there's a flip side to exercising your mental muscle: The mental strength that the sport demands and encourages leads to benefits that extend far beyond the physical. In a way, running gives back as much as—or even more than—it takes. As you work to develop your motivation and as you progress with your running, don't be surprised if you find a positive impact on other areas of your life.

Take this example: Sitting down to breakfast the day before a race, a number of female runners were discussing why they ran. Time to myself, some said. Empowerment. Sanity. When it was one woman's turn to speak, she listed a few reasons. Stress relief. Fitness, of course. And then came this: Recently, her husband had attacked her for the first time. Running was something she could do for herself in order to feel strong and in control.

# The Road to Self-Discovery

**M**any women find that running changes their lives for the better in some way, large or small. These women felt so strongly about the benefits that they made running their life's work.

● For me, running resulted in a total coming out from a caterpillar into a butterfly. Maybe nobody else could see it, but I could. It started when my 12-year-old daughter beat the whole school in the 600-yard dash—the boys, too. We saw that she had some talent and, to encourage her running, I took her to the track. I sat on the sidelines and watched her all summer. Finally my girlfriend and I started slogging around the track ourselves. At the age of 32, I realized that I could run, and even run fast. That confidence totally changed my outlook on life. It was the start of a great blossoming.

—**Henley Gabeau**, 54
Executive Director, Road Runners Club of America

● When I started running, I was married and a mother of four. And that's how I saw myself: as a mother and a wife—certainly all those things before an individual. But when I started running, I was surprised to see that the people I ran with didn't care about those other things. They related to me as *Diane*. It gave me a strong feeling of who I was, separate from all the roles I had. Ultimately, it gave me courage to make changes in the rest of my life, including seeking more supportive relationships.

—**Diane Palmason**, 61
Cofounder and Codirector, Women's Running Camps

● I was born with bone deformities and had both feet re-formed when I was 13. I first joined a running club when I was going through rehab as a kid. Women weren't allowed to run very far back then, only 400 and 800 meters, but I loved it immediately. For me, even though I did it competitively, I used running as a meditation for all those years. To this day, if I have a business decision to make, or if I have some stress, or if something is just really annoying me, I'll go out and run. If the run makes it go away, I think, Okay, it's not that important. If it's still there bothering me, then I know I need to deal with it. It's my form of stress release and meditation.

—**Anne Audain**, 42
Cofounder of the Idaho Women's Fitness Celebration
and one of the first professional female runners

The women at the table nodded their heads in understanding. Not one of them seemed particularly shocked by this stranger's soul-baring statement. In some way, they'd been there themselves. They hadn't necessarily been victims of physical abuse. But they had needed a sense of strength and control in their lives. Maybe the feeling came when they started a new job. Or when one of their children was troubled. Or when they were suffering from pointed loneliness. Somehow, running had given them strength.

It's something that women runners themselves marvel at. Get them in a group and invariably the subject will meander over to something far deeper than split times and waist sizes. For most women runners, the sport is more than a great aerobic workout: In some way, it fills a corner of their soul. Women speak of running as meditation, therapy, quiet time, an outlet for emotion, a catalyst for growth, a microcosm of their bigger picture. Running takes on these roles and more, often with powerful effects on your whole life.

Anne Audain, of Boise, Idaho, one of the sport's first female professionals and cofounder of the Idaho Women's Fitness Celebration, says that she boils the essence and benefits of running down to one word: *movement.* It's a word that comes up time and again when speaking to women about the impact of their running.

"By movement, I mean cleansing," Audain says. "By moving the body itself, you are moving not just air, food, and blood but even thought through the body. If you let things sit still, you'll get cobwebs. Movement gives you so much more energy."

And that means energy for all aspects of your life: physical, mental, and emotional. Runners quickly realize that the three are connected. Many women who enter the sport for the health or weight management benefits find themselves continuing for the mental and emotional energy. In a survey of 30 women runners of all ages and abilities, more than half said that stress relief and time by themselves were the main reasons they ran.

Marathoner Jerry Lynch, Ph.D., one of the country's premier sports psychologists and founder of the TaoSports Center for Human Potential in Santa Cruz, California, puts it this way: "A woman who embraces a running program and the movement that comes with it now has a metaphor for movement in the rest of her life." Dr. Lynch believes that many women who find themselves at a crossroads in life are ripe to discover the integration of body, mind, and spirit that running offers. Although these women focus on their bodies as the starting point for change when they begin running, the benefits can't help but move into other parts of their lives as well. Mary, 52, is a great example. After only 3 months in the sport, she decided to run a marathon. "I'm at a crossroads in my life," she explained. "I needed a change; I'm going back to school, and it's all connected for me. If I can take this step with the running, then I can take the others as well." Now that's motivation.

## HOW RUNNING HELPS WOMEN

Almost any physical activity will improve your mental state. A body of research has shown that exercise, particularly endurance-oriented activity, can elevate moods and alleviate stress in both men and women. But speak to women runners, and you'll find more going on than a simple endorphin buzz. The benefits seem to go beyond science and whatever magic is happening at the cellular level.

See if any of these comments from women runners ring a bell with you:

"Running has a very calming effect on me; it's a time when I meditate and work out unsolved problems and generate my most creative thinking."

"I feel so great about myself and my life after a run."

"It's very empowering to feel strong and to have the mental endurance to be by myself for hours at a time."

"Running makes me happy and optimistic; it helps me solve problems and get a better perspective."

"Running gives me confidence and inner peace. I am stronger and more in tune with where I'm going in life."

"It gives me a boost in my self-esteem—it makes me think I can do other things."

"I now have a confidence and a sense of competence that has filled all of my life."

How is it that an act as simple as putting one foot in front of the other can reap such complex rewards? The key might be

*I remember a run on a chill December day in New Mexico. Sitting at work, I had received a phone call: A medical test had come back positive. Could I schedule an appointment for surgery? The need for so-lace pointed out, like a slap in the face, the finality of the previous day's events: I was divorced. The signed papers had just arrived in the mail. Sitting at my desk with the phone still in hand, I felt frightfully alone.*

*I left work and I ran—a raw, primal scream of a run. I ran as the tears came in the aching beauty of a frozen pink Santa Fe sunset. I ran as long as I could, and when I could run no more, I stopped.*

*I remember a more joyous run, a year-and-a-half later. A new start in a new city, a new job I loved, on a spring day filled with impossibly warm showers shot through with sun, lightning glittering in the distance. I ran down a canyon path, unable to contain the smile on my face, the renewal in my heart.*

*Those moments in time have passed. But somehow, they exist now in the memory of those runs more than anything else does. I do not remember the en-suing doctor's appointment or moving into my new apartment with anything approaching the clarity of the emotion found in those runs. They are the photo album, the magnifying glass, the chrysalis through which life's changes are re-membered. They are so much more than runs.*

running's simplicity. The sport lends itself to a meditative quality that is not possible in many other activities. Self-propelled and in touch with the ground, not reliant on or distracted by equipment, the runner finds that her mind is free to wander or focus as she chooses.

"It is something that is unique to running. You see it somewhat in other individual sports, but particularly in running because it is so measurable," says Diane Palmason, cofounder and codirector of Women's Running Camps in Denver. Palmason, 61, holds age-group records in distances ranging from 200 meters to 50 miles. "When you accomplish something in running, it is so obvious that it is you and you alone who accomplished it. In other areas of our life, there is rarely an obvious measure. In running, when you achieve a quantifiable goal, you have every right to feel good about yourself."

When women do achieve goals in running—whether losing 20 pounds or breaking 20 minutes for a 5-K—they grow far beyond those results, and sometimes beyond what men would experience in similar situations.

Although men have grown up developing positive self-images through sports, most middle-age and older women have yet to experience similar affirmation. Women who come to sports later in life find it their playing ground on which to develop confidence and control. With girls today encouraged to play sports, future generations of women probably won't have to wait until middle age to make such gains.

Running can have such a positive effect in a woman's life that clinical psychologist Leon J. Hoffman, Ph.D., includes the sport as treatment in his practice in Chicago. "Unfortunately, in today's world, affirmation is crucial," says Dr. Hoffman, a member of the American Running Association. "Some women have problems because they have been trained to be funnels, not cups. For these women, when the applause stops, the depression sets in. But running can fill that. A woman can do it at her own pace, be assertive, try different things, be expressive, enjoy her body. She can give all these good things to herself, and not have to rely on somebody else or have it be in response to a man."

Sports psychologist Dr. Lynch says that running and women are a natural match. The sport requires one to be fluid, or "soft but strong," which he considers intrinsically feminine characteristics. "Women tend to find the more spiritual, deeper side of running. It is just natural for women to align themselves with the concepts of courage, companionship, and cooperation. Win or lose, when women run a race, at the end they hug, congratulate each other, and then talk about how to improve the next time, all the while learning and achieving their goals."

# 13

# Eat Right
# to Run Your Best

"LOSE WEIGHT!" "BOOST ENERGY!" "LOOK GREAT!" Every
day, women are pummeled with promises about weight and nutrition. Every week seems to bring a new diet, and with it a new guru.
We're bombarded with a parade of low-fat diets and high-fat diets,
low-protein this and high-protein that, all to be washed down with
the latest supplements and herbs. By the time you have tried one
"miracle," the industry is ready with another.

Well, combine all of those messages and it's no wonder that
many women runners don't know where to begin when it comes
to nutrition. That is, if you have *time* to think about nutrition at
all. Between rushing to get the kids off in the morning, running
errands during lunch, and collapsing in a heap at dinner, eating
well generally takes a backseat to convenience. You may be able
to get through the day on a bagel for breakfast and salad for
lunch, but by the time evening rolls around, your fat- and protein-
starved state leaves you powerless in the face of greasy take-out
food.

It's ironic: As more and more nutrition information bombards
us, our food choices and weight struggles are growing worse than
ever. The simple act of eating has become so complicated that
many women have developed extremely tedious and self-defeating

routines or thrown up their hands and said, "The heck with it—pass me another doughnut!"

## THE ACTIVE WOMAN'S DIET

Running places demands on your body that require you to pay more attention to healthy eating. It increases your energy requirements, which translates to a need for more—and better—calories and nutrients. "When you're exercising regularly, your body becomes a finely tuned machine," explains Tammy Baker, R.D., a spokeswoman for the American Dietetic Association who lives in Cave Creek, Arizona, and specializes in sports nutrition and women's issues. "It's the difference between a racing car and a regular car. You become more sensitive to nutritional imbalances because you are pushing to a greater degree. Although many of the problems are the same as with sedentary women, the repercussions will likely be more noticeable for an athletic woman."

● Take a realistic look at your eating habits. Try keeping a food journal for 3 days. Write down everything you eat and drink. You might be surprised at the results. Often, women overestimate the amount of protein and vegetables they eat, or they underestimate their intake of sweets and junk food.

● Have an expert review your diet. Most health clubs have nutritionists on hand for consultations. There are also many Web sites that offer nutritional analysis.

● Keep your pantry well-stocked. Keep plenty of healthy, convenient foods available for times when you have to eat in a pinch. Canned beans and tuna, dried pasta, frozen vegetables, nuts, and dried fruits are all good staples to keep on hand.

● Make changes slowly. If you find that your diet is out of balance, don't attempt to overhaul it overnight. Make a few healthful switches each week to give your body a chance to adapt without rebelling.

Since you can't be cavalier about nutrition when you're a runner, it's a good thing that running often makes your body start craving healthier items. This nice side effect might be Ma Nature's way of making sure that you're taking care of yourself.

The other good news is that eating well doesn't have to be complicated. It doesn't require extra hours spent in the kitchen or grocery store. By understanding your body's needs and making smart choices, you can easily eat for optimal nutrition, fitness, and weight management. While diets go in and out of vogue, the foundation of proper nutrition remains constant—and simple. You can start by ignoring all the diet books and gurus. Forget extremes, and strive instead for balance. Your primary goals should be to balance your caloric intake with your energy expenditure and to balance your meals in a healthy manner.

## A HEALTHY BALANCE

Some runners subsist on pasta, bagels, and bananas because they believe that eating plenty of carbohydrates is the key to success. They tend to exclude more calorie-dense foods, which are often high in protein and fat, from their diets. Other runners swear by protein: They'll eat plenty of lean meats and avoid refined carbs such as bread and cereal.

Who's on the right track? That's been a subject of great debate. There are proponents of just about every imaginable ratio of carbohydrates, protein, and fat. And over time, the scales have tipped in all different directions. Generations ago, runners would eat a hearty meal of steak and eggs before a race. In the 1970s and 1980s, carbohydrate depletion and loading was common before events. Most recently, high-protein diets have been in vogue.

Strip away what's hyped and hip, however, and what you should be eating as a runner is pretty much what everyone else should be eating. "Basically, you don't want to go too heavy or too lean on anything," says Susan Kundrat, R.D., a sports nutritionist with Nutrition on the Move in Champaign, Illinois. "High-protein is the big diet fad now for women starting a running program, but that can be detrimental. That might not be providing enough quick energy—carbohydrates—for running. It's especially important to avoid following a fad diet when you're starting to run. Otherwise, if you don't feel good, you run the risk of thinking that it's the running that's not working for you—that you just don't have enough energy—when in fact the pitfall might be the diet."

Most sports nutritionists advise runners to take in roughly 65 percent of calories from carbohydrates, 25 percent from fat, and 10 percent from protein. To do so, simply follow the USDA's Food Guide Pyramid. The foundation of your diet should be grains and grain products: bread, rice, cereal, and pasta, the less refined the better. After that come fruits and vegetables, and be sure to get a good variety of both, since they provide different vitamins and phytochemicals (literally, plant chemicals—a variety of substances found in plants that can help fight cancer, heart disease, and

# smart
## tips

Eating a healthy, balanced diet doesn't have to be an exercise in tedium. You don't need to carry around a kitchen scale or calculate calories from package listings. Strive to take in a sampling of healthy fat and protein every day along with a larger dose of complex carbohydrates (grains, fruits, and vegetables) with each meal. You often can accomplish this with creative additions to old favorites. Little adjustments throughout the day add up. Here are some tips to help you begin. Once you get the hang of it, you'll naturally think of others.

● Spread toast lightly with peanut butter instead of butter. Unlike butter, which contains high amounts of artery-clogging saturated fat and virtually no vitamins and minerals, peanut butter contains heart-healthy monounsaturated fat and a good dose of vitamin E.

● Add fresh fruit and yogurt to cereal and oatmeal. The fruit will provide lots of phytochemicals, which are healthy for your heart and fend

stroke). Eat meat, fish, eggs, nuts, beans, and dairy products in small portions, as accents to your meals, and use sweets and fats sparingly.

Few women—few Americans, for that matter—eat such a balanced, healthy diet. Women tend to fall into two camps: those who eat too many carbohydrates to the exclusion of fat and protein and those who eat too much fat and processed food, denying themselves healthier complex carbohydrates. Most such patterns come from misguided notions that certain foods are good and others bad. Beef, eggs, and dairy products are just some of the foods that have gotten a bad rap over the years. In fact, there's a place for all of these in a runner's diet.

Today, nutritionists believe that one of the keys to any healthy diet is to consume a wide variety of foods. A number of studies have shown that people who eat a wider variety of foods on a

off muscle soreness. The yogurt supplies appetite-suppressing protein and a good dose of bone-boosting calcium.

● Mix steamed vegetables into your pasta. On its own, pasta contains few nutrients. The veggies add plenty of the vitamins you need.

● Add frozen vegetables or a can of crushed tomatoes when cooking rice. Rice supplies plenty of energizing carbohydrates. But, like pasta, it's weak on nutrients.

● Crumble tofu into your pasta sauce. Soy products contain isoflavonoids, which may ease menopausal symptoms, boost bone health, lower heart disease risk, and prevent breast cancer.

● Toss canned beans and greens into soups. Both supply plenty of appetite-suppressing fiber.

● Add canned tuna, nuts, and chickpeas or other beans to salads. All provide quality sources of protein with no artery-clogging fat.

daily basis consume more vitamins and minerals along the way than their counterparts who eat a limited number of items day after day. Excluding foods or whole food groups can lead to nutritional deficiencies, not to mention periods of rebellious bingeing.

# SPECIAL CONCERNS FOR WOMEN WHO RUN

Adhere to the basics outlined above and you'll be well on your way to good nutrition. Following is a more detailed look at some of the items of special concern to women runners.

## Caffeine

It may have a bad reputation, but only some of that is deserved. In addition to causing the jitters, moderate doses of this stimulant can interfere with iron absorption and contribute to dehydration and stomach distress. On the other hand, attempts to link regular caffeine consumption to cancer, heart disease, and osteoporosis have proved inconclusive. The bottom line: It's perfectly safe to indulge your buzz; just limit your daily intake to three servings or less of coffee, tea, or soda.

Beyond health issues, caffeine is a proven performance enhancer that's banned in high doses by the International Olympic Committee. Nancy Clark, R.D., author of *Nancy Clark's Sports Nutrition Guidebook*, says the latest research suggests that caffeine functions primarily as an energy enhancer because of its effect on the brain, as opposed to any direct effect elsewhere in the body. In other words, exercise may seem easier after a dose of caffeine, but in fact, physical function remains unchanged. Other studies suggest that caffeine encourages fat burning, which can in turn spare your body's glycogen reserves on the run. But before you hit Starbucks on the morning of your next race, you should know that caffeine's impact varies dramatically from one person to another. Although some runners won't leave for a workout without downing a cup of coffee, others won't go near the stuff. For them, it brings on a racing heart, dizziness, nausea, dehydration, and diarrhea.

Some runners wonder whether they should avoid coffee before races because of caffeine's diuretic effect. If you are a regular coffee drinker, this is likely to do more harm than good, bringing on side effects of withdrawal that can include headaches and jitters. Just

## Energy Bars and Gels

Energy bars were originally created to provide easily digestible fuel for athletes during and after strenuous workouts. Now used by everyone from busy executives to weekend warriors, they have become a multimillion-dollar industry.

Although there's certainly no harm in these products, nutritionists point out that they don't contain anything you can't get from ordinary food—at a far cheaper price, to boot. Such supplements are really not necessary for low-mileage runners who work out for less than an hour a day. But energy bars are convenient. "If it's the bar or nothing at all, then it's a fine alternative," says Tammy Baker, R.D., a spokeswoman for the American Dietetic Association who lives in Cave Creek, Arizona, and specializes in sports nutrition and women's issues. "It depends on your lifestyle. For junk-food junkies, this might be the healthiest thing they eat all day."

Sports nutritionists caution you to read labels. Be sure that what you're getting from an energy bar fits into your overall dietary profile for the day. Originally, energy bars contained primarily carbohydrates with a small amount of protein. These kinds of bars are best for consumption before or during runs. Many newer varieties, in the interest of improving flavor, contain a whopping number of calories from sugar and fat. Some are really candy bars masquerading as sports fuel in order to capitalize on the fitness craze. They're fine—if you're looking for a candy bar. Other bars attempt to deliver a full range of nutrients, carbohydrates, protein, and fat. Often high in calories, they can serve as meal replacements in a pinch. All energy bars are best washed down with water for easier digestion.

Gels are the latest energy food. They provide easily transportable, quick bursts of fuel. Though they don't sound or look particularly appealing, gels taste a lot like cake frosting and slide down easily. They consist primarily of carbohydrates and are readily absorbed by the digestive system. For high-mileage runners, gels can be a godsend during a workout. Many marathoners now count on them and stash a packet or two in their shorts. If you've never tried a gel before, be sure to experiment on some long runs before your race. Try taking one after an hour or so of running and another every 30 minutes thereafter. In races, plan to eat them before water stops, since they are best digested when chased down with a swig of water.

keep your consumption to less than a cup before a race or a hard workout to avoid digestive difficulties.

## Calcium

This is one of the most important minerals in a woman's diet, yet most women take in only half the amount they need. Calcium is essential for young and old women alike to maintain healthy bones. Although your bone mass peaks by age 30, you need to continue to optimize your calcium intake to keep your bones from weakening. Calcium may also prevent high blood pressure and colon cancer. And some evidence suggests that it may help you lose weight. Furthermore, runners who do not consume enough calcium are more susceptible to muscle cramping.

Dairy products are the most concentrated and convenient source of calcium. Low-fat milk and plain yogurt in particular are excellent choices. Although other foods such as vegetables and fish do contain some calcium, you'd need to eat a very large amount of those foods to get the necessary daily dose. If you are a vegan or if you are allergic to dairy products, consider calcium-fortified products such as orange juice and soy milk.

You should take in a total of 1,000 milligrams of calcium per day if you are under age 50, or 1,500 milligrams if you are over 50. Since your body can absorb only about 500 milligrams at a time, spread out two or three servings of calcium-rich foods throughout the day.

## Fat

The very mention of this three-letter word can make almost any woman cringe. Most women see fat as the enemy, something to be eliminated at all costs—from your body and your diet. But for every woman who rigorously strips her diet of every iota of fat, there's another who merrily orders another cheeseburger with fries. Neither approach is optimal for health or fitness.

Too much of the wrong type of fat in your diet can contribute to heart disease and body fat. But eliminating all fat has its own set of health consequences. Some types of fat are actually good for your health—especially if you run. Depriving yourself of these good fats can even affect your skin and hair and leave you perpetually hungry. "When women severely restrict the fat in their diets, they have more of a tendency to binge and, in turn, develop other eating problems," Kundrat says. "Also, when women have a real fat phobia, their intention might be to eliminate calories, but they end up avoiding protein, calcium, magnesium, zinc, and plenty of other important nutrients because a lot of the foods that contain fat are also good sources of these other nutrients. What might start as a well-intended low-fat diet can snowball into an unintended nutritional problem."

How can you tell the difference between good fat and bad fat? Consult the list on page 168.

## Timing Is Everything

**T**he more you run, the more you will want to concern yourself with the relationship between what you eat and when you exercise.

If you run for a half-hour or so a few times a week, this is a fairly simple proposition. Eating a high-carbohydrate snack, such as a banana, and sipping a glass of water shortly before a run will fend off hunger, dehydration, and any related tiredness.

If you're a more competitive or high-mileage runner, things get a little trickier. Since it can take a day or more to fully replenish liquids lost during high-intensity workouts, maintaining a hydrated state becomes a full-time proposition. You should drink throughout the day and before you head out for a run. A good-size snack, such as a banana and a bagel, eaten an hour or so before running will help to ensure that you'll get through a longer workout.

After a rigorous run, you need to replenish energy as quickly as possible. Several studies have shown that your body is most receptive to rebuilding glycogen stores within a 30-minute window immediately after exercise. If you eat soon after you complete your run, you can minimize ensuing muscle stiffness and soreness. You'll primarily want to eat quickly absorbed carbohydrates such as fruit, but don't ignore protein altogether. According to Nancy Clark, R.D., author of *Nancy Clark's Sports Nutrition Guidebook*, the combination of protein and carbohydrates enhances the transport of glucose to the muscles. She recommends a ratio of 1 gram of protein to 3 grams of carbohydrates. Eat a bagel spread with peanut butter, or drink a shake made with fruit and yogurt.

*Monounsaturated fats.* These are found in avocados, nuts, and olive oil. Make them the predominant fats in your diet.

*Omega-3 fatty acids.* Found in fish such as salmon and mackerel as well as in flaxseed, this fat can prevent heart disease and cancer; it may help you lose weight; and it might even reduce muscle soreness. Try to eat fish once or twice a week. Use flaxseed oil on salads, and add ground flaxseed to your favorite recipes.

*Polyunsaturated fats.* These fats are found in most cooking oils. Treat them as neutral: They neither help nor harm your health.

*Trans fats.* Found in margarine, many baked goods, and many processed foods (including crackers), these fats are just as bad for your health as the saturated fat in bacon and butter. Limit them as much as you can.

*Saturated fats.* Found in most animal products, saturated fats encourage heart disease. Limit them as much as possible.

If you need to cut back on your overall fat intake, don't attempt to drastically change your eating habits overnight. Rather, gradually adjust what you eat so your body and appetite don't rebel. Try making a few minor changes each week. Substitute a baked potato for fries. Switch to low-fat cream cheese on your bagel.

Just as important, switch to eating healthier sources of fat most of the time: Choose olive oil over butter, fish over beef. Remember, moderation is the key. If you love the taste of butter on your toast, you don't have to give it up. Just make sure that the rest of your day isn't filled with similarly saturated fat sources. If, on the other hand, you have a fat phobia, sneak nutritious sources of fat into your regular recipes: Toss some walnuts or almonds into your cereal or pasta. Sauté veggies lightly in olive oil.

## Iron

Few women take in enough iron, and some of these women become anemic. Anemia can easily go undetected because the symptoms—extreme fatigue, dizziness, and shortness of breath—mimic those of exhaustion. To prevent anemia, you need 15 milligrams of iron a day. Although the iron recommendation isn't any higher for runners, taking in that basic amount becomes even more crucial.

Iron helps to combat the increased breakdown of red blood cells due to exercise, Baker explains.

Although plenty of foods are fortified with iron these days, the type of iron they contain is poorly absorbed. Lean cuts of red meat remain the best source of iron around. So, if you don't eat red meat, you'll have a difficult time getting enough iron, says Kristine Clark, R.D., Ph.D., director of sports nutrition at Pennsylvania State University in University Park. Clark says that women runners should take a daily vitamin and mineral supplement and take a second look at red meat. "To stay away from red meat is a ridiculous concept for athletic females," she says. "Not only can you now buy very lean red meat, but in some cases it's leaner and lower in fat than poultry."

If you're dead set against eating red meat, you need to be especially diligent about your iron intake. Dried fruit, beans, chard greens, and kale are all good sources. Also consider taking a multivitamin with 100 percent of the Daily Value for iron.

## Protein

Many good protein sources are also high in fat. That fact has made many runners slash beef, cheese, and nuts from their shopping lists. But you need these foods to repair the muscular breakdown that comes from exercise.

Sports nutritionists recommend that you consume two to three servings of protein-rich foods a day. Protein is available in plenty of healthy foods, including beans, fish, soy products, and low-fat dairy products. And don't forget the importance of variety and moderation in eating: If you're active, you can feel free to dine on beef, cheese, and nuts as long as they don't make up the foundation of your diet.

## Vitamin and Mineral Supplements

Nutritionists often repeat the following mantra: "Try to get all the nutrients you need from real food, not from pills." Your body absorbs the nutrients from food better than from supplements. That said, take a multivitamin anyway.

Runners have greater needs for many vitamins and minerals. Think of multivitamins as insurance and peace of mind. The re-

*Reading books and magazines is one way to learn the importance of proper fueling. Having the pavement rise up and smack you in the head during an afternoon run is another. Although such a dramatic demonstration packs a potent punch, I'd advise you to learn from others' mistakes— okay, my mistake.*

*It happened when I was notching up my training in preparation for a marathon. I was running twice a day most days of the week. I was also working 10 hours a day, which left precious little time for luxuries like, say, eating. I'd run a long track session in the morning, then have a bagel and coffee at work.*

*Now, it's not as if I was ignoring my diet. In fact, I was pretty proud of myself: I'd stashed a jar of peanut butter in my office in order to make sure I had some protein and fat along with that bagel. And on the day in question, I'd grabbed a banana before leaving home, for good measure. So I ate my bagel, peanut butter, and banana at my desk, worked most of the day, and headed out in the early afternoon for my second run, which was supposed to last an hour.*

*Ten minutes into the run, I felt fine. After 20 minutes, I was getting dizzy and weak. After 25 minutes, I turned around, worried that I'd have to walk in order to get back. Next thing I knew, I had to sit on the ground. The trudge back to the car was one of sheer determination, during which I cursed my idiocy. Let's see: a bagel, 250 calories; peanut butter, 200 calories; a banana, 100 calories. Heck, that's less than I should have had all day if I hadn't run at all, much less after running more than 10 hard miles in the morning!*

*Upon reaching the car, I fumbled around in the glove compartment and sucked down the two packets of Gu I had stashed there. I felt better within a few minutes. Except for the residual embarrassment, that is. Amazing. Calories out, calories in. Energy out, energy in. What a concept. It's one I haven't ignored since.*

ality is that few of us can eat optimally day in and day out. But consider multivitamins a supplement to your healthful eating habits—not license to cheat on the rest of your diet.

## Water

Although it's not a substantial source of nutrients, water is of crucial importance to runners. Even many sedentary people are chronically dehydrated without realizing it. They may suffer from headaches and exhaustion. The loss of fluids during exercise can exacerbate this problem, leading to muscle cramps, dizziness, gastrointestinal distress, and, in extreme cases, a dangerous and potentially life-threatening inability to regulate body temperature.

Make it a habit to drink before and after runs, as well as throughout the rest of the day. Don't wait until you are thirsty to drink: You will already be in a state of dehydration at that point. Also keep in mind that intense exercise can diminish the urge to drink. This is one case where you should overrule your body and drink despite its protests.

For most runners, water or juice is an adequate hydrator. If you log a lot of miles, you might want to replenish your electrolytes by drinking one of the many sports drinks on the market. For the average recreational runner, these drinks aren't necessary, but they won't hurt. "For most people, the key is getting in the fluids," Kundrat says. "If you like the taste of a sports drink and that means you'll drink more, then that's fine."

Kundrat recommends that you start by monitoring your fluid intake to see if you are anywhere near the recommended eight 8-ounce glasses of water a day. Then strive for an additional quart or so a day to make sure that you replenish the fluids lost during exercise. To do this, make a habit of downing an extra glass of water before and after a run.

# 14

# Lose Weight on the Run

MANY WOMEN COME TO the sport of running with the goal of losing weight. That's great: Running is one of the most efficient sports for weight loss, burning an average of 100 calories per mile. (This figure varies depending on your speed and size.) It also tends to moderate your appetite and encourage a shift to a healthier lifestyle.

If you wish to take off some pounds by running, follow these tips for sensible weight loss and optimal overall health.

**Follow the training programs in this book.** If your goal is to lose weight, follow the training programs in this book for either the beginning or the intermediate runner, depending on your experience level. The same programs that help you get in shape will also help you gradually take off pounds. Consistency is the most important aspect of training when it comes to losing weight. Try to run or walk/run three or four times a week, and supplement your program with other active pursuits on your off days. Although it's true that longer or faster running will burn more calories, you should not attempt more strenuous workouts without first working up to them with the more basic training schedules. Taking on extra workouts in order to lose weight faster presents the same pitfalls as any rapid increase in a training program: increased risk of injury and burnout.

**Don't starve yourself.** Some women think that because they are burning calories while running, they can double their rate of weight loss by also cutting back what they eat. But severely restricting calorie consumption while running is not a recipe for successful weight loss. In fact, it can have the opposite effect. Taking in too few calories will cut the amount of energy you have left to run. By dropping your consumption below what your body needs to function, you can also cause your metabolism to slow down.

"Women who cut way down on calories at the same time they increase their exercise intensity run the risk of injury and exhaustion and won't see the benefits of a running program as quickly," explains Susan Kundrat, R.D., a sports nutritionist with Nutrition on the Move in Champaign, Illinois.

Kundrat specializes in working with female athletes, and she advises women to make changes gradually. "A lot of women who start exercise programs want to make sweeping changes in diet at the same time because they are very motivated, but

## How Many Calories Do You Burn in a Day?

**N**ancy Clark, R.D., author of *Nancy Clark's Sports Nutrition Guidebook*, offers the following formula to calculate how many calories your body uses per day.

**1.** Multiply your body weight by 10. This gives you your resting metabolic rate, the number of calories your body uses just in functioning.

**2.** Calculate how many additional calories your body uses during the day in the following manner. Multiply the figure you arrived at in Step 1 by 20 to 40 percent if you are sedentary, 40 to 60 percent if you are moderately active, or 60 to 80 percent if you are very active.

**3.** Determine how many additional calories you'll expend running. You can use a figure of 100 calories per mile.

**4.** Add the numbers you arrive at in Steps 1, 2, and 3 together. This figure is your total daily calorie expenditure.

it's important not to make those changes all at once," she says. "Rather, let your body get used to the changes that come with exercise. Make sure that you're getting enough fuel. Then, once you are feeling good with your workouts, you might want to assess where you are, determine what your goals are. You might wish to lose body fat or get stronger. Then you are in a position to make changes that can complement your exercise routine."

If you are running primarily to lose weight, let the exercise do its work gradually. Eat consciously, without being too restrictive. Listen to your body, eat when you are hungry, stop when you are full, and make wise and healthful choices when you do eat. By doing this, you will ensure that you have adequate energy to run. Follow this formula and you are more likely to lose body fat gradually, in a safe, conservative manner. You'll be more apt to keep it off, too.

**Watch your calorie intake.** Although I just told you not to *severely* restrict your food intake, you should pay attention to your overall calorie consumption. That's because it's the total number of calories consumed that has the greatest impact on your weight. Fad diets continue to offer all manner of formulas to achieve weight loss, but the bottom line is that whether you eat grapefruit or steak, the total number of calories you consume will determine the pounds you gain or lose.

You can watch your calories in a general sense by recording what you eat each day and by not overindulging in high-calorie treats or huge portions. If you prefer a more precise method, use the formula on page 173 to determine your daily caloric requirement. By eating this number of calories per day, you should roughly maintain your weight. In order to lose weight healthfully while running, restrict calories by no more than 10 to 20 percent of this number.

Once you've reached your target weight, the calories burned while running can negate many sins of overindulgence. In fact, plenty of runners who have been at the sport for years say that one of the great bonuses is that they are able to eat more.

*W*eight management doesn't have to be considered a deprivation game. Maintaining an appropriate weight—which depends on your body type—feels good, increases energy, and allows you to be your healthiest self. Although I definitely watch what I eat, I prefer to think of this as health management rather than weight control. That way, fresh, nutritious foods become positive indulgences. Like summer's blueberries over oatmeal. Or an autumn curry of sweet potatoes and carrots. Treats like these from the good earth are every bit as sinfully delicious as a gooey dessert. But instead of feeling guilty after eating them, you can relax knowing that you have indulged in a different kind of luxury: that of caring for yourself.

**Make wise food choices.** Although dieting per se is frowned upon by more and more nutritionists, healthful food choices are of the utmost importance for anyone who's attempting to lose weight. Follow the guidelines for healthful eating outlined in chapter 13. Make your choices wise ones, optimizing the use of the calories you do take in. That means minimizing junk foods, fast foods, and empty calories from soda and the like.

**Treat yourself.** If you make wise food choices, you can still indulge occasionally. If you allow yourself to indulge a craving now and then, you will be less likely to feel deprived and eventually binge. Remember, you aren't supposed to be dieting, but making a change for the long haul. How likely is it that you'll be able to forgo cheesecake for the rest of your life? So go ahead and have a small piece—just don't make it an every-meal or everyday occurrence. Follow the 90/10 rule: Make healthful choices 90 percent of the time, and allow yourself a splurge during the remaining 10 percent.

**Eat out less often.** Restaurant food and fast food are filled with hidden fat and calories. By eating at home, you maintain greater control over what you eat and what goes into every dish. You will also be less tempted to indulge in fattening appetizers and desserts. When you do eat out, be sure to make special requests, such as ordering salad dressing on the side or vegetables without butter.

**Supplement running with strength training.** Muscle tissues require more calories to function than fat does. That means that by building muscle, you can boost your metabolism and burn more calories, facilitating weight loss. Strength training can help you build muscle, and it's a good complement to any running program. As an added boost, it also helps visibly tone your body.

# 15

# Body Image Issues

IT IS THE BEST OF TIMES and the worst of times for women's bodies. Why the best? Acceptance of women's participation in sports and fitness activities has changed the spectrum along which the female body is measured. Women are no longer held up to an ideal of beauty that is rooted in fragility and helplessness. Muscle, strength, and athletic ability are celebrated, as is variety among body types.

Which brings us to the worst: Relentless media images of ever-increasing perfection skew the standards of beauty. The particularly au courant look—a lean body with large breasts—is a genetic impossibility for all but a few women. Yes, muscles and strength are acceptable, as long as they come in an attractive package. In fact, the fitness craze has upped the ante, since now women needn't just be trim, but toned, too. Fat is, as ever, taboo.

Compounding these expectations is a damning belief that a woman should be able to create any body she chooses—the self-help craze run amok. She just needs to work out hard enough and demonstrate enough discipline—or have enough money. Stubborn pockets of the body that resist the effects of training can be enhanced or made to disappear, thanks to cosmetic surgery. The message to every American woman: If you're not happy with something, you can change it.

That message is a dangerous one. Striving for a healthy body and seeking perfection are very different things. Not understanding the distinction is a recipe for frustration. Sure, stomach crunches will flatten your abs, running will tone your thighs, and liposuction can trim the rest, but nothing will alter your fundamental body type, bone structure, and height.

## LOVE YOUR BODY

For the vast majority of women, the increased physical fitness and awareness that come from running counteract negative messages and contribute to a healthy body image. "Exercise can help a woman develop a body in which she feels in control: strong, powerful, and toned," says Carol Otis, M.D., a former physician with USA Track and Field and with the University of California, Los Angeles, cross-country and track teams. Through running, you'll start to see your body as a finely crafted mechanism. You'll learn to appreciate your strength and abilities. Running, for so many women, is the answer to a lifetime of body battles.

Coming to terms with your physical self can, in turn, contribute to a sense of well-being. Women runners, when compared with their sedentary counterparts, are typically less depressed and less anxious and have more energy and greater self-esteem, according to David Brown, Ph.D., a behavioral scientist with the Centers for Disease Control and Prevention in Atlanta. And indeed, many women who began running later in life can pinpoint a fairly obvious shift in outlook that occurred once they took up a more active lifestyle.

For a smaller number of women, however, exercise becomes a double-edged sword. These women take such positive elements a step further, into the dangerous realm of unrealistic expectations. If I am this fit now, they wonder, then how much more will I gain by losing a few more pounds? Or by running still more miles? Look, they say, pointing to thighs, hips, and tummies, I still have fat to lose! Suddenly a healthy pastime becomes a knife of obsession with which they attempt to carve a better self.

"When women use exercise to reshape their bodies, it can be a form of punishment," says Nancy Clark, R.D., author of *Nancy*

*Clark's Sports Nutrition Guidebook*, who has worked with a wide spectrum of female runners on body image issues. "Someone who runs for more than an hour a day might be training for a race, which is fine. If not, it might be a mode of punishment." These women come to view their bodies as "the enemy," as objects that need reforming.

Clark says that if you are one of these women, it's important to realize that the problem doesn't lie with your body at all. "Your body is perfect the way it is. It's your relationship with your body that's not perfect. You want to work on loving yourself from the inside out."

Body dissatisfaction tends to be more prevalent in women than in men, in younger women than in older women, and in sports such as gymnastics and rock-climbing, in which a certain look or weight is beneficial to performance. Because of this correlation, some say that some sports actually contribute to self-critical thinking and behavior. But today, it's largely accepted that personality traits—not particular sports—are the cause of such body image issues. "If these women didn't run, they'd be beating themselves up in some other way," Clark says. "They'd be the ones saying, 'My hair is the wrong color,' or, 'I'm not pretty enough.'"

When women have profound body image dissatisfaction, it can show up through either excessive exercise or restrictive eating. Such beliefs and accompanying behaviors are now considered symptoms of a psychological problem that lies elsewhere. "Such behaviors are smoke alarms that mean there's a fire somewhere else," Dr. Otis says. "It's often the case with the compulsive runner or the person who uses exercise as punishment that there are family issues, relationship issues, or a history of abuse."

Extreme body image dissatisfaction and its ensuing behaviors can be episodic, coming and going depending on the stage of a woman's life. Times of extreme stress and changes in relationships with family or partners can exacerbate the psychological factors that lead to body image dissatisfaction. So can times of transition, such as when a girl enters puberty, when a young woman leaves for college, or when an older woman's children leave home.

One factor that can exacerbate such tendencies is what Dr. Otis calls a sport-body misfit. This is especially prevalent in activities that put a premium on a certain look, such as ballet and gymnastics, but it can also be seen in runners. "When a woman is born with a shot-putter's body and she wants to be a good distance runner, that's a sport-body misfit. It puts her at greater risk for body image dissatisfaction."

Dr. Otis says that this phenomenon is most prevalent in a level of runner sometimes called the sub-elite. Recreational runners don't have a problem because they do not focus on performance, and top professionals in the sport tend to have bodies

---

## ( IN YOUR OWN WORDS )

## Through the Looking Glass

*W*hen I first started running, a lot of people told me that I was too big. This began my attempt to change the body I was given to fit the image of the sport. Fortunately, I gave that up and have pursued running for many years. I now appreciate my body. It also helps that people tell me all the time that I have nice legs—definitely a product of all the running.

**Jane, 44, Fort Collins, Colorado**

*W*hen I was little and ran, it felt good to go fast and I was so proud of what my body could do. When I was in high school and college and facing the body image battles, running was a psychological challenge. I could not overcome my competitive need to be better each time I ran, and I would try to reach perfection rather than appreciate my body for what it was capable of. Now, I am at peace with my body and with running, and I am thrilled at how it feels to be able to move so freely. I go fast when I feel like it and slow when I don't, and I always feel better about myself when I am done.

**Erin, 24, Durham, North Carolina**

*B*eing in shape has an enormous effect on my body image. I know intellectually that this is a body that has done its work: It's had two children, weathered many a life storm, and stayed relatively healthy and attractive. But when I get to the high end of my weight scale, I do start feeling extremely self-critical. Conversely, when I'm in shape, I feel sassy and sexy and unstoppable. And yes, at my age, these feelings are still extremely important to me.

**K.C., 51, Casper, Wyoming**

that lend themselves to success. But because sub-elites are attempting to achieve high marks in a sport for which their bodies might not be built, chances are scant that they will be able to break through to the uppermost levels of competition. That serves to compound their frustration and determination, adding to body-related unhappiness. And in fact, Dr. Brown confirms that the self-esteem benefits of running begin to drop off among high-mileage, competitive women runners, who actually have an increased rate of mood disturbance. "For someone who's born

*I* always felt that I was "big." I've never been overweight, but I am much taller than the average woman. As a teenager, I became anorexic. My body image remained poor for many years after I recovered the weight. I started running after age 30 and toned up. I feel better about myself than I ever have. I still struggle some days with poor self-image, but I think that former anorexics will always have a distorted body image, and for the most part I have a very healthy attitude about it now. I attribute most of the way I feel about myself today to running.

**Kelly**, 39, Bloomington, Minnesota

*M*y body image has been positively affected by running, and I'm much healthier because of it. But in the running community, I find myself unnerved by competitors' comments that I have "so much muscle." Nonrunners, however, are in awe.

**Ann**, 36, Ann Arbor, Michigan

*A*fter struggling with an eating disorder in my teens, I'd say that running saved my life. Without the desire to run, I wouldn't have had any reason to grow into my body again. Running has given me a way to enjoy my body, and it fosters a quiet confidence in my strength, a way to understand that there's no easy distinction between mind and body.

**Renee**, 36, Silver City, New Mexico

*W*hile running up a steep mountain trail, I feel the strength of a less-than-perfect-looking body. My "mirror" is the way my legs feel when they churn up a steep hill or glide down a pine-covered trail.

**Sharon**, 46, Marblehead, Massachusetts

with the applelike endomorph's shape, all the running in the world won't turn her into Grete Waitz," Dr. Otis says. "If you are born with a short, stocky frame, exercise won't change that. But you will develop a strong, toned body that matches what your inheritance is. It's important for women to recognize more images of what 'normal' is and for them to choose role models from this wider range."

## BURNING MOTIVATION

Women don't have to be competitive to suffer from unhappiness with their bodies. Many recreational runners enter the sport in order to lose or stabilize their weight. Some of these women never get past this mind-set. To them, physical activity is little more than a calorie burner. These women may also carefully measure and restrict what they eat and calculate how much they are losing on the run.

But what they are losing is far more than weight. These women, who are essentially restricting themselves to negative motivations, may also be losing out on everything else that physical activity has to offer: greater self-esteem, relaxation, pride of accomplishment, and more.

Furthermore, they might not even be accomplishing their weight-loss goals. If a woman restricts her eating severely, she won't have enough energy to run. Chances are that she'll feel lousy during her workouts; she may even need to slow or stop early. As her body tries to conserve precious energy, her metabolism will slow down, meaning that she will burn fewer calories throughout the day. She could be setting herself up for failure, should her body not respond in the manner she had hoped or as quickly as she had planned. If weight loss is the only motivation, then this kind of disappointment can even end a running career.

Though it's fine to use running as a method of weight control, ideally it shouldn't be the sole source of motivation. You should instead focus on improving your relationship with your body. You should also seek out other, healthier motivations and goals for your running. For example, other similar reasons to run that have a healthy twist might include:

- To be as healthy and strong as possible
- To encourage healthy forms of socializing
- To indulge in a pastime for your own pleasure
- To get to know your body better
- To develop your mental and emotional fitness

## Beat the Body Image Blues

If you believe that you are obsessing about your body, take these steps, as outlined by Carol Otis, M.D., a former physician with USA Track and Field and with the University of California, Los Angeles, cross-country and track teams.

- Resist comparing yourself with anyone else.

- Emphasize health rather than weight.

- Understand what your body type is. Look at people in your family to get an idea of what a realistic goal is for you.

- Understand what it means to be healthy for your body type. For example, some women will naturally become very lean when they run, while others retain more body fat. Both types can be at optimal health while at different weights.

- Choose "body-appropriate" role models. If you have a larger frame, instead of hanging a picture of a very thin cross-country runner on your wall, find a shot of a woman who represents your body type in its fit stage.

- Emphasize the positive. Instead of loathing your thighs and pinching for cellulite, recognize how strong your quadriceps are.

- Choose clothing that's appropriate for your body and for your comfort level. You don't have to wear tights or bun-huggers. Try looser pants and longer shorts.

- Practice yoga or engage in a stretching program. Both have been shown to make women feel good about themselves.

- Start to get outside help early. If you feel that you'd be fitter or faster if you lost a few pounds, work with a sports nutritionist. Consultations are available at health clubs and at many Web sites, or you can call a specialist where you live.

By taking a more holistic approach to running, you can open yourself up to the entire range of benefits that the activity has to offer. Increased self-esteem, discipline, and well-being add up over time to a lifestyle that's conducive to healthy weight management, without negative self-criticism.

## EATING DISORDERS

Although headlines about anorexia and bulimia are alarming, the overall percentage of female runners who suffer from a clinical eating disorder remains small. Numbers are highest among competitive high school– and college-age athletes. Eating disorders are illnesses with serious health consequences, and they should be treated professionally. Left untreated, an eating disorder can lead to potentially life-threatening malnutrition, heart trouble, and bone loss.

Anorexia nervosa is an intense fear of fat that is diagnosed when a patient weighs at least 15 percent less than the normal

## Where to Turn for Help

For further information about eating disorders, contact these organizations.

American Anorexia Bulimia Association, Inc.
165 West 46th Street, Suite 1108
New York, NY 10036
(212) 575-6200

National Eating Disorders Organization
6655 South Yale Avenue
Tulsa, OK 74136
(918) 481-4044

National Association of Anorexia Nervosa and Associated Disorders (ANAD)
P.O. Box 7
Highland Park, IL 60035
(847) 831-3438

weight for her height and frame. A person with anorexia severely restricts her caloric intake and suffers from a distorted body image, continuing to feel fat even when emaciated. Eventually, she will suffer from symptoms of starvation. Ensuing lethargy and feelings of worthlessness make her less likely to seek treatment.

A person with bulimia, although she also may restrict calories and exercise obsessively, indulges in binges in which she rapidly consumes large amounts of food. She also displays counteractive behavior, such as self-induced vomiting and the use of diuretics or laxatives. Bulimia can go undiagnosed and unrecognized by friends and family because women who suffer from it typically are not underweight and therefore do not fit the expected profile of a person with an eating disorder. A person who suffers from bulimia will eventually develop telltale symptoms, including worn tooth enamel, tooth decay, puffiness in the face, and a chronic sore throat.

Compulsive exercising is now also recognized as a form of purging and is therefore considered a symptom of bulimia. Women can manifest this compulsion in many sports; however, running is a popular outlet due to the high number of calories burned. Women who undertake this form of purging can be acting in an attempt to burn off calories or to "punish" themselves for eating or for being the wrong body type.

"It is important for family and coaches to pay attention," says Steven Ungerleider, Ph.D., a sports psychiatrist in Eugene, Oregon, and author of *Mental Training for Peak Performance*. "Often, people who are close to the runner will suspect something but be in denial. Parents might hear through the grapevine that something isn't right. If I hear, for example, 'My girl's doing great, but she's so tired and not looking good and her coach expects more,' those are red flags."

Women who suffer from eating disorders tend to be perfectionists and might come from dysfunctional families. Their behavior often begins as an attempt to control or numb psychological pain by blocking it with physical pain. Many suffer from depression. "In

Body Image Issues   **185**

a way, eating disorders and compulsive exercise are an attempt to self-treat depression or poor body image," Dr. Otis says. "These people do need psychological help to deal with these issues."

Today, most experts agree that horror stories about coaches bringing on eating disorders with off-the-cuff comments about a runner's weight are largely mistaken. Although an athlete herself might claim that such an event was a trigger, experts will agree that other psychological factors have made her prone to an eating disorder. Nevertheless, coaches, parents, and others close to the ath-

## TRAINING LOG

*It was Saturday morning, and we'd just run an 18-miler. Our group—my coach, two male runners, and three females—headed to a bustling breakfast joint to refuel, rest, and socialize. The guys ordered the skillet special: eggs, potatoes, veggies, cheese, and plenty of other goodies on the side. One of the women ordered a bagel, hold the cream cheese. The other two ordered short stacks of plain pancakes, hold the butter. After 18 miles. This prompted one wise young man to comment: "What's with you women, anyway?"*

*What's with us, anyway? We were women in our twenties and thirties, a group of local- to national-level competitors, not particularly elite but quite serious about our training. None of us were suffering outright from bulimia or anorexia. We ate several times a day, usually healthy choices, and didn't binge or purge.*

*We did, however, constantly restrict our food choices, constantly limit our calories, constantly monitor the sizes of our thighs, and constantly compare our bodies with those of other runners. (Perhaps not unrelated, most of us were constantly crabby.) And we were not alone.*

*A professional female runner in her forties once told me that she doesn't know a single competitive woman who hasn't had "issues" with food. I had no trouble believing her.*

*My own flirtation with disordered eating didn't last long—I love food far too*

lete should be cautious not to contribute to a problem by applying additional pressure for performance.

If you believe that you or someone you know has an eating disorder, seek help from a physician who specializes in such issues. The American Psychiatric Association recommends psychotherapy in order to understand what has triggered the eating disorder, to correct distorted body image, and to change obsessive behaviors. Nutritional counseling is advised as well, in order to learn healthy eating patterns. Doctors may prescribe antidepressants and other

much to deny myself of it for any length of time. It reared its head for the year-and-a-half in my midthirties during which I became very serious about my training. But looking back, it's clear to me that it wasn't the running, per se, that brought on my hypercritical diet. Rather, it was my own struggles with body image brought to the surface in a culture of thinness that we women runners perpetuated and secretly admired. "Eat, eat," we would urge each other on. "You're looking too thin." But the speaker of such thoughts would never be caught in her own infraction of consumption. It was a silent game of diabolical one-upmanship. She just wants me to get fat and slow, the thinking went. I'll show her. Thus the bagel, hold the cream cheese.

Every woman's experience is different. For every problem I had withholding dessert and agonizing over the heredity that gave me puffy inner thighs, I had equal and greater triumphs of body image. As a runner, I'd come to love the strength and endurance of my body, and, for the most part, liked the package it came in. When I dropped my plans to compete, I suddenly gained perspective. When I dropped my miles and gained a little padding, I didn't mind feeling curves in new places. I was more than just a machine built for speed; I was a woman built for a dozen different roles and challenges. Seeing my body in a new light, I blinked at the darkness of the tunnel I'd been in—even if just for a brief while—before.

medications to combat depression, boost self-esteem, and reduce obsessive-compulsive behaviors.

## DISORDERED EATING

More common among the general population of athletic women is what has come to be known as disordered eating. This term refers to a wide spectrum of ineffective and potentially harmful eating behaviors. Clark explains it this way: "Normal eating is eating when you are hungry and stopping when you're content. Hunger is seen as a simple request for fuel. But a disordered person will respond to that request by saying, Oh no, I'm hungry. I'm going to get fat."

Although they do not suffer from anorexia or bulimia, these women are inordinately concerned with their eating habits. They tend to restrict calories, banish certain foods from their diets, fast for periods of time, weigh themselves often, worry constantly about weight loss, and fit their social and eating patterns around these concerns. Sometimes, disordered eating habits will develop into a clinical eating disorder, but not necessarily.

In some cases, disordered eating results from a lack of education about nutrition. Clark says that she often sees women runners who diet at breakfast, diet at lunch, "blow it" at night—and then do it again the next day and the next. "That's because they don't know that it's okay to have 600 calories each for breakfast and lunch. They have a flake of cereal for breakfast and a piece of lettuce for lunch. They don't know that the signs of what they see as an eating problem are actually hunger."

In more serious cases, disordered eating is a symptom of other psychological difficulties, much the same as with more severe eating disorders. "It's not that these women don't know how to eat, but rather that they have other issues going on, and this is how the problems are manifested," Dr. Otis says.

It can be difficult for some runners to determine the difference between a healthy concern about performance and disordered eating. Dr. Ungerleider recalls experiencing such problems himself. "When I was training for marathons, there were times when I'd come back from a long run of 18 miles and still be very picky about what I'd eat—and I had a background in sports psychiatry!" If you think that you are developing patterns of disordered eating, Dr. Ungerleider recommends becoming educated in sports nutrition and taking the following steps:

- Honestly assess your current situation: Are you spending more time thinking about food than you used to? Have you changed your eating habits? Are you going through an especially stressful time?

- Examine any training and weight-loss goals to ensure that they are realistic.

- Check in with somebody who is close to you: a coach, training partner, or parent. Talk about your concerns and see whether they have noticed any potentially harmful behavior.

- Consult a sports nutritionist or physician. Make sure that your diet is adequate for your level of activity.

The bottom line for every woman: Treat your body with the respect it deserves. For some women, that may mean becoming educated; for others, it might mean getting help. For all of us, it means loving, nurturing, and feeding the legs and lungs that carry us through our lives.

# 16

# Caring for Your Body

YOUR BODY TALKS TO YOU constantly. It whispers during every footfall of a run. It tells you about uneven ground, about humid air, about a wee bit too much impact on your shins. If you learn how to listen to these subtle messages—many runners don't—you can avoid most running ailments.

The longer you run, the more adept you will become at interpreting your body's attempts at communication. Experience will help you discern the difference between everyday discomfort and impending injury. "It's not as if your left arm turns blue as a signal the day before you overdo it," says David Martin, Ph.D., exercise physiologist and sports science chairman of USA Track and Field. Your body offers more subtle messages, such as a twinge in your thigh, or a pain in your shin, or a slight burn on your big toe.

If you sense such messages and react right away, you can stop an injury in its tracks. A combination of corrective strengthening and flexibility exercises, proper shoes, and corrective inserts can solve many problems. But left untreated, the same injuries can lead to severe discomfort and tissue damage, eventually requiring a break from running, or even surgery.

The lesson? Don't ever try to "run through" an injury, ignoring symptoms until they become debilitating. Even when your pain diminishes on a run—which it sometimes does, as the injured site warms up—don't consider it license to ignore your body's plea for help. Lewis Maharam, M.D., a team physician for USA Track and Field, goes by this rule of thumb: It's okay to self-treat an injury as long as the pain does not alter your stride. When pain makes you limp, see a doctor.

If you've been injured before, you know that seeing a doctor isn't always as easy as it sounds. Running injuries are complicated. Many doctors, especially those who don't run or even exercise at all, don't want to spend the necessary time to get to the bottom of your problem. So you end up getting advice that doesn't work.

To avoid frustration, seek out a doctor who specializes in sports medicine or, better yet, in running. Fortunately, such doctors aren't hard to find. Many communities now have offices or centers that specialize in sports medicine. To find a good specialist, ask long-time runners for recommendations, or inquire at your local running store.

Some running injuries are cut-and-dried; others defy diagnosis. You can increase your chances of a proper diagnosis by providing honest, accurate information about your training. If you don't feel satisfied with the information or attention you receive from one doctor, look for another.

To keep an injury from happening again, make sure that you understand the underlying cause. The majority of injuries are caused by bad training. That's right: running too far too soon and wearing old shoes. If your doctor tells you to stop running but doesn't offer any training tips, get another opinion. When you stop running, your symptoms might go away. Odds are, however, that your injury will only rear its head again when you start running again.

If you have a stress fracture, for example, you will have to stop running—or run in a swimming pool—until the fracture heals. But you should also work with your doctor, following through with bone density tests and an analysis of your diet and hormone levels. Only then will you learn why the fracture occurred in the first place.

With all injuries, take the following precautions.

**Reduce your mileage.** You can continue to run with certain injuries. Just reduce your training to the basics: Plan to cut back by half or one-third and do that running at an easy pace. Avoid terrain such as hills, which can exacerbate biomechanical problems. Also avoid extremely hard surfaces such as concrete and extremely soft surfaces such as sand.

**Train smart.** You may have gotten away with not warming up or cooling down until now, but it's time to break yourself of that bad habit. Precede each run with a gradual warmup and follow it with a cooldown and stretches.

**Stretch lightly.** Be cautious not to overstretch the injured site. Overstretching is a common mistake that can worsen an injury. Don't stretch to the point of pain, and don't jerk. Slowly ease yourself into a stretch, and hold it for 15 to 20 seconds.

**Take painkillers with caution.** Anti-inflammatories can often speed the healing process, but never take them before a run. If you do so, you'll cut off important physical messages, essentially gagging your body's ability to tell you when you've done too much. Take anti-inflammatories only after a run.

**Cool it off.** Icing an injury after a run is one of the simplest yet best therapies to reduce inflammation. A bag of ice cubes works fine; strap it on with an elastic bandage to free up your hands and go about your business. Or try an old runners' stand-by: a bag of frozen vegetables, which conforms well to your body's curves. Or fill a polystyrene foam cup with water and freeze it. Just peel away the edges as needed to massage the ice into your sore muscles. It's easy to hold and control, thanks to the foam insulation.

**Consider seeing a physical therapist.** Physical therapy is an often-overlooked but important part of treatment for most running injuries, says Thomas Shonka, D.P.M., a former president of the American Academy of Podiatric Sports Medicine who has a practice in Boulder, Colorado. Dr. Shonka points out that good physical therapists will do more than just administer treatments such as ultrasound or electrical stimulation. "They can be the ones to crack the whip and be sure you do the flexibility and strengthening exercises you need," he says. "It's not exactly glamorous stuff, and lots of runners won't do it at home left to their own devices. But that's the important work that will get you back on track and keep you healthy down the line."

**Cross-train.** If you have to cut back on your running (or worse, stop altogether) your mood can easily plummet. It's not uncommon for injured runners to feel angry or depressed. Maintaining a positive attitude can be the most challenging part of injury rehabilitation. To keep your mood up, find some form of exercise to maintain your fitness. The type of injury will dictate what type of exercise you can do safely. Consider running in a swimming pool, cycling, or swimming. You can also use your downtime to work on strengthening with weights, to focus on rehabilitative exercises that your physical therapist has recommended, or just to take a relaxing break.

**Resume your training slowly.** After your injury has healed, resume running gradually. The last thing you want is to undertake a sudden leap in training intensity that wreaks new havoc. After a prolonged layoff, your muscles, tendons, and bones will need to readapt to the stresses of the sport. Carefully monitor your injury's progress, backing off should the pain resume. If you have been cross-training, you can start your training again by alternating days of running and cross-training. This will minimize stress on your body.

How much you run when you resume training will depend on how much time you've had to take off. Use these guidelines.

*One week off:* Resume at previous distance.

*Two weeks off:* Resume at half of previous distance.

*Three weeks off:* Resume at one-quarter of previous distance.

*Four weeks or more off:* Start from scratch, alternating jogging and walking until your body has had a chance to adapt. You'll progress more quickly than a true beginner, but you'll still need to take the time to ease back into your full workout schedule.

**Adjust your expectations.** The big race you were training for might have to wait. The PRs you were hoping for might have to come next year. Stubbornly maintaining goals and accelerating a training schedule to get "back on track" can lead to a cycle of disappointment and further ailments. Injuries, much like races that don't go as planned, usually contain lessons. Heed them and you'll become a wiser, healthier runner.

# A GUIDE TO WHAT AILS YOU

The following list includes most common running injuries and conditions, especially those that plague women in particular.

## Achilles tendon pain

Most runners call it tendinitis, but doctors now call it tendinosis or tendinopathy. Regardless of the name you use for this degenerative condition, the result is the same: frustrating pain that can hinder your running and hang around for years.

Achilles tendon problems typically begin as an inflammation of the lining through which the tendon glides, eventually involving the tendon fibers themselves. Chronic inflammation and deterioration in the tendon area can weaken the fibers, eventually leading to partial or complete rupture.

Pain and inflammation are the first signs of Achilles tendon trouble. Eventually, the tendon area will become tender to the touch and visibly swollen. Upon movement, it may elicit a crunching feeling like that of packing snow.

*Cause:* When your calf muscles are tight, you exert too much force on your Achilles tendon, which connects the calf muscles to the bones of the foot. The more speedwork and hill training you do, the more strain you apply.

*Treatment:* At the first signs of Achilles aggravation, stop doing hills and speedwork. See a podiatrist to get a heel lift for your shoes. Warm up and cool down thoroughly during every workout. (More advanced cases of tendon deterioration may require a break from training to allow the tendon to heal.) Ice, anti-inflammatories, and ultrasound (administered by a physical therapist) can promote healing. Massage can accelerate bloodflow to the area and break up adhesions from the scar tissue that develops as you heal. Future maintenance should include flexibility exercises, particularly for the lower leg. One to try is the wall lean: Face a wall, standing an arm's length away, and place your hands on the wall. Step back with one leg and hold that leg straight while you lean into the wall. For an optimal stretch in your calf, keep your weight on the outside of your foot.

## Acne

Women runners can be plagued by skin breakouts on the face, hairline, upper back, chest, upper arms, and rear end.

*Cause:* Sweat production combined with hair follicles or friction from rubbing clothes is a formula for acne. Increased temperature and humidity exacerbate the problem, as do products such as sunscreen and makeup, which sweat off onto the skin and clog pores.

*Treatment:* To fend off exercise-induced acne, follow these steps from Wilma F. Bergfeld, M.D., head of clinical research in the department of dermatology at Ohio's Cleveland Clinic and former president of the American Academy of Dermatology:

- Minimize use of makeup and hair-care products before running. Although special makeup products are being developed for and marketed to women who exercise, the best makeup for running is no makeup at all. If time allows, wash your face before running. After running, wash your face again before reapplying makeup.

- Use a sunscreen specifically formulated for the face on your face and neck. Choose a gel or lotion for the rest of your body, instead of a cream-based product.

- Wipe acne-prone areas with an astringent pad or towelette immediately after running. (Once your body's natural oils cool, they harden, leading to plugged pores.)

- Change out of sweaty exercise clothes immediately after running, and shower or bathe as soon as possible.

- Cleanse acne-prone areas thoroughly. Gentle exfoliation can help, but don't scrub to the point of aggravating your skin.

- If you are generally prone to acne, consult with a dermatologist about the use of prescription medication.

## Allergies

The sneezing, coughing, and watery eyes of seasonal allergies can make you feel like taking a nap instead of running outdoors.

Fortunately, there's a new prescription medication arsenal that can stop allergies without making you feel drowsy or hurting your performance.

*Cause:* Specific irritants—such as pollen or dogs—trigger an immune system reaction, resulting in allergy symptoms.

*Treatment:* Avoid allergens whenever possible. Run early or late in the day, when winds and pollen counts tend to be lowest. Weather patterns and pollen differ in every location, so ask a local allergy expert when it is best to be outside in your area. If rearranging your schedule does not provide sufficient relief, see a physician. Prescription medication can alleviate most symptoms, and it is preferable to over-the-counter medication, which tends to cause drowsiness.

## Asthma

Exercise can reduce asthma symptoms because it improves lung capacity. But since running and other vigorous exercise can serve as a stimulus for asthma attacks, you need to take precautions during workouts.

*Cause:* When a person with asthma encounters cold air, smoke, pollution, or other stimuli, an inflammatory reaction causes airways to narrow.

*Treatment:* Thoroughly warm up before and cool down after runs, advises Stuart Stoloff, M.D., a family physician in Carson City, Nevada, who specializes in airway diseases. Plan to jog very slowly for 5 to 10 minutes before and after your workout. If the air temperature is very cold, cover your face with a bandanna or scarf to warm and humidify the air before it enters your lungs. Finally, ask your doctor about a prescription asthma medication. As with allergies, prescription medication is preferable to over-the-counter drugs.

## Back pain

If you have back pain, you might be suffering from more than tight, overworked muscles. When pain radiates down into your buttocks or one of your legs, chances are that you have aggravated the sciatic nerve.

*Cause:* Sciatica can be caused by any number of mechanical stresses on this nerve, which runs from your lower back through your pelvic area and down your legs. Such stresses can result from bad biomechanics, damaged vertebrae, or even osteoporosis—any of which can put pressure on the disks in your spinal column.

*Treatment:* Strengthening and flexibility exercises for your trunk and legs can sometimes help eliminate the causes of sciatica, as can attention to biomechanics with proper shoes and inserts. Do the back extensions, crunches, and hamstring stretches offered in chapter 18, being especially careful not to strain your back. In some cases, chiropractic adjustments may also help. If you suspect that you have sciatica, see a sports medicine specialist, physical therapist, or chiropractor.

## Birth Control Pill Side Effects

Researchers disagree about the impact of birth control pills on athletic performance. Though most studies have shown these pills to have no effect on performance, some research indicates that women on the Pill may have a slight reduction in aerobic capacity. "For elite athletes, the impact could be significant, enough to lose a race," says Jerilynn Prior, M.D., professor of medicine in endocrinology and metabolism at the University of British Columbia in Vancouver, Canada.

On the other hand, some runners feel that birth control pills may help performance by reducing menstrual symptoms. These runners prefer to take birth control pills on a varying schedule in order to control and time their cycles so that they do not have to race during their periods. Although it is safe to manipulate the timing of your periods by altering the pill cycle, experts generally agree that this practice should be reserved for major competitions and done only a few times a year.

*Cause:* The same hormones that the Pill regulates to prevent pregnancy can affect the way your body feels and functions. As with the Pill's side effects, this effect is highly individual.

*Treatment:* Ultimately, you need to decide for yourself whether birth control pills make sense for you. For each runner who swears by the convenience of the Pill, there is another who insists that she feels and performs better without it. If you run recreationally, you probably don't have to worry about any athletic impact of the Pill. On the other hand, if you race competitively and don't want to risk sacrificing aerobic capacity, you might consider using another method of birth control, such as the diaphragm. If you wish to stay on the Pill, talk with your doctor about getting a very low dose version to minimize side effects.

### Black Toenails

Often surfacing after a race, especially a marathon or one with lots of downhills, black toenails can ruin your chances of looking good in a pair of sandals.

*Cause:* Repetitive trauma to your toe causes a blood blister under the nail. Since the blister can't breathe, it takes much longer to heal than a blister elsewhere on your body.

*Treatment:* Make sure that your shoes fit properly. Keep your toenails trimmed. If you do a lot of downhill running, try to lace your shoes tighter along the tops to prevent your feet from slipping forward.

### Blisters

Although they're not exactly genetically predisposed, some unfortunate runners seem to be plagued by blisters, while others can run merrily mile after mile without generating so much as a hot spot on their feet.

*Cause:* Friction, typically between skin and sock.

*Treatment:* Buy shoes that fit. Then, buy socks made specifically for running. Look for socks made of synthetic fabrics such as Teflon and CoolMax, which wick moisture away from your feet, preventing the sock from bunching up and causing blisters. Also, look for socks with no seams and a smooth surface. Some runners prefer double-layer socks specially created to deter blisters. (The idea is that any friction occurs between the two sock layers instead of between your skin and the sock.) Blister-prone women can also spread petroleum jelly or specially made runners' lubricant on problem areas. Just go easy: Too much will leave you sliding around in your shoes.

If it's too late and the blister has raised its nasty head, take the following steps: Leave the skin covering intact, since it serves as protection. You can drain extremely painful blisters to alleviate pressure. Synthetic skins (now sold over the counter specifically for this purpose) can be placed over the blister to protect against infection and to provide a layer of cushioning. These pads might also speed healing. If possible, run in a different pair of shoes until the blisters calm down, to avoid aggravating the same spots.

## Bone Bruises

Technically speaking, bone bruises are deep contusions. They commonly occur on the outer covering of a bone. Runners will often use the phrase to describe a pain, typically in the foot. But in fact, *bone bruise* is not usually the technical medical diagnosis. The actual injury can be anything from plantar fasciitis to a stress fracture.

*Cause:* True bone bruises are caused by impact with an unyielding object. Trauma typically occurs when the bone is not padded with overlying tissue—think of whacking your shin on a table. In runners, the cause is usually stepping on a sharp rock.

*Treatment:* Again, actual bone bruises are rare in runners. If you feel a deep pain in your foot that does not improve within a few days, see a podiatrist. What you think is a bruise might be a symptom of another injury. The treatment for a true bone bruise is time away from running. If you can run without altering your stride, continue training. Otherwise, cross-train or pool run until the pain subsides.

## Breasts That Ache and Sag

Running, or more precisely, the bouncing action that occurs from impact during running, does not injure your breasts. When it is unchecked, however, that repetitive motion can contribute to sagging.

*Cause:* The skin that supports your breasts is susceptible to stretching over time from gravity and motion. Running exacerbates this stretching—but only when your breasts are not adequately supported. According to LaJean Lawson, Ph.D., adjunct professor in exercise and sport science at Oregon State University in Corvallis and a consultant to the intimate apparel industry, this is a purely cosmetic concern—no harm is done to the mammary glands.

*Treatment:* Wear a properly fitted sports bra. The larger your breasts, the more support you will want in a bra. For more on choosing a sports bra, see chapter 2.

## Chafing

When your clothing doesn't fit correctly, it moves around as you run, slowly wearing away small bits of skin. At the end of your run, you're rubbed raw. Chafing most often occurs around the bra line, on the inner thighs and under the arms.

*Cause:* Repeated motion—specifically, skin rubbing against loose fabric or other skin. In humid climates, the constant presence of sweat can exacerbate the problem.

*Treatment:* Use petroleum jelly or one of several specially formulated runners' lubricants. Spread a thin layer of lubricant on the affected area before you head out for a run. Wear only sports bras made of synthetic materials such as CoolMax that wick moisture away from your breasts and dry quickly. Look for sports bras with smooth seams. Jump around in the store when trying on sports bras to make sure that the seams don't rub against your skin.

## Colds and Flu

Several studies have shown that runners are more susceptible to colds and flu when they are training heavily and especially after they have completed a strenuous, long-distance event such as a marathon.

*Cause:* A weakened immune system is easier prey for the common cold and flu, both of which can result after you inhale or come into contact with the virus.

*Treatment:* Whether you run when you are sick should depend on the severity of your symptoms and on your own judgment. If your nose and head are stuffed up, an easy run can help clear your congestion. If you have a fever, if your muscles ache, or if congestion has moved into your lungs, you are better off taking a break until these symptoms subside. Some doctors refer to this as the above-the-neck test. If symptoms remain in your head, go ahead and run.

If symptoms reside lower in your body or all over your body, give it a rest. Most important, know yourself. If you are sick, chances are that your immune system has been weakened due to stress or fatigue. A day or two of rest might be just what the doctor ordered.

## Corns and Calluses

Some runners like to show off ugly feet as a sort of battle scar of training. But there's no need for roughing it, and with a little attention even runners can have beautiful feet.

*Cause:* Skin toughens as a result of friction and pressure from repetitive motion in running shoes. Ill-fitting shoes exacerbate the problem.

*Treatment:* Keep corns and calluses under control by going over hot spots with a pumice stone in the shower. For overall comfort, slather on a foot-massage product after running or before bed. Look for products specially formulated for athletes; they are meant to cool burning feet and rejuvenate aching muscles.

## Damaged Hair

Your hair might not seem to be at risk from running, but exposure to the elements can take its toll over time. A few precautions can ensure that your locks stay as healthy as the rest of you.

*Cause:* Your hair reacts to the elements much as skin does, meaning that it can become dehydrated and damaged due to sun and wind exposure. And, much like skin, fair hair is more susceptible to damage than darker hair.

*Treatment:* Protect your hair from negative environmental effects by wearing a cap when running. Putting long hair in a pony tail or cropping hair into a short style can keep tresses healthy. Treating your hair with protein- or silicone-enriched products can rejuvenate and strengthen it to some extent. Minimize the use of styling products before running, though, since these tend to sweat off onto your face, blocking pores and contributing to breakouts.

## Dehydration

Although mild dehydration can negatively affect athletic performance, more severe dehydration can cause illness and eventually be life-threatening. Symptoms of dehydration include headache, dizziness, nausea, and cramping. Thirst is not an adequate measure of hydration; many people are chronically dehydrated and do not know it.

*Cause:* Waiting until you are thirsty to drink.

*Treatment:* Runners can avoid dehydration by drinking regularly throughout the day, as well as before and after workouts. For recreational runners, plain water will suffice. But women who train strenuously will need to replace sodium along with fluids to avoid hyponatremia, a dilution of blood sodium that results from ingesting too much plain water. Women who run for more than an hour-and-a-half at a time should consume a sports drink that contains sodium. If you are training for a marathon or a longer distance, or if you're cross-training for a triathlon, you definitely fall into this category.

## Diarrhea

If you have to make frequent pit stops during your run, don't fret: It's not unusual for runners to be afflicted by diarrhea and other gastrointestinal distresses.

*Cause:* Troubles usually occur during lengthy or strenuous exercise during which blood is pulled to the muscles, leaving an inadequate supply in the intestinal tract. These problems are more common in untrained runners than in highly fit athletes. The bad news: Research has shown that women are afflicted more often than men. The good news: A little preemptive attention can alleviate most problems.

*Treatment:* Maintain proper hydration; dehydration exacerbates reduced bloodflow. During marathons and long runs of several hours, consume a sports drink to maintain electrolyte levels. Don't eat foods that are high in fiber before working out: Fruit, vegetables, legumes, and whole grains are notorious troublemakers. If you must have coffee or tea—both of which pack a double whammy of diuretic and laxative effects—try to give yourself a half-hour before running, which should allow time to hit the bathroom before hitting the road. Finally, avoid nonsteroidal anti-inflammatory drugs, or NSAIDs, such as aspirin and ibuprofen, which can also exacerbate alterations in bloodflow to the gut.

## Frostbite and Hypothermia

Since your body generates significant heat during aerobic activity, you can work out comfortably in most climates throughout the winter. And despite what your mother may have told you, your throat and lungs will not freeze when you run in extreme cold. On the other hand, cold air can leave you at a higher risk for frostbite, hypothermia, and strained muscles.

*Cause:* Mother Nature.

*Treatment:* Wear a hat to cover your ears, and wear mittens to cover your fingers. Petroleum jelly can help protect exposed parts of your face. On extremely cold days, monitor your fingers, toes, ears, and nose. They should warm up after a few minutes of running. You can help them along by wearing special winter running socks made partially of wool and by tucking disposable heat packets (sold in most sporting goods stores) into mittens.

If you become wet from rain or are soaked through with sweat while outdoors in cool temperatures, you will have an increased risk of hypothermia, a lowering of the body's temperature. This can occur even in temperatures above the freezing level. To stay as dry as possible, wear proper wicking fabrics that will help keep sweat off your body while running. Do not hang around outside if you are damp; change your clothes and get warm as quickly as possible.

Finally, use common sense. If the weather is so cold that you can't run comfortably, you are at greater risk of pulling a muscle. Warm up slowly and run at only an easy pace on very cold days. Save the hard workouts for the coming thaw. Beware of ice on the street. When you are done running, head indoors and change out of wet clothes.

## Heat Illness

Running in hot or humid weather increases your risk of heat injury, otherwise known as hyperthermia. There are three levels of hyperthermia, listed here in order of increasing severity.

Heat cramps are felt as muscle spasms. Hydration and rest are usually adequate to treat this level of hyperthermia.

Heat exhaustion is typically felt as a headache, weakness, dizziness, and a decrease in coordination. Although your body temperature will be elevated, your skin will feel cool to the touch. Treatment entails rest, hydration, and cooling your body with water.

Heatstroke symptoms are the same as those of heat exhaustion, except that instead of being cool, your skin is hot and dry. Because your body temperature can rise dangerously, if you are suffering from heatstroke you should be taken to the emergency room, where you will be treated with intravenous fluids and cooling methods.

*Cause:* Hot or humid weather that creates conditions in which your body can't adequately cool itself.

*Treatment:* To avoid hyperthermia, stay well-hydrated, wear loose-fitting, lightweight clothing, and run in the morning or evening on days that are very hot or humid. According to Dr. Maharam, runners should be particularly cautious in the "85-85" danger zone, when the temperature exceeds 85°F and the humidity exceeds 85 percent.

### Heat Rash

These tiny, itchy bumps that typically appear on the trunk usually occur when you are overheated and dehydrated.

*Cause:* Your body temperature has increased, and your sweat glands are failing to equalize it.

*Treatment:* Though not harmful in itself, heat rash is a signal from your body that it's time to cool down and hydrate. Cortisone cream, sold over the counter, can help if the bumps persist after you have cooled down.

### Iliotibial Band Friction Syndrome

The iliotibial band is a long span of muscle and thick tissue that runs from your hip to your knee. As with so many biomechanically related running injuries, iliotibial band troubles tend to come on slowly. Increasing pain outside your knee is a cue to take action.

*Cause:* When it becomes tight or overstressed—often the case in runners who over- or underpronate—friction and tension result where the iliotibial band attaches to the outside of the knee. This causes pain and inflammation.

*Treatment:* Ice, anti-inflammatories, and physical therapy such as ultrasound can alleviate pain and inflammation. Although the iliotibial band itself does not stretch, you should regularly stretch the muscles around it. Cross your left foot in front of your right; then, keeping your right leg straight, lean from your hip into the wall and hold this position. Switch sides and repeat the stretch on the other side. Proper shoes and orthotics are a must to fend off the problem once and for all.

## Incontinence

We women are more prone to incontinence because of our anatomy. Although it's not uncommon—it's estimated that about one-half of all women experience some level of urine leakage—it is annoying and disconcerting.

*Cause:* Women who suspect that they experience more trouble while exercising may be correct. Although running does not cause incontinence, the activity—as well as that of other exercises and sports—can induce urine leakage in women who are already prone to it.

*Treatment:* Many women find relief by strengthening the muscles in the pelvic area with Kegel exercises. To do these, contract your pelvic muscles as if you were attempting to stop a flow of urine. Hold for a few seconds, then release for a few. Repeat for up to 5 minutes. For the greatest effectiveness, do these exercises in a variety of positions: sitting, standing, lying down. There are also several devices, both over-the-counter and prescription, that help control leakage. Talk to your doctor about what method might work best for you.

## Medication Side Effects

A running program should generally have no effect on either prescription or over-the-counter medications, according to Dr. Maharam. On the other hand, some medications might have an effect on running performance. Typically, these effects are minimal and of peripheral impact—for example, affecting weight, appetite, or energy level as opposed to directly affecting strength or endurance.

*Cause:* Drugs that seem to be affecting your desire or ability to exercise. As with any medication, any such impact will be highly individual.

*Treatment:* Speak to your doctor if you are concerned about the effects of any drugs you are taking.

## Menstrual Problems

Although some women complain of discomfort during their periods, it is generally accepted that menstruation does not negatively affect running performance. In fact, the menstrual cycle overall is believed to have limited impact on exercise performance. Women have run well, set records, and won championships at all phases of the menstrual cycle. Clinical studies have found no change in heart rate, strength, or endurance during the female cycle. Although some research has shown a slight decrease in aerobic capacity during the latter portion of the monthly cycle (after ovulation), the significance of the finding is questionable.

*Cause:* Menstrual symptoms are the result of hormonal changes that occur with the female reproductive cycle.

*Treatment:* Exercise can improve your feelings of well-being before and during your period. Today, some doctors even prescribe exercise for women who suffer discomfort at this time of the month. Research has shown that moderate exercise can alleviate physical premenstrual symptoms, including breast tenderness and fluid retention. Working out regularly is also thought to relieve anxiety, depression, and other mood disturbances characteristic of premenstrual syndrome. (Some research shows that these benefits tend to become less pronounced in women as they approach menopause, due to ovarian hormonal changes.) Exercise can also contribute to changes in the menstrual cycle itself, most typically resulting in a shortening of the luteal (post-ovulatory) phase.

A potential problem for runners is the cessation of menstruation. Women who run strenuously may be at higher risk of experiencing irregular or absent periods. The term *athletic amenorrhea* has even been coined to describe the phenomenon.

*Cause:* In years past, intense exercise was considered a possible sole cause of menstrual disturbances. But today, exercise is thought to be just one piece of a complex puzzle that typically involves a multitude of emotional and physical stresses. Training stress, performance pressure, low body fat, and inadequate intake of calories and nutrients are all possible contributing factors.

These elements and others create an equation of energy balance, and when the equation tips toward the negative—whether from running itself or from associated stresses—some women will experience menstrual irregularities. Young runners, those who train at intense levels, and those with a history of menstrual irregularities are most prone to disturbances in their menstrual cycles. Other women are able to train at high levels and never experience such problems.

One of the most serious health consequences of amenorrhea is osteoporosis. (It happens because female hormones, which help protect the calcium in bone, are in shorter supply during amenorrhea.) An early onset of osteoporosis can lead to a greatly increased risk of stress fractures and acute fractures. And since decreased bone density is not easily reversed, those serious implications might last for the rest of your life.

An additional concern women runners might face is a lack of ovulation. Because women can menstruate even when they are not ovulating, the mere presence of a period is not a sufficient gauge of a healthy menstrual cycle, Dr. Prior points out.

*Cause:* Lack of ovulation can signal insufficient levels of progesterone. A progesterone deficiency can lead to overstimulation of the uterine lining, putting you at risk for endometrial cancer. (Researchers disagree as to whether lack of progesterone alone also leads to loss of bone mass.)

If you suspect that you are not ovulating, track your temperature as if you were attempting to conceive. A woman's body temperature is generally lower at the beginning of her monthly cycle and higher for the final 2 weeks. The increase in temperature occurs at the time of ovulation. To track this cycle, take your temperature first thing in the morning—before rising—with a basal temperature thermometer. (These are made for tracking the menstrual cycle and are sold in drugstores.) If your results don't follow the above pattern, chances are that you are not ovulating. Complete lack of premenstrual symptoms, such as breast tenderness and cramping, is another clue. If your condition points toward any such abnormality, consult with a physician to determine the cause and a course of action.

*Treatment:* If you suffer from any kind of menstrual disruption, whether amenorrhea or lack of ovulation, investigate the cause with your gynecologist. "Athletes can never assume that menstrual problems are due to exercise," says Mona Shangold, M.D., director of the Center for Women's Health and Sports Gynecology in Philadelphia. "They are not immune to other problems. There might be other serious causes that have serious consequences." Any condition that causes abnormal periods merits investigation, regardless of whether it is exercise related.

Although cutting back on training can help to restore some women's cycles, this shouldn't necessarily be your first or only response. If you are experiencing any menstrual abnormalities, consider the following steps:

- Track your periods, recording dates, duration of flow, and any accompanying symptoms.

- Evaluate your diet, preferably with the help of a nutritionist. Make changes in your eating habits to ensure that the bulk of your calories is coming from healthful food sources, not from junk foods. Be especially careful to take in enough calcium, protein, and fat.

- See a gynecologist to determine or rule out causes of menstrual irregularities not related to exercise. Discuss with your doctor whether hormone replacement therapy is an appropriate option for you.

- Evaluate your training to ensure that you're getting adequate rest and recovery and to make sure that you aren't showing other signs of overtraining, such as slowing times, mood disturbances, trouble sleeping, and weight fluctuation.

## Muscle Cramps

Muscle cramps can feel like anything from a slight twinge to a severe and debilitating bunching of a muscle. They can occur almost anywhere in your body.

*Cause:* Cramps are believed to be caused by a combination of dehydration, low electrolyte levels, and possibly a lack of flexibility.

*Treatment:* Thoroughly warm up before and cool down after workouts. Stay well-hydrated, drinking a sports drink that contains electrolytes if you are engaged in workouts that last more than 90 minutes. Engage in a regular stretching program.

## Osteoporosis

Weight-bearing exercise, such as running, can help build and maintain bone levels in women. But women who exhibit abnormal menstrual cycles, which can result from the combined physical and mental stresses of overtraining and disordered eating, can find that these positive effects on bones are negated.

*Cause:* Several studies have shown that women who have disrupted menstrual cycles suffer more stress fractures than their counterparts with normal cycles. These women also typically exhibit lower levels of bone mineral density. Although it's generally accepted that hormonal disruptions and premature loss of bone density are linked in female athletes, the cause and effect relationships are not clear. For example, some researchers theorize that the type of girl or woman who is drawn to intense athletic performance is more likely to experience and exhibit increased stress in all areas of her life and thus that her hormone levels might be affected even without the exercise. Similarly, women with lean body types might be more drawn to strenuous activity; they, too, might be prone to hormonal fluctuations even without exercise.

*Treatment:* Experts agree that women must act to protect themselves from early-onset osteoporosis, which can leave a 20-year-old athlete with bones as brittle as those of a 50-year-old woman. That's particularly important because it's generally accepted that, once she is past her mid-thirties, a woman can no longer build bone but only maintain her reserves.

If you train at an intense level, you should take every precaution to ensure that you are not losing bone mass. Eat a properly balanced diet: In addition to consuming all the important nutrients and calcium in particular, you should make sure that you are consuming enough overall fat and calories to sustain your level of exercise. Also, monitor your menstrual cycle, watching not just for irregularities in your period but in ovulation as well. If you have abnormalities, consult with a physician. He or she might recommend hormone replacement therapy.

It's also a good idea to have a bone density test. New technology has made quick, simple screenings possible at a wider range of locations—from health fairs to race expos—and at a lower cost. These screenings, while fine for a general indication of bone health, should not be considered a replacement for a comprehensive analysis, which involves x-ray technology and must be done at a hospital or doctor's office.

## Plantar Fasciitis

Most people can go their whole lives never knowing what *fascia* is. Lucky for them. Many runners learn all too painfully about these fibrous sheets of connective tissue, thanks to the ones in their feet. Plantar fasciitis manifests itself as pain on the bottom of your foot—typically, directly under your heel. Although it starts slowly, the condition can become so debilitating that even walking becomes difficult. Pain tends to be worst in the morning, particularly during the first few steps out of bed.

*Cause:* The plantar fascia is a sheet of tissue that runs underneath the length of your foot and connects to the bottom of your heel bone. Because the fascia is not elastic, problems arise when other forces tug on it, meaning that something has to give. "The plantar fascia is not designed to stretch," explains Dr. Shonka. "It's a strong, thin band that is meant to help support your arch." This means, he says, that when excessive pronation or supination or an overly tight Achilles tendon and calf exert force, "the plantar loses this tug of war." The pain and injury come into play when the fascia is actually tugged away from the bony attachment at the bottom of your heel. In advanced cases of plantar fasciitis, x-rays show a spur extending from the heel bone where scarring has built up bony deposits.

*Treatment:* Once plantar fasciitis has set in, ice, anti-inflammatories, and ultrasound can promote healing in the inflamed area. Proper attention to biomechanics and stretching of the calf and Achilles area are crucial to ending the tug placed on the fascia. See a podiatrist for a foot and gait analysis: Arch supports, heel pads, orthotics, or a change of shoes may be appropriate. One currently popular treatment for runners with plantar fasciitis is a "night splint" that holds your foot in an upward flex while you sleep. Many runners once hobbled by the injury swear by this device, which works by keeping the calf stretched. It also eliminates the most damaging tugs on the foot early in the day.

Long-term treatment should include flexibility exercises for the calf of the afflicted foot, especially for its lower section. Take care during this therapy not to further tug and aggravate the fascia. When doing the against-the-wall calf stretch on page 230, relax your back foot and roll it to the outside, then lean into the wall to stretch the calf. It's important to keep the weight on the outside of your foot and not to let your foot roll inward. Done correctly, the stretch should be felt in the lower leg, not in the foot.

## Razor Bumps

Irritated skin around the bikini line is an annoying side effect of running to which some women seem more prone than others.

*Cause:* Bumps or inflammation in this area usually result from plugged hair follicles, which are exacerbated by sweat and rubbing.

*Treatment:* When shaving this area of your body, always pull the razor *with* the direction of hair growth, recommends Dr. Bergfeld. "Shaving against the grain can bury skin detritus and other blockages in the follicle," she explains.

If that doesn't work, investigate other forms of hair removal. Depilatories and lasers have the benefit of keeping hair away for longer periods of time. No matter what method of hair removal you use, wait at least several hours or overnight before running, in order to allow any trauma to the skin to settle down.

## Runner's Knee

You'll feel this around, under, or in front of your kneecap.

*Cause:* Poor biomechanics is the primary cause of runner's knee, which is medically known as chondromalacia patellae. When it is properly functioning, your kneecap glides up and down in a smooth groove of cartilage. When your kneecap gets pulled out of that groove and tracks improperly, the underlying cartilage is aggravated and begins to degrade. Overpronation of the foot is a leading cause of this mistracking because it leads to an internal rotation of the lower leg. Some sports medicine specialists believe overpronation—and thus runners' knee—can be particularly problematic in women, due to the greater quadriceps angle that results from their wider hips.

*Treatment:* Act at the first sign of trouble. Although at first it might seem possible to run through the pain, the discomfort eventually can become severely debilitating, and repeated motion can exacerbate the injury. Detected early, runner's knee can almost always be solved with physical therapy and proper attention to biomechanics. Since damaged cartilage does not heal, however, some advanced cases can require surgery.

Have a podiatrist perform a gait analysis to see whether you need orthotics. Changing your shoe—typically to a more supportive model—and temporarily reducing intense training may also help. Don't run on cambered road surfaces; their slant can exacerbate pronation. Use ice and anti-inflammatories. Stretch your outer thigh using the thigh stretch on page 232, and strengthen your inner thigh with the squat exercise on page 238, to keep your kneecap tracking correctly.

## Shinsplints

Much like the term *bone bruise*, *shinsplints* is a catchall slang term, not a real medical diagnosis. Runners use it to describe any pain between the knee and the ankle.

*Cause:* Rapid increases in training intensity. Shinsplints are most prevalent in less-trained and younger runners. Tibial fasciitis is one of the most common medical diagnoses when such shin pain does occur. This results from a tugging on the outer covering of the bone when the connecting muscle-and-tendon unit is overworked.

*Treatment:* Alleviate inflammation with ice. Stop doing speedwork and other intense training until the shin pain subsides. Pay attention to your biomechanical needs. That means getting orthotics if your feet tend to overpronate. Don't increase your training mileage or intensity too rapidly. It's also crucial to maintain flexibility throughout your calf and Achilles area. "The inter-

**M**y first serious running injury was a textbook case—not only the problem but also my reaction. My knee had become progressively more painful, but I didn't want to stop running. So I didn't. I simply ignored the problem, hoping each morning that it would be gone. It wasn't. My knee finally froze so completely that I could no longer run. That's when I got depressed. (How effective!)

It's not uncommon for runners to react poorly to injury. Our fix has been taken away, and nothing else will do.

At the time, my injury seemed interminable. But doctors quickly diagnosed runner's knee, fitted me with orthotics to control my overpronation problem, and got me up and running again. When I resumed training gradually, I was free of pain.

Having learned from that experience, I'm now prepared to be a better patient when the sidelines beckon. Rather than hoping for divine intervention, I take action. I cut my mileage. I ice. I get massages. I see a physician and then follow up with whatever treatment is necessary to solve the problem. In the meantime, I stretch, I pool run, I lift weights.

But there's one more thing. Once I know that I'm doing everything possible to solve the problem, I let it go. I don't count the days until my next run. Instead, I garden. Read. Clean the house. Have lunch with a friend. In short, I do all the things I never have time to do when I'm training hard. Because as much as we'd like them to, fretting and pouting don't heal tissue and bone. Believe me—I've tried.

The interesting thing is that all of that activity and action make it hard to be too blue, anyway. Taking control of the healing process blunts the sense of loss that typically comes with injury. And pursuing other activities is a healthy reminder that there is life beyond running. When I finally get around to training again, it feels that much sweeter.

play of calf and Achilles and foot arch are critical," Dr. Shonka explains. The tighter the calf and Achilles, the greater the tugging on connecting muscles and tendons.

## Side Stitches

Sharp pains in your side or abdomen can come on suddenly and are usually felt just under the bottom of your rib cage as a sensation that makes it difficult to breathe. Stitches occur most commonly in novice runners and in more highly trained runners when they are exerting themselves to a point that exceeds their fitness level.

*Cause:* Side stitches are typically caused by cramping in the diaphragm.

*Treatment:* Stitches can almost always be alleviated immediately by stopping your run. If you don't want to stop, slow your running pace. Use your fingers to press into the stitch. Exhale forcefully when the foot on the opposite side of your body from where the pain is strikes the ground. (Inhale for three steps, exhale on the fourth, then inhale for three steps again, and so on.) To avoid stitches, warm up properly, breathe deeply from the belly while running, and leave a half-hour between eating or drinking and working out.

## Skin Damage and Wrinkles

Left unchecked, environmental and physical factors can take their toll on your appearance.

*Cause:* Sun and wind are the main factors you face that contribute to the aging of skin, says Dr. Bergfeld.

*Treatment:* You can minimize negative effects with these proper skin-care steps.

- Always wear sunscreen when you are running. Look for a product with an SPF of at least 15; UVA and UVB blocks; and water repellency so that sweat doesn't melt the sunscreen off your skin. If you are prone to acne, seek out gels and lotions; creams contain more oil.

- Moisturize with a good lotion after running and bathing. New products containing alpha hydroxy acids, vitamins, and retinols have been shown to reduce visible signs of wrinkling.

- Try to maintain a stable weight.

- Stay hydrated.

- Run early or late in the day, when the sun's rays are the least powerful.

- Wear a mesh baseball cap to reduce your face's exposure to sun.

- Look for running clothing made from new, high-tech fabrics that are formulated to provide extra sun protection. Check the hangtags.

## Stomach Upset

This is typically the bane of the beginning runner, but any runner can suffer from gastric distress from time to time. Although they are not dangerous, such stomach troubles can be painful enough to stop a run.

*Cause:* Stomach upset usually results from eating the wrong foods or from eating or drinking too much shortly before a run.

*Treatment:* Although you can solve the problem by abstaining from food and drink for several hours before running, such fasting is ultimately not healthy, especially for runners who are doing workouts or races of several hours in duration. You can train your stomach to better withstand food and drink, though. To do so, start by abstaining from eating and drinking for several hours until you are able to run without trouble. Then gradually reintroduce food an hour or so before running. Start with only a few bites of bread and a few sips of water. Increase this amount incrementally until you are able to drink a glass of water and eat a small meal, such as a bagel or an energy bar, without gastric distress. Avoid spicy foods and those that are high in fiber.

## Stress Fractures

Stress fractures in runners are found most commonly in the lower leg and foot. Although the metatarsals (the long, slim bones that make up the midsection of the foot) are most prone to fracture, any bone in the foot is susceptible.

*Cause:* Stress fractures tend to occur when training intensity is increased too quickly. "Bone is constantly remodeling according to the stresses placed upon it," explains Dr. Shonka. "When a runner gradually ramps up her mileage, bone strength increases in response to that stress. But when she does too much too soon, she can exceed the ability of her bone to adapt to stress." Women with low bone density as a result of poor nutrition or irregular menstrual cycles can be at higher risk of stress fracture.

*Treatment:* In most cases, stress fractures begin as a break in the outer covering of a bone. Left unchecked, this can spread and eventually result in a complete fracture of the bone. Therefore, it is crucial to diagnose a stress fracture at the earliest possible time. You'll typically sense a gradual onset of pain when you are developing a stress fracture. At the first sign of symptoms, consult with a podiatrist to confirm the presence of a fracture. Although a stress fracture generally won't show up immediately on x-rays, after approximately 10 to 14 days, evidence of bone growth on the injured site will be visible. Bone scans can confirm the injury right away, but the expensive process is not readily available and thus best left to runners who compete at a very high level.

The only cure for a fracture is time and rest, but that doesn't mean that you must become passive and out of shape. Cross-training can maintain your fitness, provided that the exercise does not mobilize or exert force on the injured area. (Pool running is generally good because it generates no impact.) Make sure to eat properly, since inadequate nutrition—especially a lack of calcium—can slow healing.

## Vaginal Itching

Some runners seem plagued by discomfort in this area, while others never have trouble.

*Cause:* During exercise, your groin area produces a large amount of sweat. Because it also tends to be poorly ventilated—think tights and cycling-style shorts—it is a prime location for bacteria production.

*Treatment:* As soon as possible after exercise, change out of sweaty running tights or shorts and take a shower. Look for shorts and tights that have wicking fabric in the crotch panel. Dr. Lawson recommends synthetics, such as high-tech forms of nylon and polyester, as opposed to cotton, which tends to hold onto moisture.

# 17

# Safety

SAFETY PROBABLY ISN'T the first thing on most women's minds when they run. But here's a wake-up call: In a 1998 survey conducted by the Road Runners Club of America (RRCA), 73 percent of female respondents reported that they had experienced a "frightening or uncomfortable incident" while running.

"I want women to run," says RRCA executive director Henley Gabeau. "But I want them to run safely." Gabeau, who herself was accosted on a run in 1981, has made it both a personal and professional crusade to address the unique challenges that women runners face. "I hate to talk about it because it's a negative subject, while running is such a positive thing in women's lives. But in this day and age, the reality is that there are more women out there running, so you can't ignore it." Most of the incidents reported by women in the RRCA survey were verbal in nature, leading to no physical harm. But even catcalls and leers can contribute to a feeling of vulnerability, a feeling that women can and should work to minimize.

No activity is 100 percent safe. And there are no actions that can create an absolutely guarantee of security. According to Gabeau and other experts, though, a little precaution and a lot of common sense go a long way toward ensuring your safety on the run. As with every other activity you undertake, you must make choices and judgment calls. Ultimately, those choices will depend on your own comfort level.

Gabeau, for example, still prefers to run alone, choosing not to sacrifice her personal time for the potential safety of running with a partner. She takes other precautions, however, including varying her routes, carrying a canister of pepper spray, and informing someone of her whereabouts. "We all take chances every day, and we all make choices every day," she says. "In the end they are not 'right' or 'wrong' but personal decisions. You can't go through any part of life without common sense, and that's what it boils down to."

## STACK THE ODDS

Here's a look at some of the most important precautions you can take when running.

**Follow your intuition.** Your first line of defense when faced with a questionable situation should be to follow your instincts. "That feeling that something is wrong is there for a reason—it's there to protect you," says United States Park Police Lieutenant Kelcy M. Stefansson, who travels the country giving safety talks to women. "I've learned to trust my intuition. I count on it in my job and when I'm out jogging."

Gabeau offers this vivid example of instinct at work: A few years back, a female runner was hit by a car and found herself slightly injured. The two men who were in the car that hit her offered her assistance, but something about them made her distrustful, and she declined. Two days later, the same two men were arrested for abducting and murdering a different woman.

"We're all conditioned to be polite at all costs," Gabeau says, "but if the hair stands up on the back of your neck, you should trust and act on that." That means not being embarrassed to take action when something concerns you. If you are uncomfortable about somebody following you, change course, cross the street, or duck into a store.

**Project a confident attitude.** Your demeanor can become an important part of the safety equation. "If you project a confident attitude that shows that you are aware of what is going on, you are less likely to become a victim," Lieutenant Stefansson says. "Perpetrators are looking for somebody they can control and take charge of."

"I put a lot of stock in attitude," Gabeau says. "I encounter women on the trail who won't even look at me when I pass. These women come across as passive." Not only do they look weak and vulnerable, she points out, but not making eye contact tells a potential attacker that they probably won't be able to identify him in a lineup, because they'll most likely never really get a good look at him.

Although some situations might call for a different response, it's generally important to look people in the eye so they know that you have seen them. Pay attention to details and identifying marks. "You are not so much staring them down as you are basically looking at them as if to say, 'I can identify you,'" Lieutenant Stefansson explains. More extreme measures might even involve action (moving away from a person) or verbal contact (telling somebody to give you space). "But being confident is the first step that might avoid everything else beyond that," Lieutenant Stefansson says.

**Pay attention to logistics.** Of course, no matter what your demeanor and level of alertness, you should do everything possible to eliminate opportunities for trouble. Run during daylight hours, stay away from lonely areas, and run with partners whenever possible. Avoid overgrown trails, and leave plenty of distance between you and bushes or parked cars.

**Ditch the stereo headset.** Safety experts continually warn that one of the worst things you can do is run with a stereo headset. By cutting off your sense of hearing, you put yourself at a disadvantage and eliminate your ability to react quickly. Don't believe it? Experiments have been done in which a stranger was able to run up to women listening to their headsets and touch them from behind; the runners had no idea that a person was coming up behind them. "With headphones, you are not aware of anybody approaching you," says Lieutenant Stefansson. "You can't hear a potential attacker or, for that matter, a dog or oncoming traffic. You have five senses; why cut one off? Would you run with a blindfold on?"

**Leave contact information.** Tell someone in your household where you plan to run, or write down your planned route in your log. Carry identification and change for a phone call while you run.

**Run in familiar areas, but alter your route pattern.** If you run the same route every day, your predictable pattern could be an invitation to an unwelcome interruption. Also avoid a pattern in which you run the same routes on the same days of the week—a pattern in which, for example, Tuesday is Mesa Trail day. Better to mix it up.

**Leave the jewelry at home.** This is especially true when traveling in new cities where you are not certain of the environment in which you'll be running.

**Ignore verbal harassment.** Let catcalls and any other remarks go unanswered. Responding could escalate the situation.

**Run against traffic.** This is not only safer in traffic, but it also allows you to observe the passengers in oncoming automobiles and to spot trouble early.

**Carry a personal alarm and/or pepper spray.** These can scare off a potential attacker. Be sure to get training if you plan to carry pepper spray.

**Be proactive.** Report suspicious behavior to the local police department. Your intuition can help determine when somebody is up to no good. "There will be something that indicates to you that all is not right with the picture," Lieutenant Stefansson says. It might be an out-of-place vehicle parked in the same spot for days, or a man watching people on the bike path, or somebody dressed for running who is not exercising.

"You hate to be suspicious of everybody, but, here again, you should trust your intuition," says Lieutenant Stefansson. It might save somebody else a troubling incident down the road.

In Gabeau's case, other women had reported the man who attacked her in 1981. In several incidents, he had grabbed women or tugged on their clothing and attempted to wrestle them to the ground. "What made me mad at the time was that the police hadn't alerted the community," she recalls. It's one of the reasons that she advocates strongly for a network of women taking action and reporting suspicious behavior. Lieutenant Stefansson agrees, saying that changes in law-enforcement attitudes over the last few decades work to your advantage: "Before, the thinking was, Let's not alarm the community. Now it's accepted that people should know about incidents and suspicions so that they can protect themselves.

"Obviously, it's best to identify a person before an incident takes place. But police can't be all places at all times. You can be the ears and eyes that protect another woman."

Gabeau is philosophical about her brush with danger. In her case, the offender jumped out from behind a tree after she came around a blind corner. After exposing himself, he grabbed her by the shoulders. Luckily, and partly because she was sweaty, she was literally able to slip away unharmed. She has learned from what she sees as her mistakes. "I was extremely regular; I ran the same route every day," she says. "And looking back, I knew that I'd seen him out there before. So now, I try not to be too predictable."

But the experience hasn't frightened her away from running. Far from it. "I'm 55 now," she says. "And I plan to be out there even if I'm 99 and running with a cane."

## OTHER THREATS

Although potential attackers are probably your largest threat, you do have other potential hazards. Here's a look at some of the most common threats and how to handle them.

### Animals

Most of the time when you cross paths with a dog while you are running, the dog isn't likely to bite. He may annoy you by barking, thus destroying your serenity, or by following too closely, thus making you feel like he's going to trip you. But most dogs don't attack.

That said, some do. You never know when a barking annoyance will turn into a snapping menace. Never yell or physically attempt to threaten a dog, says Leslie Sinclair, D.V.M., director of veterinary issues for companion animals for the Humane Society of the United States. "If you make a threatening motion, some dogs will back away, but others will escalate the aggression. And you never know which kind of dog you are dealing with."

Dr. Sinclair suggests that you take the following steps when dealing with a threatening dog.

- If you are approached, don't run away. It could prompt the dog to give chase.

- Stand still with your hands down at your sides.

- Back away slowly, still facing the dog.

- Avoid direct eye contact, which the dog might perceive as a threat, but do keep watch on him.

In most cases, a dog will lose interest, Dr. Sinclair says. Should an attack occur, roll up into a ball on the ground. This action should help the dog lose interest and can protect you from harm. Self-defense sprays can work on dogs in the event of an attack, and a personal alarm can be useful in alerting others that you need help.

## Drivers

Try to avoid heavy traffic when possible. Besides the safety hazard, it's just plain unpleasant to breathe in auto emissions and to have to worry about cars. When you do find yourself faced with traffic, don't count on cars to do the right thing. Too many drivers are so busy doing other things—talking on cell phones, eating fast food, looking at scenery—that they don't pay attention to runners or other pedestrians until it's too late.

Some runners talk about running offensively as opposed to defensively. This means that you must be the one to make the first move to avoid trouble, rather than relying on a driver's judgment. Whenever possible, run facing traffic so that you can see what oncoming cars are doing. In addition to facing the oncoming traffic, you should keep an eye out for particularly hazardous driving maneuvers—for example, when a car is aggressively passing another car by moving onto a road's shoulder and not looking out for runners. Or when a car is turning right, and therefore the driver looks only to the left, not seeing a runner who is coming from the other direction. Also be wary of people backing out of driveways or pulling out of parking lots and into traffic. Finally, wear reflective materials if you must run at night.

## Terrain

Run cautiously when you are on uneven surfaces. Trails with rocks and tree roots can lead to twisted knees and ankles. Be especially careful running downhill on trails; acceleration can make it difficult to control your foot placement. Keep your eyes focused several feet in front of you so that you can anticipate the next few

## TRAINING LOG

*I do not feel 5 feet 2 inches tall when I run. I do not feel as if I'm 103 pounds. I do not feel like a red-haired freckle face. Okay, that's what I am. But inside, I feel like a lion, a warrior, and, should someone decide to infringe on my revelry with hostility, sometimes I feel like what I've instantaneously become: an angry runner.*

*For whatever reason, it is not hard to conjure these attitudes when I run. I've seen my share of suspicious creatures, and when I do, I'd like to believe that I look at them as if to say, "You have found the wrong target."*

*Does this help? Who knows? I wonder myself. When it comes to safety, experts say that attitude has much to do with what comes your way. It's probably true to an extent.*

*I run smart, I pay attention, I run proactively, keeping an eye out for trouble and trusting my gut. I would never wear headphones, I vary my routes, I take note of license plates. But I don't follow all the rules. I have run at night—alone. I have run in strange cities, exploring areas with which I am not familiar. I am fully aware as I do these things that I have increased my risk. And that, should real danger rear its head, all the attitude in the world may not help a 5-foot-2-inch freckle face.*

*The risks that I take are by choice and with understanding. I take them because without a certain level of choice in my life—whether in my running or in any other pursuit—I could not feel free. My choices might seem brash and foolhardy to some; to others they might seem prudish and meek. But they are right for me.*

*In the end, we must all find our personal level of comfort. We must be smart, educated, and aware and take the precautions we choose. And then we must walk out the door and run to our heart's desire.*

footfalls. If necessary, slow your pace and walk down precarious slopes.

Be especially cautious when running on ice. Choose snow-covered sections of road when possible; they offer more traction than slick pavement. And, although it might feel pleasant, it's best to avoid running barefoot, even on the grass or on the beach. Glass and other garbage present a threat to your feet.

## Weather

In many parts of the country, weather can be highly unpredictable. Since runners can be out on the road for several hours, it's possible for you to head out for a workout under sunny skies and end up in a hailstorm several miles from home. Even a small amount of protection can help keep you warm and dry if you get stuck in or decide to wait out a storm. If it's a season of changeable weather, tie a lightweight jacket layer around your waist before you leave the house. A baseball cap is a simple, easy bit of protection that can keep your eyes and face free of rain, hail, and snow. If the precipitation never comes, then the cap can serve to keep the sun out of your eyes.

Should conditions turn downright dangerous, follow the common-sense rules that you would whenever you are outdoors.

*Lightning:* If lightning is still far off in the distance, try to get home by as short a route possible. If lightning is already nearby, do not continue running. Take shelter in a building or under a roof. Do not stay outside in the open or under a tree, which could be a target.

*Hail:* Although you can run through a brief shower of light hail, you will want to take shelter for protection should the storm turn ferocious. The duration of a hailstorm is typically brief, so you can probably take shelter for a few minutes and then proceed to run home when it eases up.

*Ice storm:* When rain freezes underfoot, running can become dangerous. Should the footing become too treacherous, chances are that it won't be getting better anytime soon. Your best bet is probably to call it quits. Walk home if you are close, or use a nearby phone to call a friend for a ride.

# 18

# The Well-Rounded Runner

YOU MAY FEEL LIKE RUNNING is the only exercise you want or need. And yes, running is one of the best full-body workouts around, burning among the greatest number of calories in the least amount of time. So why do anything else? Isn't running enough?

No. It's not. When you run, you do the same motion over and over again. This can tighten your hamstrings and weaken your quadriceps. Sometimes your back can experience too much stress, especially if you don't strengthen your abs. And any less-than-perfect stride—feet that roll in, knees that bow out, hips that tilt forward—can strain an assortment of muscles, tendons, ligaments, and joints.

That is, unless you become a well-rounded runner.

Of course, some enviable women—runners who have perfectly aligned bodies and perfectly shaped feet—can run for a lifetime with no problems. They never get blisters, never strain a muscle, never have the slightest ache, even though they do everything wrong—wear old shoes, increase their miles too quickly, and so on. Such women were blessed with superior genes.

And then there's the rest of us.

You don't have to accept soreness and injury as a given. You don't have to cut back on your miles or intensity. Rather, you simply need to complement running with the right mix of the following elements.

*Cross-training.* Within any training program, your body needs time to recover from running. But that doesn't mean you can't exercise. Cross-training options that don't pound, such as cycling, swimming, and stairclimbing, can do more than help you burn extra calories on a nonrunning day. They can help you strengthen muscles that tend to get weak when you run. Cross-training also provides a way to maintain your fitness when you're injured. Cycling and swimming, for example, are usually still possible when you are suffering from a stress fracture.

*Stretching.* Stretching improves your flexibility, which, many studies show, can actually strengthen your muscles, help you recover faster from workouts, reduce injuries, and improve your range of motion.

*Resistance training.* Stronger muscles can put up with more stress than weaker muscles, so they are less likely to get injured. Weight training can also equalize strength imbalances that could otherwise lead to aches and pains down the road. As a bonus, it also adds power to your stride, which will make you faster.

*Drills.* Basically an exaggerated style of running, the various drills mentioned later in the chapter will make you stronger and may even make running feel easier.

*Pool running.* When you run in a swimming pool, the water's resistance creates a full-body workout, while the buoyancy eliminates the impact on your legs. Plus, pool running is the best recuperation strategy for injured runners since it simulates regular running.

*Massage.* Besides the fact that it feels good, massage can help you recover faster from your hard efforts and reduce injury.

## MORE THAN JUST RUNNING

In addition to preventing injury, becoming more well-rounded will improve your performance and make running *feel* easier. Women runners often suffer from weak midsections, for instance. By shoring up core muscles with other activities, you can avoid slumping forward at the waist—a common mistake when fatigue sets in. Such an improvement in posture will not only keep lower-back, neck, and shoulder pain at bay but also will enable superior pushoff for an optimal running stride.

Spicing up your running routine with other sports and activities can also stave off boredom, boost motivation, and inspire you to take on new challenges. "There's no reason to do the same thing over and over," says biomechanics specialist and seven-time Ironman Triathlon champion Ray Browning, of Boulder, Colorado. Browning says that he once added up all the activities he could do around the house that counted as "working out" and arrived at more than 70. "Some women like to work out in the gym with a trainer or with friends," he says. "For them, a more structured environment is great. Others tend to come from another perspective; they prefer to do exercises on their own and be creative." For these women, hauling firewood or mowing the lawn might develop all the upper-body strength they need.

The process of learning a new skill can prove to have value beyond the obvious physical aspects. "To learn another skill, you really have to pay attention to how your body moves and think of what you're doing," Browning explains. "You then carry that same psychology back to running." A runner often can't tell that she is tight in the shoulders, for example—even when her shoulders are scrunched up around her ears. But when the same runner takes up swimming, she can feel that tightness in the new activity. "It boils down to the fact that we're more receptive when we're learning something."

So how well-rounded do you need to become? How much time will this take? It depends on your goals. All runners should do some flexibility work year-round. If you are a recreational runner, you can also maintain the same strength-training program year-round, optimally two or three sessions per week. If you are a competitive runner, you should concentrate your strength exercises in the winter or off-season. Competitive runners can lift three or four times a week during this base building phase. As spring and summer approach and you intensify your running workouts, back off of the heavy lifting. Cut the frequency of your weight workouts or drill sessions to twice a week. Your goal at this point is not to build more strength but to maintain what you have. If you do track sessions or other quality workouts, be sure to do drills or weights on these hard training days. Otherwise, you'll be making your easy running days too difficult.

Here's a closer look at the six elements that make a strong runner.

# CROSS-TRAINING

Cross-training has been bandied about as the best thing to happen to athletes since spandex. Used loosely, the term applies to any sport or exercise that supplements your primary sport. You don't have to cross-train rigorously to get results. If you run four times a week, hike with your family on the weekend, and swim one morning with friends, you're cross-training. Anyone from the recreational fitness jogger to the professional can benefit from some break in the routine of her running program. Older runners, especially, swear by mixing other sports in with running to reduce stress on their bodies.

Which activities you choose for cross-training ultimately depends on your goals and needs as a runner. Here are some options.

- If you want to develop seldom-used muscles, gravitate to sports that focus on lateral (side-to-side) motion and upper-body strength. In order to develop your inner thighs, arms, and trunk, look to sports such as inline skating, tennis, racquetball, basketball, and martial arts.

- If you need a stress release, look to swimming and rowing. Both are relaxing and provide a non-weight-bearing break in the routine. They're also quiet, meditative activities that produce a mind-set similar to running's.

- If you want to become faster, weight training, drills, and activities that are closely related to running, such as cross-country skiing and snowshoeing, are best. Some runners swear by the benefits of cycling. They say that it's an intense leg strengthener that at the same time allows your joints to rest from impact for a day. Other runners feel that cycling further tightens already taut leg muscles. They think that cycling can overdevelop your leg muscles in a way that interferes with your running performance. Most runners who find cycling to be beneficial are older runners looking to reduce stress on their joints.

The bottom line: Choose a sport or activity that you love. "The main criterion when choosing another activity to supplement running—or any fitness program—is to pick something you find fun," Browning says. "It should make you giggle, feel great when you walk back in the door. It shouldn't be another chore. It's less important to tie it in to running than to be sure that it provides a mental break." And that holds true for the jogger and the elite racer alike. In fact, Browning says that while the hard-core runner may obsess about the performance benefits of her cross-training, she's often the one who could most benefit from a mental break in her routine.

If you're a recreational runner, supplement your 3- or 4-day-a-week running program with 2 or 3 days of other activities. If you're a competitive runner, maintain your 4 to 6 days of running per week. During the off-season, you can let a rigorous cross-training session such as snowshoeing take the place of a quality workout. During a sharpening or racing phase, however, keep cross-training at a lower intensity and substitute it 1 or 2 days a week for an easy run or an off day.

## STRETCHING

Runners are notorious for barely being able to touch their toes, thanks to the tightening effects of the sport. But it's not necessary for you to suffer from an ever-progressive scrunch: Stretching regularly can keep your limbs flexible. And the more flexible you are, the less prone you will be to injuries. Your performance will also benefit from a greater range of motion and a more efficient stride. Besides, as any cat can tell you, stretching just feels good.

Stretching is best done after a workout, when your muscles are warmed up. (If you are injured and suspect that you've a pulled muscle, do not attempt to stretch it. That will only make matters worse. Let the muscle rest for a few days before stretching that part of your body.) When you stretch, do so gradually, and hold positions for 15 to 20 seconds. Do not bounce and never force yourself beyond the point of comfort. Rather, maintain a position at which you feel slight tension. If this becomes painful or difficult over the 20-second period, back off slightly until you reach a point at which you can hold the position.

Once you're in a position, you'll often find that moving slightly to the left or right, higher or lower, stretches a slightly different muscle. The key is to maintain good form; otherwise, you won't be stretching the desired body part at all. For example, try to keep your back straight, but not rigid, when stretching your hamstrings and buttocks. Finally, listen to your body. Stretching should never be painful. If it is, you are pushing too far and running the risk of a pulled muscle.

**Calf stretch**

Stand about one stride's length away from a wall. Put your palms against the wall. Position your right leg close to the wall and extend your left leg back. Keep your left leg extended and your foot pointed forward. Lean into the wall. Make sure that your rear foot stays flat on the ground and that your ankle does not collapse inward. Hold for 15 to 20 seconds, then switch legs.

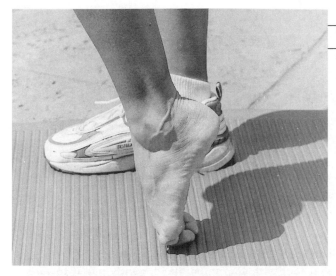

Stand with your body weight on your right foot. Curl the toes of your left foot under, and bring your heel off the ground. Roll onto the top of your left foot. Very gently press your toes into the ground to stretch the outside of your shin. (Be careful not to force this; don't proceed if you feel any discomfort in your foot or ankle.) Switch legs.

Hamstring stretch

Lie on your back. Raise your right leg off the floor as high as you can while keeping your knee straight. Gently use your hands to pull your leg toward your head. Do not raise your lower back off the ground. You should feel the stretch along the back of your upper leg. Move your leg slightly to the left and then to the right to stretch different portions of your hamstring. Some women like to wrap a rope or towel around the foot and gently pull on that for better control. Hold for 15 to 20 seconds, then switch legs.

Thigh stretch

Roll onto your right side. Bend your bottom leg at the knee, hugging it to your chest (1). Bend your upper leg at the knee, bringing your foot behind you. Holding that foot with your upper hand, gently pull it toward your butt (2). Keep your back and trunk as straight as possible. You should feel the stretch in your quadriceps, along the front of your top leg. Hold for 15 to 20 seconds, then switch sides.

Butt and lower-back stretch 1

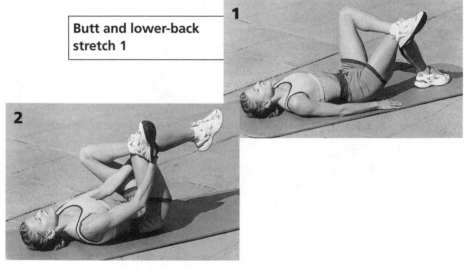

Lie on your back, bending your right leg at the knee. Cross your left leg in front so that your left ankle rests above your right knee (1). Keeping your legs in that position, raise your right foot off the ground. Thread your arms through the opening of your legs so you can hold on to your shin (2). Use your hands to pull your legs even closer to your chest. Hold for 15 to 20 seconds, then switch legs.

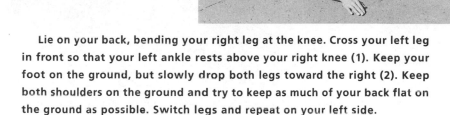

**Butt and lower-back stretch 2**

Lie on your back, bending your right leg at the knee. Cross your left leg in front so that your left ankle rests above your right knee (1). Keep your foot on the ground, but slowly drop both legs toward the right (2). Keep both shoulders on the ground and try to keep as much of your back flat on the ground as possible. Switch legs and repeat on your left side.

**Inner leg and groin stretch**

Sit on the floor with your knees bent and feet pressed together. Hold on to your feet with your hands, and drop your knees toward the floor. Lean forward at the waist, keeping your back straight, to intensify the stretch.

**Hip and waist stretch**

Stand with your arms at your sides and your legs spread about 2½ feet apart. Slowly lean to your left as your left hand slides down your leg. Try to keep your body aligned, bending neither forward nor backward. Raise your left arm straight toward the sky. Switch sides.

**Abdominal stretch**

Lie on your stomach on the floor, with your legs a few inches apart. Place your palms down on the floor just outside your shoulders (1). Straighten your arms as you raise your upper body off the ground, arching your spine and stretching your abdominal muscles (2).

Back stretch

Kneel on the floor (1). Drop your buttocks to your feet, and slowly drop the rest of your body forward. Let your chest relax toward your knees while stretching your arms straight in front of you, palms on the floor (2).

Arm stretch

While standing, raise your right arm toward the sky, then bend your right elbow and drop your hand behind your head. Use your left hand to gently pull your right elbow to the left. You should feel the stretch in the back of your upper arm. Hold for 15 to 20 seconds, then switch sides.

**Shoulder stretch**

Stand with your legs slightly apart, and grab a door frame or exercise station post with your right hand. Step back until your right elbow is straight. Twist your body away toward the left to feel the stretch in your biceps and shoulder. Hold for 15 to 20 seconds, then switch sides.

# STRENGTH TRAINING

The program here is adapted from the one that strength and conditioning specialist Neal Pire of Midland Park, New Jersey, recommends for runners. Pire, who oversees fitness instructor certification programs and trains athletes and nonathletes alike, swears by simple strength-training routines.

"Runners," he says, "tend to want things to be concise and goal-oriented. Otherwise, they just won't do them." Focus on the basics, he says, and you're more likely to maintain your program. You don't need to use every machine at the gym or spend an hour a day there to develop strength and stability. Remember, your goal is to complement your running and develop balanced muscle groups, not to chisel yourself into a bodybuilder.

As more recreational athletes have added resistance training to their regimens, options have grown beyond the traditional health club machines. Gyms are still popular for their selection of weight machines, but free weights, dumbbells, resistance tubing, and plain old body weight are all good alternatives. The exercises listed here can be done at home with strap-on weights or resistance tubing, available at sporting goods stores.

If you are a serious athlete, concentrate your resistance training in the off-season. At this time of year, you can add a strength workout three times a week. During the competitive season, maintain your strength on just two workouts a week. If you are a recreational runner, you can maintain your strength routine year-round with two or three sessions per week.

Here are some strength-training tips.

- Do each exercise in sets of 8 to 15 repetitions, except where noted in the captions. Your last repetition in each set should feel difficult to accomplish—what's commonly known as lifting to the point of exhaustion. Rest 1 minute between sets.

- If you're a beginner, adopt the program very gradually to avoid intense muscle soreness. Start with one set of each exercise, repeating that workout two to three times a week until it's comfortable. Then try to increase to two and then three sets per workout over time.

- Maintain good form. Be careful to work only the body parts specified and not to "assist" with the rest of your body. For leg and arm exercises, keep your back in a neutral position, bent neither forward nor backward. Consider hiring a personal trainer to check out your form for a session or two at home or at the gym.

- Train your legs as you see fit. Some serious runners would never go near a weight with their precious legs for fear of injury. Others maintain that resistance training is a key element to their running success. In the end, there is no right or wrong, only the decision that is best for you. If you run just for fitness, you can safely add weight training for your legs. If you are a more serious distance competitor, keep leg weights light and beware of any strain on your joints and muscles.

**Squat** 1

2

Stand with your feet shoulder-width apart and your arms out front for balance (1). Bend your knees and lower your butt slowly toward the floor. Stop once your thighs are parallel to the floor. Keep your back straight and your head up (2). Return to a standing position and repeat 15 to 20 times.

**Leg curl** 1

2

Put on 2½-pound ankle weights and stand erect (1). Bend your right knee to curl your right leg up behind you, bringing your heel close to your butt (2). Then slowly lower and repeat. Switch legs.

Leg extension

Put on 2½-pound ankle weights and sit on a chair (1). Extend your right leg straight out in front of you (2). Slowly lower and repeat. Switch legs.

Calf raise

Stand on the edge of a step. Rest a hand on a railing or wall for balance. Let your heels drop slightly (1) and then raise them to a level position (2). Once you can easily do the exercise with both feet, switch to one foot at a time.

**Pushup**

Lie facedown on the floor with your hands resting palms-down beside your shoulders (1). Keep your back and legs straight as you push your palms into the floor to raise your body (2). Once your arms are straight, slowly lower yourself back to the starting position. If this is too difficult, bend your legs and then raise your body, keeping your knees on the floor.

**Pulldown**

At a lat-pulldown machine, grab the bar with both hands overhead and shoulder-width apart (1). Then sit with your arms still fully extended. Pull the bar down to shoulder level (2). Raise the bar and repeat.

**1**

**Biceps curl**

**2**

You can do this exercise while sitting or standing. Hold a pair of light (5 pounds each) dumbbells (1). With your palms facing away from your body, bend one elbow and curl that hand up so that your palm almost touches your upper arm (2). Don't move your shoulders or upper arms. Also, keep your back straight and motionless. Lower your arm and repeat. Switch arms.

**1**

**Lateral raise**

**2**

Hold a pair of light dumbbells. Start with your arms at your sides, palms in (1). Keeping your elbows slightly bent, raise one arm out to the side until your upper arm is parallel to the floor (2). Lower and repeat. Switch arms.

**Triceps extension**

Sit on the edge of a heavy, stationary chair or bench. Put your palms on the front edge of the seat, beside your butt. As you use your arms to hold your body weight, bring your buttocks forward, off the chair (1). Then slowly lower your butt toward the floor until your arms are bent at a 90-degree angle (2). Push yourself back up and repeat.

## Upper abdominal crunch

Lie on your back, knees bent and feet flat on the floor. Cross your arms in front of you and rest them lightly on your chest. Keeping the small of your back flat on the floor and your face pointed up toward the sky, bring your shoulders off the ground (1). Without letting your shoulders touch the ground, pulse slowly up and down without resting, counting off each pulse for a total of 20. For best results, do one set of 20 crunches like this straight up and down, and then twist your trunk slightly to the left and the right for one set of 20 total (2).

## Lower abdominal crunch

Lie on your back, knees bent and feet flat on the floor. Cross your arms in front of you and rest them lightly on your chest. Raise your upper body off the ground to the point at which your shoulder blades no longer touch the floor. Keeping the small of your back flat on the floor, curl several inches farther forward (1). Lower yourself by only a few inches, not letting your shoulder blades return to the floor. Pulse up and down in this manner by a few inches for the first set of 20, then twist your trunk slightly to the left and the right for one set of 20 total (2).

**Back extension**

Lie facedown on the floor, hands placed under your chin and legs straight (1). Squeeze your thigh, buttock, and lower-back muscles as you raise your arms and chest off the ground (2). Lower and repeat.

# DRILLS

Although they sound Spartan, drills are the same silly hopping, skipping, and jumping exercises you knew and loved as a kid. They're a great way to combine fun and games with challenging bodybuilding work.

Drills force you to develop both sides of your body equally, calling into play both large and small muscle groups, says Diane Palmason, cofounder and codirector of Women's Running Camps

**Bounding**

Run slowly with a greatly exaggerated stride. Concentrate on the pushoff motion with each foot. Try long bounding, where you see how far you can leap with each stride. Then try high bounding, where you try to

in Denver. Palmason, a world record holder in the 60-plus age group who coaches women of all abilities, encourages all runners to do drills on a regular basis. "Drills are an exaggeration of the motions you use in the act of running," she explains. "They develop strength specific to running patterns, where you transfer weight from one foot to another."

Although you don't actually hop while you run, for example, a hopping drill can develop your pushoff strength. That power will then translate to a longer stride when you run. Other drills develop your buttocks and hamstrings, counteracting what Palmason calls runner's shuffle. "You see a lot of runners using a very sloppy style, shuffling along and relying on their quads to drag themselves forward. But if you have strength in the back of your leg, then you can pick up that leg and move it forward in a more efficient range of motion." Still other drills develop the muscles along the sides of your legs that tend to absorb the shock of running. "And," she adds, "unlike with weight lifting, you're doing the work in a dynamic way. That means that you develop all the tiny muscles in the foot and ankle."

For maximum results, do drills two or three times a week. If you do them only once a week, you'll be starting from scratch each time. Worse, you'll feel sore after each session because your body

jump as high as you can with each stride. Speed does not matter. The slower you go, the better your pushoff will be. Use your arms in an exaggerated manner, pumping high in front of and behind you.

**Run quickly with light steps, lifting each knee as high as possible.**

will never quite adapt. Start with a few minutes and build up to 10 minutes or so in total, doing each drill for 50 to 100 yards.

To do them, find a soft surface, such as grass or dirt, that will minimize impact. Palmason encourages you to adapt such exercises, changing the drill session each time. "Just be sure that whatever you're doing, you're focusing on good form and extension. There's no point in doing sloppy drills. Other than that, do what

Butt kick

**Run quickly as you try to hit your butt with your heels.**

**Don't worry about how much ground you cover.**

feels good to wake up those muscles, get that bounce into your step," she says. Be creative: Leap from side to side, jump over low things; think of the things you did as a child. For optimal benefits, mix flexibility exercises into the strength drills to counteract tightening. For example, follow a skipping exercise with a "rag-doll" run in which you let your arms flop limply at your side. And be sure to stretch gently after the session.

**Don't worry about how much ground you cover.**

## Striding

Run in a slow, exaggerated motion, pumping your arms and

## Sidewinder

Run sideways, placing your rear leg first in front of and then in

## Hopping

Hop on one leg for several steps, then hop on the other. Switch

leaping from leg to leg to make your stride as long as possible.

back of the lead leg. Switch sides and lead with the other leg.

back and forth every 10 steps or so.

# POOL RUNNING

Sad to say, most runners discover the pool only when an injury forces them to do so. In the pool, you can duplicate your running stride, getting many of the same benefits of running on land without the impact. But don't wait for disaster to strike to try this great strengthener: Pool running can also provide a safety break in a high-mileage running routine or serve as a cooling relief session on hot days.

Although you can pool run without a flotation device, you'll probably feel more comfortable using a buoyancy vest designed to keep you afloat and in the correct position. Many pools now provide these pool-running vests, which are also increasingly sold in running and sporting goods stores.

When running in the water, keep your body erect. Try as hard as you can to approximate your road running posture. The biggest mistake runners make in the water is leaning forward from the waist, which results in more of a crawl than a run. Performed correctly, you will move forward at a very gradual rate.

Just as you would on the road, you can vary the intensity of your workout by varying the pumping frequency of your stride. In fact, due to the monotonous view, you'll probably find pool running most enjoyable when you play around with different "speeds." Bear in mind that "speed" while pool running refers to your stride frequency, not to your movement forward. Some runners do whole speed workouts in the water, with a warmup, intervals, and a cooldown. Just don't attempt to base your workout on a heart rate: The cooling effect of the water will keep your heart rate slower than on land.

While the resistance of the water gives you an intense strength as well as endurance workout, it can tire you out. The harder and faster you attempt to stride, the greater the force of the water working against you. Don't be surprised if you tire quickly the first few sessions. Build up gradually as you would with any new activity.

# MASSAGE

Sports massage serves a different purpose than traditional relaxation massage. A good sports massage therapist can loosen up tight muscles, finding potential trouble before it turns into an injury.

This kind of body work is typically deeper than other forms of massage, and it can cause greater discomfort.

For best results, look for a massage therapist who specializes in sports massage. Some even work solely on runners. These therapists will know the trouble spots that plague runners, and they can give you the most comprehensive massage. A good massage ther-

## TRAINING LOG

*I*nspired by my multitalented friends, I decided to break one summer's running ennui by racing my first triathlon. I'm in good shape, I figured. How hard could it be? Here's how hard: After performing well in the running leg (unlike most triathlons, this course put the run first and the swim last), I noodled along with my underdeveloped quads as 500 cyclists swarmed past me. I wasn't in dead last yet. No, that milestone occurred when an 11-year-old boy passed me as I flailed in the water. While the other competitors ate bagels, I chowed on postrace humble pie.

Running will make you fit, all right, but it's not the only game in town. I faced a decision after that race: Do I attempt to branch out and master this triathlon thing or stick to running? For me, the answer was clear. Running was my true love, and I would remain a runner. I resigned myself to the fact that I'd never be breaking the wind for anyone on a bike ride and that my swimming is at best a survival skill. But the race did point out the imbalances in my body. Afterward, I began to do more strength training and flexibility work to ensure that I was fit in a well-rounded manner.

Not everyone needs to be a multisport athlete. Some personalities like to delve deeply into one area, while others prefer a smattering of different stimuli. Both can be well-rounded. You are a well-rounded runner if you are aware of your body's strengths and weaknesses. You are a well-rounded runner if you work to develop your fitness in a holistic manner from which you derive enjoyment. You are a well-rounded runner if you are strong yet supple. And if you can complete a triathlon without someone offering you swimming lessons along the course, well, that's just icing on the cake.

apist will ask how much pressure you are comfortable with. You should never be afraid to speak up if something hurts.

If you aren't used to deep massage, your body may feel sluggish and sore the day after the session. This feeling should dissipate within a few days, and it will become less noticeable with ensuing sessions.

Always communicate with your massage therapist about your running schedule. That way, you can get the right type of massage at the right times. Just before and after a tough workout or race, for example, your massage therapist should never go deep. A deep massage before a race can make you feel sluggish. A deep one right after can actually cause more harm than good. But a light rub that warms up your muscles is perfect. In general, you want to leave at least 3 days to recover from an intense massage before a race.

If you are a competitive runner who trains heavily, consider having a massage every week—if time and money allow. On the other hand, if you put in fewer miles, you may wish to schedule a massage only when you have increased the level of your training or when you have engaged in other activities that have left you sore or tight.

You can also try self-massage. Using your hands or specially designed massage devices, apply gentle pressure where your muscles are tight. Applying friction by rubbing horizontally back and forth across the muscle can help loosen up knots. You can even hire a sports massage specialist for a session or two to teach you how to best self-treat your trouble spots.

# The Pregnant Runner

LAURIE COULDN'T FIGURE OUT why she wasn't running faster. "Here I was racing at sea level after training at altitude, and I didn't feel any faster," she recalls. "I'd just gone for a run with a friend and I was telling her how crummy I felt: sluggish, heart racing, just tired. She thought she recognized my symptoms. We were at the train station in Chicago and she made me stop in the drugstore and get a pregnancy test. We checked it right there in the ladies' room at Union Station, and sure enough, I was pregnant!"

Other than the part about the train station, Laurie's experience is similar to that of many women runners. Because the sport teaches you to listen to every message from your body, runners often receive the first clues about their pregnant condition from their workouts. Something may simply feel amiss. Your pulse may race, you may breathe more heavily, or you may have to work harder to hit the same times. After a few days—or weeks—of wondering what's wrong, all the pieces fall into place when you take a pregnancy test and find out that you're "running for two."

Although physicians used to frown upon exercise for pregnant women—especially upon weight-bearing activities such as running—today, many experts consider exercise healthy for both you and your child. A body of research shows that moms who exercise through their pregnancies tend to have fewer physical complaints and fears, feel more positive about their pregnancies, retain a better self-image, be more prepared for labor, have a decreased incidence of Caesareans, and recover more quickly after delivery. Douglas Hall, M.D., an obstetrician in Ocala, Florida, who specializes in developing workout programs for expectant mothers, explains that exercise can counteract some of the debilitating effects of pregnancy. "Women who work out during their pregnancy overall have a better, more positive pregnancy experience," he says. "They take control of the process instead of the pregnancy controlling them."

Because of the tremendous number of variables that go into each pregnancy, it's harder to measure the impact of exercise on the fetus. Experts agree, however, that no research indicates that moderate exercise is harmful to a developing fetus, provided that you do not exercise to exhaustion and that you heed any warning signs from your body. Indeed, babies born to mothers who exercise can reap the benefits of a mom who took the time to care for herself. "A woman who exercises through her pregnancy tends to take an active role overall in her health, instead of taking the attitude, I'm just trying to get through this. And that can make a difference to the child," Dr. Hall says. "Babies don't come out a blank canvas. They reflect what their mothers have put into the pregnancy already."

Even with a go-ahead from the medical community, you probably have countless questions and concerns: How much is too much? Will my body temperature or breathlessness harm the fetus? How do I know if I'm hurting my baby?

The first answer to all of those questions is to relax. Your body has an amazing array of adaptations that protect your growing child against harm. The second answer: Listen to your body during pregnancy. Listen constantly and listen carefully. Although your body gives off warning signals during exercise to ensure the safety of the fetus, it's up to you to heed the messages that are being sent.

## INITIAL REACTION

If you have been attempting to conceive, discovering that you are pregnant is joyous news indeed. But for some women, especially serious runners, the first reaction might not be so clear-cut. After years of enjoying the fringe benefits of running—time to themselves or time socializing, improving fitness, and a trim figure—it's no wonder some women are ambivalent upon discovering that they are pregnant.

Laurie, who became pregnant at the age of 28, had the reaction of a runner who dearly loved competing. "I'd just been getting back into good racing shape. In fact, I'd just traveled to go on a racing circuit, and I was really fit at the time," she recalls. "So to be honest, my first reaction was, I can't believe this is happening! I was shocked. I wasn't unhappy; I just didn't know how to feel. After a short while, I was thrilled, but my first reaction was definitely, I don't know how to react!"

She's not alone. The value placed on career, independence, and even thinness in our culture mean that pregnancy can be a loaded emotional issue. For athletic women, questions can be compounded. Because those feelings of ambivalence can be a great source of guilt, it can be comforting to realize that you are not alone. Above all, don't berate yourself if you find that your first reaction is one of fear, uncertainty, or disappointment. Take comfort in the fact that—provided that other variables in your life are favorable—such extrinsic reservations about the pregnancy typically disappear within a few weeks.

"I had been working very hard to get in shape when I found out that I was pregnant," says Mya, who was 29 when she had her first child. "But I couldn't be disappointed. I knew that I could still run well later. You look at other women and see that they regain their old fitness and even more."

## A SHIFT IN PRIORITIES

When you become pregnant, your running goals should change overnight. If weight control or faster times were a priority before, they shouldn't be anymore. Whereas you might have been pushing yourself to the limits of fitness before, now you simply want to pamper yourself for optimal health, well-being, and relaxation.

"The women who have a hard time are those who retain the idea that they must be as fit as possible," says Dr. Hall. "During

# Wisdom from Moms Who Have Been There

*Sometimes, running can get rough for a month or so, depending on how your body feels. But things keep changing throughout the pregnancy. So even if you have to take a break, try it again later. You might be able to go back to it. I ran better at 8 months than 2 months before!*

**Laurie**, 30, Boulder, Colorado

*Find a doctor to work with who believes in exercise during pregnancy, because so many still don't. And don't push yourself trying to get fitter once you find out that you are pregnant. Run however much feels comfortable, based on the level at which you were when you got pregnant.*

**Mya**, 38, Denver

*Even if you're tired, take the time to exercise—even if it means letting other chores go undone. This is one thing you are doing for your health and your sanity, and you shouldn't ignore it. Besides, the running will give you more energy.*

**Shirley**, 43, Santa Fe, New Mexico

*As I began to show, I struggled with whether to strip off my T-shirt and let it all hang out so that I could be comfortable, or whether to cover up and skip the strange looks from folks on the trail. I was surprised to learn how shocked people were at the sight of a bare pregnant belly. I typically chose to tolerate the looks, knowing that the baby could sense the sunlight through my uncovered belly.*

**Lisa**, 29, Boulder, Colorado

*After the first two babies it was like, Boom! My fitness came back fast. But after the third one, no way. I thought I'd be back within 6 months, but my body wasn't ready. I was comparing too much with what I'd experienced before instead of listening to my body, and I was sorry after that. I kept having setbacks. But now, if I have a fourth child, I'll know what to do. After the first two, I told women who wanted to start running, "Just go for it." Now I tell them, "Relax, listen to your body, and just take your time."*

**Nadia**, 31, Boulder, Colorado

pregnancy, you want to be as strong as necessary but not as strong as possible. It can be hard for an athletic woman to change her goals suddenly, because she won't feel like she is doing enough. But it's a very important distinction."

Here are some ways to help you change focus.

**Pamper yourself.** Instead of dreading the weight gain, fitness loss, and discomforts of pregnancy, look on the bright side. You have a good excuse to indulge completely in your well-being. Appreciate it while it lasts. In fact, these 9 months can be a time to develop good health habits that you can carry beyond pregnancy. With your baby's health foremost in your mind, you might, for instance, begin eating correctly and getting enough sleep for the first time in your life. "When you are pregnant, you take such good care of yourself," says Nadia Prasad of Boulder, Colorado, an Olympian and 1995 French national 10,000-meter champion who has run through three pregnancies. "Your runs then become such times of celebration and joy."

**Just get out there.** Symptoms during the first trimester can make exercise sound less than joyous for some women. Nausea, exhaustion, and dizziness make it tough to function, much less run. Most women say that running during the first few months of pregnancy is even more difficult than running during the final months before delivery. But they all agree that mustering the wherewithal to get out the door—even if it's for only a little bit of exercise—is just the thing to boost your energy.

"I was lucky; I didn't have a lot of symptoms. The only thing that affected my running was that I was so tired," Mya says. "But running helped that because it gave me a burst of energy. If you're running before you become pregnant, don't stop. It will help give you energy and let you feel more in control."

**Give your training diary a rest.** Ah, control. You'll quickly learn to go with the flow. Planning workouts, especially in the first trimester, can be a lesson in futility. One day can differ from the next dramatically in terms of energy levels and other factors that affect running, such as heart rate, blood pressure, breathlessness, and dizziness. It's hard to ignore the demands of the little one growing inside you, and in fact, you shouldn't try. Consider those symptoms to be signals telling you to take it easy.

# Risk Factors

**M**ost women can continue to exercise at a mild to moderate level during pregnancy. For some women, however, the additional stress of exercise might put them at higher risk of suffering some negative consequences for themselves or their babies. Women with the following conditions are generally advised to refrain from exercising:

● Pregnancy-induced hypertension

● Preterm rupture of membranes

● Preterm labor during the prior or current pregnancy

● A cervix that dilates prematurely

● Persistent second- or third-trimester bleeding

● Inadequate fetal growth

Although some physicians discourage exercise for women with a history of premature labor, three or more miscarriages, or multiple-birth pregnancy, others feel that there is no evidence proving that exercise is indeed harmful in these cases.

In addition, the American College of Sports Medicine advises you to carefully monitor your body's reactions while exercising. Consider any of the following as signs to discontinue exercising and consult a physician before resuming:

● Bloody discharge from the vagina

● Any gush of fluid from the vagina

● Sudden swelling of the ankles, hands, or face

● Persistent, severe headaches or a visual disturbance

● Swelling, pain, and redness in the calf of one leg

● Elevation of pulse rate or blood pressure that persists after exercise

● Excessive fatigue or any palpitations or chest pains

● Persistent contractions (they may suggest the onset of premature labor)

● Unexplained abdominal pain

● Insufficient weight gain

"For some women, the experience can be frustrating because they can no longer run at the level they desire," says Judy Mahle Lutter, president of the Melpomene Institute for Women's Health Research in St. Paul, Minnesota. "But it's time to listen to your body and be wise." Lutter's own daughter was disappointed because discomforts kept her from exercising to the extent that she wished during pregnancy. "As with so many women, she found that she needed to stay active because that's who she is. Working out was a stress reliever." It's easier to continue, Lutter says, when you understand that the usual rules don't apply. "Understand that things will happen—you'll get a backache or something else that a run might ordinarily help—and now the run is making it worse. If things don't feel good, that's probably reason to stop for the time. But that doesn't mean that you have to give up on exercise entirely."

## LISTEN TO YOUR BODY

To keep your baby safe, never make your exercising body compete with the baby for adequate bloodflow, heat dissipation, oxygen delivery, and energy. That means never reaching the point of exhaustion and breathlessness.

Amazingly, your pregnant body's natural adaptations lessen the possibility of training to the point of risk. Several studies have shown that most women will naturally stop or slow down in a workout before they reach a point of dangerous intensity. Since your core temperature rises during pregnancy, for example, you will feel overheated and uncomfortable earlier in your workout, making you more likely to back off. Likewise, the elevated heart rate early in pregnancy will force you to run more slowly. Follow these guidelines to keep your baby safe.

**Stay at a moderate level of exercise.** Let your perceived level of exertion be your guide. Don't run to the point of breathlessness or overheating. When in doubt about the intensity level of your running workouts, err on the side of caution. Keep in mind, however, that most of the medical community thinks that exercise at a moderate intensity poses no risk to your baby if you are already used to such workouts.

**Don't worry about past actions.** If you, upon discovering that you are pregnant, remember with horror an intense speed workout or long run that you did unintentionally beforehand, relax. Just like those one or two glasses of wine you might have had before you realized that you were pregnant, a few harder workouts shouldn't have hurt you. Once again, your body likely would have

Take these precautions to keep you running comfortably through your pregnancy.

● Drink plenty of fluids to counteract the dehydrating effects of exercise.

● Dress in comfortable layers to ensure adequate ventilation. You might overheat more quickly than you are used to.

● Consider running smaller loops and staying close to home. That way, if fatigue strikes early, you can easily walk home.

● Wear sunblock. Sun exposure can exacerbate the "mask of pregnancy," a pigmentation darkening that affects many women during pregnancy.

● Try using a special maternity belt once you begin to put on weight in your midsection; some women find the extra support beneficial. These are available in most maternity stores.

The Melpomene Institute for Women's Health Research in St. Paul, Minnesota, publishes information packets on exercise during pregnancy. The Institute updates these packets regularly, based on the latest research. For information, contact the Melpomene Institute, 1010 University Avenue, St. Paul, MN 55104, or visit its Web site at www.melpomene.org.

signaled you to slow down before allowing you to hit a level that could be damaging to the fetus.

Nadia's experience with her second daughter should be of some comfort if you are worried that you trained too hard early in your pregnancy. "I had been doing 100 miles a week, all my hard workouts, everything," she recalls. "I had just run my best time yet in the 10-K, a 33:40. What finally made me realize that something was wrong was that I was getting more and more tired on my long runs. And at the end of workouts, I felt like throwing up. I got tested and realized that I was 5 months pregnant."

At that point, she hadn't yet gained any weight. She dropped her mileage, cut back her intensity, and began doing some of her workouts in the pool. Four months later, she gave birth to healthy, happy Anita. This story *isn't* meant as license to go out and put the pedal to the metal, though. Remember, your first priority is the baby. It's likely, however, that your body and your baby are a good bit more resilient than was once thought.

**Postpone major running challenges.** Save the marathon or PR attempt for another time. You should not be doing training that extends you to your limits, and trying to run fast or far will do just that. If you've been training to run a marathon, it's best to stop and cancel your race plans. Even if you were to run the race slowly, you'd still be exerting yourself for several hours.

**Put away the heart-rate monitor.** The increase in maternal heart rate renders general heart-rate formulas invalid for pregnant women. Although guidelines from the American College of Obstetricians and Gynecologists used to recommend that pregnant women keep their heart rates under 140 beats per minute while exercising, the 1993 revised guidelines recommend instead that women base their exercise intensity on perceived exertion, stopping before the point of exhaustion or breathlessness.

**Alter your workout for comfort when necessary.** Partly because of the jostling involved in activities such as running, doctors used to tell women to rely primarily on non-weight-bearing exercise during pregnancy. Today, it's generally considered safe for women who are already running to continue to do so as long as they remain comfortable. How long to continue is a judgment call, and one that is different for every woman. Nadia reports stopping at around 7 months with all of her three pregnancies, because the manner in which she was carrying felt awkward. Mya, on the other hand, was still running up to 4 miles at a stretch 2 weeks *past* her due date! When running no longer feels comfortable, consider walking, running in a pool, or swimming in order to maintain your fitness. Should you go through a setback that stops you from running early in your pregnancy, don't count yourself out for the duration: You might be able to pick it up again at a later stage. Consult your doctor first, though.

## EATING FOR TWO—AND THEN SOME

As a pregnant woman, you need about 300 extra calories per day—slightly less in the first trimester and slightly more in the second and third. If you run throughout your pregnancy, you need to be extremely vigilant about meeting your energy needs. That can be especially tough if nausea is interfering with your appetite.

Here are some ways to solve the problem.

**Graze.** If you are experiencing nausea, food aversions, or a loss of appetite, eating several smaller meals a day can be more comfortable than three large meals.

**Separate liquids from solids.** Drink liquids separately from meals—at least a half-hour before or after—and don't have items such as soup with meals. In some women, the combination of liquids and solids strains the digestive system.

**Never run when you are hungry.** An hour before your run, try something plain, such as a piece of toast or some crackers.

**Always have breakfast, lunch, and dinner.** You should never skip meals, especially if you are exercising. This is not a time to worry about keeping your trim, runner's figure, or a time to try to "bank" weight loss as a hedge against the inevitable gains coming a few months down the road. You should gain between 25 and 30 pounds. Some runners who start their pregnancies in an extremely thin state report shooting up several pounds almost instantly as their bodies attempt to pile on the appropriate reserves.

"It was a struggle at first, thinking of gaining all that weight," says Laurie. "I've never been more than 5 pounds over my racing weight in my life. Then, immediately, in the first 3 weeks, I put on 10 pounds. It was as if my body was saying, You need the extra weight. That was a shocker—I thought that I was going to gain 80 pounds at that rate! But it leveled off. It worried me a little at first, but I wasn't going to let it take control of my emotions and the baby's health. I kept eating extra like I was supposed to."

**Relax.** Some women runners who continue to train throughout their pregnancies report difficulty maintaining the proper weight during the final few months. "At 7 months, I'd put on 28 pounds, but then I started losing weight," says Shirley, an artist in Santa Fe, New Mexico. "Sienna was 9 pounds when she was born, so she was taking a lot of energy inside there. My body fat was actually disappearing in the last few months. I ate and ate and ate but didn't gain."

After gaining all that weight early on, Laurie was having a similar experience at 8 months. "I made myself eat then, even when I wasn't hungry, because I'd stopped gaining," she said. "It felt like the extra energy requirement with running had slimmed down my hips and legs, and all the food I was taking in was going straight to the baby." Although experts advise you to shoot for regular and consistent weight gain over the course of the pregnancy, such fluctuations are not cause for alarm. You should continue to ensure that your overall weight gain is sufficient and that your caloric needs are being met.

## DISCOURAGEMENT FROM LOVED ONES

Although books, doctors, and magazines might all be telling you to go for it, you can bet that someone in your family or circle of friends won't be so enthusiastic about your running. Old attitudes die hard. And, from that other person's perspective, it can be awfully hard to watch the pregnant woman you love take on tiring pursuits.

"People did try to talk me out of my running," Shirley says. "My husband was freaked that I would consider joining a team to do the running portions of the Mt. Taylor Winter Quadrathlon (an event consisting of biking, running, skiing, and snowshoeing up and down a mountain). He was appalled. He'd seen me dissolve into tears because I was so tired, so he condemned me for adding to the stress with running. He was just concerned for the child and for me. And it was, in fact, a hard time because I was so tired. But I needed to continue to run for myself. When he saw that in the second trimester I had more energy, he was fine with my running."

If people you love are discouraging you from running, ease your mind by:

**Remembering that they mean well.** After all, you know how worried you are about ensuring the optimal health of your baby.

**Reassuring your concerned loved ones.** Let your husband or mother know that you *are* keeping your child's best interests child at heart. Explain to them the health benefits for both the child and you. Finally, let them know how important your fitness is to you, both physically and emotionally.

# The Myth of Pregnancy and Performance

**R**umors abound about the performance-enhancing effects of pregnancy. And in fact, women have run personal records during and after their pregnancies. Although reputable research on this subject is scanty, a number of possible explanations have been put forth, including hormonal shifts, increased aerobic capacity, and a higher pain threshold due to childbirth. Reports have even circulated that coaches in Eastern Bloc countries in the 1980s—a period tainted by admissions of improper drug use—tried to capitalize on such "pregnancy effects," encouraging their female athletes to become impregnated and then abort the fetuses.

"There is no solid research about performance improving after pregnancy," says Judy Mahle Lutter, president of the Melpomene Institute for Women's Health Research in St. Paul, Minnesota. "It's a case-by-case basis. Most of the reports of improvement come from elite athletes. But for women on a more recreational level, it's hit or miss. Some say that they become stronger, and plenty of others say that they never quite get back to their former strength or stride. While improvement is a physical possibility, it shouldn't be expected. And it is even less likely for nonprofessional runners because they suddenly have the added responsibility of a child, meaning less time to train and a shift in priorities."

## Breast-Feeding Concerns

**W**hether you breast-feed or not might impact the rate at which your body returns to "running normalcy" after giving birth. But that means different things for different women, and it's impossible to predict the manner in which your body will respond. Some women claim that the caloric requirements of breast-feeding help them drop extra pounds in a jiffy. Others believe that breast-feeding encourages their bodies to hang on to extra adipose tissue. As with most other factors surrounding your pregnancy, this is a decision you should make with the baby's best interest in mind. If you do choose to return to your running program while you are breast-feeding, monitor your baby's weight gain. Insufficient gains could be a sign to cut back on exercise. To ensure adequate milk production, be sure to consume enough calories from healthful sources, and don't drop weight too quickly.

Some research indicates that your postexercise breast milk may contain lactic acid. Although this won't harm your baby, some babies get fussy about the different taste. If your baby doesn't like your postexercise milk, simply use a breast pump to extract some milk before your run. Or just wait it out: Your lactic acid levels will return to normal within an hour after your run.

*Being a good listener.* Sometimes it takes an outside observer to see things clearly. Pregnant women who are pushing themselves to accomplish everything at their pre-pregnancy rate risk overdoing it. If you've been running yourself down, your mom, your hubby, or whoever it is could be right: It might be time to take a day off from running, housework, and everything else and just take a nap.

## ON THE COMEBACK TRAIL

According to the American College of Obstetricians and Gynecologists, many of the same physiological factors that limit your ability to run during pregnancy persist for several weeks after you give birth. Follow these guidelines for a successful return to running.

**Beware of setting expectations.** Don't create a time frame in which you'll return to your former self. This could force you to overdo it or to be disappointed if you fall short of your planned schedule. You'll notice that there's no training schedule in this chapter for returning to running. That's because of the great variety in experiences women have after giving birth.

**Start gradually.** Let your body decide when it's ready to go for a spin around the block. Your first sessions should be easy walks of short duration. Don't set goals for time or pace. When you can complete these sessions with no trouble, gradually increase your time and integrate brief intervals of slow jogging. Follow the rules for beginning runners, gradually working up to a half-hour or so of walk/runs. Only when you can comfortably jog again for at least a half-hour four or five times a week should you consider picking up the pace. If you experience complications such as heavy bleeding at any time, lay off the running for at least several days before trying again.

**Remember that you're different from other women.** Lutter points out that women vary dramatically in their post-pregnancy experiences and that measuring yourself against others can be a setup for disappointment. Although some literature says that you can return to your former fitness in 6 weeks, "for plenty of women, it's more like 6 months," she says. "Their babies are still up all night, the women are supertired, and it's not realistic. It's better for a woman to assume that the process will last at least 6 months. Then, if she happens to be back in 2 months, it's gravy."

**Listen to your body.** Just as women have different experiences returning to running after childbirth, the same woman can have different experiences from one pregnancy to another. Resist comparing yourself with where you think you should be or with where you were in a previous pregnancy. Just as in training during pregnancy, listen to your body and proceed at a pace that feels comfortable.

Mya was able to begin running 3 weeks after she had a Caesarean. After a few weeks of training, she felt up to entering a race. She ran it as 6-week-old Michael watched from the sidelines. Shirley's experience was more challenging. "I tried to start running 6 weeks after giving birth, but my breasts hurt too much from breast-feeding. So I quit and waited until about 10 weeks. I ran a race shortly thereafter, and I didn't feel very strong, but I felt very light. Between breast-feeding and running, I was burning a lot of energy."

Nadia experienced both extremes. She began running a mere 1 week after her first and second pregnancies. (Six weeks after the birth of her second daughter, she managed to click off a half-marathon in 1 hour and 11 minutes.) But the birth of daughter number three, Nyla, was a more difficult affair, and Nadia's comeback was significantly slowed. "I made things worse by trying to meet the expectations of the previous pregnancies and by not listening to my body," she says.

## TRAINING LOG

*Never let it be said that I don't research my subject matter thoroughly. Over the course of writing this book, I learned that I was pregnant. My life, my work, and my running would never be the same.*

*I'm embarrassed about my first thoughts: What will happen to my figure? What will happen to my time alone to run? And what of my quest for the Olympic Trials?*

*A week passed. We'd first seen our baby on an ultrasound, a blurry pulse vibrating in my womb. It might as well have been a lifetime. My life and my running had already inexorably been changed, and the questions of only a week ago no longer seemed important. I was no longer concerned about muscle tone; my body instead became a source of nurturing. I ate five, six times a day, as hunger dictated. My "training" had become exercise for the health of the baby and myself. I ran as my body told me. When my heart raced, I stopped. When I felt good, I would walk and jog for up to an hour. When I felt bad, I would skip it altogether.*

*And the Olympic Trials? Somehow the idea of whipping my body into shape after giving birth seemed not only stressful, but rather beside the point. My dreams had become consumed with other priorities, of health and fitness not only for myself, but for my child.*

*Pregnancy gave me a gift I never could have expected. I'm left with sheer wonderment at and respect for the other things my body is capable of. My running, always a celebration of movement and strength, now is also a celebration of life.*

Most of the women I interviewed for this book reported a change in focus after the birth of their children. Even the most serious competitors who planned racing comebacks acknowledged that baby now came first. The general consensus was that if the running came around to its former level, great, but it was no longer necessary. Recreational runners began to focus less on body perfection. For most women, moderation seems to be the key after a baby enters the picture. This means neither pushing all-out in runs nor sacrificing your workouts to all the other demands that compete for your time. Just because your pregnancy is over, you needn't forget everything you've learned about taking care of yourself. Your children will be relying on you for years to come, and a healthy, happy mother will be better able to meet their needs.

"When I had my baby, I thought, I want to return to my running career, but mostly I want my kids to be happy. That comes first," says Nadia. She sums it up with the love of a woman who is clearly inspired by both her children and her running: "Every time you come back from your run and you see your baby, it's like the sun in the house. It gives you energy. Life becomes more full, more grounded. You no longer run just for yourself; you run for your baby, you run for your family. You feel as if you can do anything."

# 20

# The Younger Runner

WITH A MARATHON BEST of 2:26:40, Kim Jones has finished within the top three in some of the country's most competitive races. But the running accomplishment of which she is most proud isn't a race or a time but rather her daughter, Jamie.

After a solid high school career that included a state championship and a top 10 national ranking, Jamie headed off to a promising career as a freshman at the University of Colorado. "I always tried to be very careful," says Jones of raising her daughter as a runner, "because I knew that she had the talent to be great."

As it turns out, Mom's caution and careful attention paid off. Jones provided a textbook case of how to do everything right when it comes to raising a daughter who runs. Jamie started running in first grade for a series of short races held within the school system. "They never 'trained,' they just played," Jones recalls. "The races were a mile or so on the grass in the park." Jamie showed promise early, clocking a 5:50 mile in grade school and winning the city-wide race. But Jones made sure that Jamie stayed active in other sports, including softball, volleyball, and basketball. "I encouraged her in everything, in those other sports as much as anything. Deep down, I was hoping that she'd go for running, but I never directed her that way." As it turned out, Jamie chose the sport on her own, deciding after middle school to focus on running.

Keeping athletics fun, encouraging a child in all areas, and staying involved as she grows up are important aspects of support echoed over and over again by experts in youth fitness. Jones was on the right track in all those areas. As proof, her highest praise comes from perhaps her harshest critic: Jamie herself. "She helped me so much," says Jamie, who hopes to become a professional runner and beat Mom's times someday. "I never felt pressured when I was young. I learned so much just from watching her."

## GROWING UP HEALTHY

What children learn from watching their parents is, in fact, crucial. It's estimated that up to one-half of children in the United States today participate in virtually no physical activity whatsoever.

Childhood today is not conducive to physical activity. Computer games, the Internet, and, of course, television keep children glued to their bottoms for the majority of their recreational hours. With both parents working, children are more likely to spend their time indoors in a day-care setting. And fear of crime and violence means that children are less likely than ever to be outdoors when they are at home—even in the best neighborhoods.

The result is a generation of children growing up unfit and over-weight. "In our part of the world, obesity is the number one chronic health problem," says Oded Bar-Or, M.D., director of the Children's Exercise and Nutrition Centre and professor of pedi-atrics at McMaster University in Ontario, Canada. "And it's getting worse and worse." Dr. Bar-Or points out that exercise is the sim-plest solution to that growing problem: The more physically active a child is, the less likely it is that she will become overweight.

Beyond the obvious physical impact, girls in particular benefit from physical activity in ways that can affect the rest of their lives. According to the Women's Sports Foundation in East Meadow, New York, girls who participate in athletics are:

- less likely to become involved with drugs

- less likely to engage in sexual activity

- less likely to get pregnant

- more likely to graduate from high school and college

- more likely to have higher than average grades

"Girls who do sports are able to look at their bodies in a different way," says Lynn Jaffee, program director of the Melpomene Institute in St. Paul, Minnesota, which specializes in girls' and women's health. "Instead of viewing it as a question of How thin am I? or How pretty am I? it's, How strong am I? How fast am I? They view the body as a competent thing rather than only as an object of attractiveness."

Those benefits continue beyond the teen years. The Women's Sports Foundation also reports that women who participated in sports as girls demonstrate higher than average confidence, self-esteem, and pride in their physical appearance. They are also less likely to suffer from depression.

# THE RIGHT START

When should you encourage your child to become active? The earlier the better. A 1989 study showed that if a girl does not participate in sports by the time she is 10 years old, there is only a 10 percent chance that she will be active in athletics when she is 25. This may be changing slowly with the greater numbers of women discovering sports and the greater acceptance of older women in sports. But clearly, the earlier your daughter becomes active, the better off she is physically, mentally, and emotionally.

That doesn't mean that you should take your child to the track and start timing her as soon as she can walk. In fact, forget "running" altogether, at first. Physical activity for children needn't be—shouldn't be—structured until they are at least in middle school. Instead, sports should remain play. That way, it becomes a regular part of daily life. Here are some ways to incorporate healthy pastimes into your child's routine as she grows.

## The Preschool Years

**Play outdoors.** It's important to get your child into this habit early on. Setting this pattern early might help to avoid a video-game habit later.

**Be creative with activity.** Tossing a ball, doing somersaults, and jumping in leaf piles are examples of fun pastimes that build coordination.

## Grade School

**Encourage natural child's play.** Child's play is, after all, pretty much running around. "When I was brought up, my mother would shove us out the door and we'd run around the fields," recalls Priscilla Welch, of Tabernash, Colorado, whose world-best 2:26:51 marathon as a masters runner ranks among the sport's greatest performances. "But it was playtime, not hard miles on the roads."

Kim Jones recalls a similar experience. "I grew up in a household of 11, and we had to share one bike," she says. "If we wanted to go to the beaches, which were a mile or so away, we would just run. It wasn't training—it was all natural."

**Engage in low-key contests.** A backyard can be the perfect training ground for building lifelong active habits and sportsmanship. Races, tag, ball games—just about any outdoor activity that entails moving around is all the running that a young child needs. "The goal shouldn't be fitness at a young age but rather to have fun," says Susan Kalish, executive director of the American Running Association. "If they always have fun with it, they'll always do it. You don't want young children to think of exercise as work or to have the upsetting connotations of not meeting performance goals." Welch concurs: "When you take children by the collar and structure them seriously, that's how you lose them."

**Play with your children.** Ask them to teach you the outdoor games that they play in school. Invite their friends over in order to have a baseball or touch football game.

**Turn family outings into active fun.** Take your child on walks, hikes, and bicycle outings; all are great family activities at this age. Be sure to let your child set the pace. "I started running with my daughters while they were on their bikes," Kalish says. "Then they started running when they wanted to. We go as long and hard as they want, and we play a lot of games. We might race to the creek. But if they want to stop and catch tadpoles, then we stop. I'm very careful not to push them. And I let them take the lead, literally going in front of me. That way, they stop when they want to."

**Begin lessons if your child wishes.** Let your children participate in organized league sports or lessons if they wish, but don't force them. At this point, it's best to let them choose the sport. Most important at this age is that they learn and enjoy, not that they turn into Junior Olympians.

## Middle School or Junior High

**Find active weekend and holiday pursuits.** Your child will be spending more time away at school and with friends. Make good use of family time by planning healthy activities. Hiking and cycling can be combined with camping trips.

**Enter a race together.** Walk together in a 5-K. Not only is it great exercise but you'll be exposing your child to the festivity of a race environment.

**Consider organized sports.** By now, your child may express an interest in team sports or even in more regimented training for an individual sport such as running. That's fine, as long as the impetus comes from your child and not from you or a coach. Forcing a program on your child at this stage could turn him or her off of the sport for good.

## High School

**Combine sports with community work.** Encourage your child to walk a race for charity, earning money from sponsors in your neighborhood.

**Let your child join a sports club or team.** A team atmosphere will help to develop cooperation and sportsmanship. At this age, children are old enough to handle greater training structure and competition.

**Continue to encourage healthy pastimes.** Fight the video habit with active family recreation. Teens enjoy fun activities such as swimming and Frisbee throwing without even realizing that they are getting exercise.

In addition to encouraging your children to be active, there are things you can do to make sure that they get off to the right start.

Here are some tips to make sure that your own behavior is supportive of physical activity:

**Be a good role model.** Experts say that one of the best ways you can ensure that your children get exercise is by setting a good example. Seeing you include running, cycling, or walking in your day will help your children think of physical activity as the norm.

**Provide positive feedback.** Negative criticism can turn your child off to sports altogether. "I would always give her positive feedback when she did well, but also when something went wrong," Jones says of her daughter's early forays into sports.

## Running and Growth

**M**any people worry that running might somehow stunt their child's growth. Not true, says Oded Bar-Or, M.D., and other experts in youth fitness. "The source of that notion seems to come from dated observations, in which active children were thought to grow at a slower rate than those who were sedentary," says Dr. Bar-Or, who is director of the Children's Exercise and Nutrition Centre and professor of pediatrics at McMaster University in Ontario, Canada. "At least one reason for that turned out to be simple: The children who did well in sports and thus were studied were already more mature than those who were less active. They had already gone through their growth spurt, while the sedentary children had their growth spurt yet to come—thus the perception of unequal growth. More recent studies confirm that running and other sports do not stunt growth one bit."

The process of growth during puberty and adolescence can, however, impact running performance. That's because, during growth spurts, bones grow at a rate far exceeding that of muscle. The result can be a decline in athletic performance during periods of growth, when the body is literally out of balance. "The anecdotal observation that running performance can suffer during these 'awkward phases'—when the limbs are lanky and seem to go all over the place—is probably due to a mismatch of growth between the bones, muscles, and tendons," Dr. Bar-Or explains. "For girls, muscular development catches up to the bones at the very end of a growth spurt. For boys, it can take even longer—up to a year—for the muscular development to catch up." Although it's perfectly safe to run during these times, these growth spurts are yet another reason to keep any training light during the preteen and teen years. Young bodies should be expending the lion's share of their energy on proper growth, not prepping for a marathon.

By providing a supportive environment, you'll be encouraging your child to take chances and learn.

**Be aware and involved.** Listen to your child. If he or she is feeling pressured, take action by talking to the coach, switching to a league with a different emphasis, trying a new sport, or making sure that you are available to offer support and guidance. Jones stayed involved in her daughter's training throughout high school, speaking to the coach when she had concerns. She made sure that Jamie understood the importance of proper nutrition and the importance of breaks and recovery for long-term fitness. The result was not just a successful athlete but also a strong, well-adjusted young lady. "She's learned so much about herself physically and emotionally," says Jones of her daughter. "She's more positive about everything as a result of her running." A bonus was that mother and daughter became exceptionally close due to their shared pastime. "She and I will go and run together in the morning and talk about everything," Jones says.

## THE SHIFT TO COMPETITION

There is no magic age when your child can or should start focusing exclusively on training for one sport. Most experts, however, recommend that you keep your children involved in a variety of activities for as long as possible. This keeps things fun and prevents boredom. It also helps children to develop a variety of skills at an age when they are most easily able to learn. Runners especially, Dr. Bar-Or points out, can be "born" at any age. Unlike gymnastics and figure skating, which require specific skill development at an early age, running does not need to be mastered early and does not require early specialization for later success.

High school traditionally has been the time at which youths make the transition from playing to training. But community and pee-wee programs are increasingly available for grade school age children who wish to engage in competitive running. "Organized groups can be a good way to take running from the fun, family stage to something more goal-oriented," says Roy Benson, an esteemed coach and heart-rate training expert in Atlanta who has 4 decades of experience working with runners of all ages and ability

## Staying Healthy

Injuries are, unfortunately, a significant risk for girls starting a running program. Research has found that the highest rate of injury among high school sports is in girls' cross country. This is probably because untrained girls come off their summer breaks and immediately start logging miles in the fall. The results can be shinsplints and stress fractures.

Girls can avoid injury by following the same smart training principles that apply to any beginning runner: Never increase mileage or speed too quickly, do some running on soft surfaces, and be sure to wear appropriate shoes and insoles. Most important for youngsters is to do some preliminary running over the summer so that they do not enter the fall program on "cold" legs and abruptly increase their mileage. Running a few miles three or four times a week over the summer might be all it takes to avoid a debilitating injury in the fall.

levels. He adds, however, that parents should make sure that the program has the right emphasis.

"These programs are good if they teach some of life's valuable lessons, for example, about the relationship between hard work and rewards. Or if they enhance self-image through accomplishment," Benson says. "But they can be bad if self-image is damaged because the child does not measure up to somebody else's definition of success. The worst thing is when children experience this type of unexplained failure and lose their love of running or competition because they are told that they aren't tough or good enough."

If your child wishes to concentrate solely on running—or on another sport—follow these guidelines to ensure that he or she will have a positive experience.

**Get her involved in numerous athletic events.** Most coaches agree that, even if your child shows talent, you shouldn't focus exclusively on running too early on. Standout runners of all ages have "disappeared" after promising high school or college careers, quitting the sport altogether or never living up to early expectations. The syndrome is referred to as burnout, and it's all too common in an intense sport such as running. What has happened to these promising youngsters? They have exhausted themselves prematurely—sometimes physically, sometimes mentally, often both.

**Make sure that she doesn't get too serious too soon.** "Except for the truly elite talents, most young runners have a window of 4 to 6 years in which they can give it their all," says Benson. "The elite runners can run just fast enough to win—they don't have to go into the depths of their psychic wells—and so they can prolong their running careers. But all the others, the kids *striving* to excel, must give an enormous psychological and physical effort. If a youngster is going to be good at this, he or she has to give up a lot. After giving 100 percent every day, and in every race, and basically giving up being a normal kid or teenager, eventually he or she will need to say, That's enough. So if you start them at age 10, the career might be over at 16."

**Keep the training light.** Benson and other coaches agree that it's preferable to undertrain a young runner than to overtrain her. After all, the most important aspect of training a high school runner is ensuring that she sticks around for the years to come, whether competitively or recreationally. Keeping training miles light in her early years can prolong a young girl's career. She will be fresher mentally should she decide to continue competing, and she will be less likely to suffer injuries.

Proper mileage will be different for every young girl, but Benson does offer some rough guidelines. In the first few years of high school, rookie runners—even those who demonstrate natural ability—should go very easy on mileage to avoid injury and allow bones, muscles, and tendons to slowly adapt to the repetitive stress of running. Although every girl is different, 15 to 20 miles a week is considered a conservative, low-risk estimate for a runner beginning her high school training. By the junior and senior year, an athlete's body should have adapted, and she should be comfortable with this level of training. At this point, Benson recommends, girls can move up to 30 or 40 miles a week, as their natural ability allows.

# THE COACHING RELATIONSHIP

Training, as it turns out, is just one part—and maybe the simplest part—of the equation for coaching youngsters. Developing the mind and building the positive attributes that can come with running should be the priority at this stage. These are the things that a young runner can take with her and apply later in life to anything from work to relationships.

"For grade school and high school athletes, coaching should be more about direction than workouts," says Ann Boyd, an elite runner who also coaches youths in Ann Arbor, Michigan. "It's the coach's job to give young runners the tools, with instruction and

## Fueling Small Engines

**W**hen it comes to hydration and nutrition, children do not respond just like miniature grown-ups. Although it seems like kids can keep going and going without tiring, in fact, children are more prone to dehydration and overheating than adults are. "When it comes to dissipating heat from the body, children are at a disadvantage," says Oded Bar-Or, M.D., director of the Children's Exercise and Nutrition Centre and professor of pediatrics at McMaster University in Ontario, Canada. "Children don't sweat as much as adults; they produce more body heat; and they take in more heat from the environment, since their ratio of surface area to volume is greater than that of an adult." That triple whammy adds up to a greater risk of rapidly rising body temperature during prolonged exercise such as running.

To protect against such a rise in temperature, make sure your children drink before and after exercise. If they are active for a long period of time, have them take breaks to drink every 15 minutes or so. This can be tricky, since many children turn up their noses at water. Because they are likely to drink greater amounts of a flavored beverage, a sports drink or diluted juice might be preferable.

For optimal nutrition, don't feed your children as you would yourself. Your low-fat, heart-healthy diet isn't appropriate for growing bodies. That doesn't mean to let them load up on junk food and unhealthy saturated fats. That does mean to include healthy protein- and calcium-rich foods in most of their meals—peanut butter, cheese, milk, meat—without trying to cut fat at every corner. The standard mandate to load up on fresh fruits and veggies still holds; most children take in far too little of these nutrient boosters. Finally, though it may seem impossible, try to limit sweets as much as possible to avoid development of a sweet tooth and its ensuing dental difficulties.

mental and emotional support. Proper coaching for young girls is not a matter of yelling, 'Faster, faster!'"

Parents and children must be on guard for coaches who try to wring every ounce of talent out of a young runner for the sake of the school or for personal gratification. "The best thing a coach can do is pass a runner on as a malleable prospect," Benson says.

If your son or daughter feels that he or she is not getting proper coaching, talk to the coach or athletic director about your concerns. You don't have to be an expert on training to know good coaching from bad coaching. If your son or daughter feels put down or pressured or is chronically exhausted or injured, the coach needs a talking-to. Should the coach disagree or fail to change his or her slant, you might want to get your child involved in a different running program, say, on a community or club level. "It's a matter of protecting your daughter," says Jones, who stayed very involved in her daughter's coaching. "Her enjoyment and health are at stake."

# BODY IMAGE

Eating disorders and body image issues can plague some runners even before they enter their teens. Although some research suggests that these problems are more prevalent among athletic girls than among nonathletes, no causal relationship has been proved. In other words, there is no evidence that sports themselves result in a greater risk of disordered eating. Rather, many experts believe that girls with certain body types or personality types are more likely to become athletes and that these girls already were more at risk for eating disorders.

You can contribute to your daughter's healthy attitude about food and her body by doing the following:

**Set a good example.** Eat healthfully yourself, and don't express extreme dissatisfaction with your own body.

**Stay away from inappropriate comments about weight.** Don't criticize her weight or give her ultimatums to lose weight. Negative remarks about weight at a young age can have a devastating effect on a girl.

**Ensure that she knows about proper nutrition.** If your young runner is concerned with her performance, you can have a big influence by impressing upon her the long-term training benefits of proper nutrition.

## TRAINING LOG

*I* was blessed and cursed with a father who introduced me to running. He had run as a kid, and so I would, too. No, it wasn't my idea for him to pressure the coach and athletic director to let me run with the boys' team in the mid-1970s. No, I didn't exactly appreciate being the pariah who infiltrated the boys' world in the peer-pressure land of junior high and high school. I wanted to play field hockey, for goodness' sake.

For years, I pretty much saw only the "cursed" side of what my father did for me. It would take more than a decade before I realized and appreciated the "blessed" side of things. My father, for example, never assumed that I could do less than a boy simply because I was a girl. He insisted that I have the same opportunities as my brother, at a time when that thinking was not popular. He went to bat for me when other parents were satisfied with the status quo. With, for example, field hockey.

He didn't have the benefit of 20 years of pop psychology admonishments to "Let your daughter find her way." And since running wasn't much of an option for girls back then, who knows? Chances are that I never would have found my way to running on my own. And for all the times that I've wondered whether my competitive career might have been different/better/longer had I had a gentler start in the sport, there is this flip side, too: I might never have had any start in sports if my father hadn't taken me by the hand and led me to the starting line.

Besides, that's all ancient history now. The result is that today, when I finish writing this, I will go for a run. And that at the age of 37, I am strong, healthy, and confident, thanks to the sport I learned as a child. I'm sure that's all he ever hoped running could give me. It's all I could ever hope to pass along to my own daughter.

Jones recognized the importance of providing a positive influence when her daughter was running as a youngster. "I was always very concerned about eating issues," she says. "Other girls on the team would come to the house, and you could see that they had a problem. I tried to communicate the fact that what you eat isn't important just for running, but for overall health."

If your daughter exhibits signs of an eating disorder, seek professional help. For more on eating disorders, see chapter 15.

# 21

# The Older Runner

WHEN DIANE PALMASON tells people that she is 61 years old, "they actually doubt me," she says. Palmason holds world and North American age-group records in several distances. She started running at the age of 38, and she says that her decades of fitness have helped her age with energy and grace.

"To a great extent, running has helped to keep me free of all the things that make someone *look* and *feel* 61," she says. "My overall energy, wellness, strength, and posture are better. Running has, essentially, slowed the aging process. I wouldn't give it up for anything."

Running can't stop time, but it certainly can soften the blows. The typical sedentary woman can expect her fitness to decline over the decades. The process typically starts as early as age 30, with gradually decreasing aerobic capacity, muscle mass, bone density, metabolic rate, and immunity. Fortunately, several studies have shown that aerobic and weight-bearing exercise such as running does slow these and other natural effects of aging. In addition to these physical benefits, studies also show that, as fit women age, they have better psychological health. In fact, women who engage in regular aerobic exercise programs, such as running, are less likely to suffer from:

- cardiovascular disease
- diabetes
- high blood pressure
- breast cancer

- stroke
- obesity
- symptoms of menopause
- and mood disturbances

And the good news isn't limited to those who, like Palmason, have been training since they were middle-age or younger. "Women can reap these benefits at any age," says Lynn Jaffee, program director of the Melpomene Institute in St. Paul, Minnesota, which specializes in women's health research. Even if you have been sedentary throughout your life, you'll still reap positive effects from running, whether you start running in your forties or in your seventies. Indeed, many women who start running later in life report feeling healthier and more vigorous than they did when they were years younger. "If everyone were physically active, we'd have entirely different standards of what is normal for any age," says Palmason.

## IT'S NEVER TOO LATE

At the age of 64, Mary Kirsling had never run before. One day, she decided to watch some of her family members take part in the Duke City Marathon in Albuquerque, New Mexico. Her granddaughter, then 8 years old, offered a challenge: "Grandma, I'll run the 5-K next year if you do." "Well," recalls Kirsling, "I thought, I'd better start tomorrow!" So she did. She began, as she puts it, "telephone pole to telephone pole."

"For my first few runs, I put on an old pair of sneakers and I ran down to the end of the block," she says. "I quickly realized that that wouldn't do, so I went out and bought my first pair of Nikes." Kirsling divided her 12-month window into a gradually increasing schedule, figuring out how far she'd need to progress each month in order to complete the 3.1-mile course the following year. She surprised herself by hitting the milestone with 2 months to spare. As she promised, Kirsling then ran alongside her granddaughter in her first 5-K. When it was over, she was shocked to learn that she'd finished second in her age group.

Since that day, Mary has completed 12 half-marathons. Now in her late seventies, she trains about 30 miles a week, with a long run of 10 miles and various quality workouts on the track. She

## Start with a Checkup

**W**omen who are beginning a running program at any age should have their health checked by a physician; for women over the age of 40, that's even more important. Undiagnosed heart disease is the primary concern for anyone about to begin an aerobic exercise regimen, says Lisa Callahan, M.D., cofounder and medical director of the Women's Sports Medicine Center at the Hospital for Special Surgery in New York City.

A physician will also want to look for other underlying medical conditions, such as hypertension or diabetes, and for anatomical warning signs, such as musculoskeletal problems, stiff joints, or arthritis. None of these factors will necessarily stop you from running. "But if they are addressed up front, it's far more likely that the woman will enjoy and succeed in her training program," says Dr. Callahan, a former competitive runner who now trains recreationally. "If not addressed, these are the types of problems that can cause injury or discouragement and a premature end to the fitness program."

travels the country to compete, counting her blessings as she counts the miles.

"Working as a nurse, I'd seen so many unhealthy people for so many years," she says. "I'd see some people in their seventies who were planted in their rocking chairs, and I knew I didn't want to be like that. It was wonderful when I started going to the races and seeing so many older, healthy, active people. I know it's made a big difference in my health. I recover faster when I am sick, I have more energy. Some folks in their sixties come up to me and say, 'Well, I'd be out there running too, except for . . .' and they'll mention this and that excuse. And I say, 'Well, give it a try. I did!'"

# TRAINING FOR A LIFETIME

The best part about running is that you can keep going and going. "With what we've seen women accomplish now, I can say with confidence, 'I can be a marathoner at 85,'" says Susan Kalish, executive director of the American Running Association. "I love soccer, too, but it's a contact sport, and I know that sooner or later

I'm going to have to stop because I'm going to break some bones. But I can roll with most any punch in running. Granted, my pace might be a little different, but I can be out there."

Just because you hit 40—or 60—doesn't mean that you have to revamp your training program. You simply have to be more careful about following the training rules that apply to all runners. "People talked about hitting 40 like I was headed for a cliff and about to fall off," says Lorraine Moller, 44, with a laugh. Moller, who lives in Boulder, Colorado, is a four-time Olympic marathoner and won the bronze medal in the 1992 Olympic Games. She now coaches and runs recreationally. "Women age at different rates," she says, "and there is not a line or a point at which they must change their training."

The training principles you'll follow at age 40, 50, or 60 are the same you followed at age 20 or 30. The older you are, however, the smarter you have to train, explains Lisa Callahan, M.D., cofounder and medical director of the Women's Sports Medicine Center at the Hospital for Special Surgery in New York City. Over the years, your muscles stiffen. That makes you more likely to get injured. Plus, if you do get injured at age 50 or 60, your body may take up to twice as long to heal.

"The principles remain the same for all ages, but acting on them is more crucial," says Dr. Callahan. Masters competitors attest to the extra attention needed for the less obvious points of running. "You can definitely get away with things earlier that you can't do when you are older," says Jane Welzel, 45, of Fort Collins, Colorado, a five-time Olympic Marathon Trials qualifier and a masters runner standout with more than 50 marathons under her belt. Welzel says that she hasn't changed her routine much over the years, but that's because she always performed strength and flexibility work as part of her workouts. "If you don't already have the discipline of good nutrition, stretching, and everything else, now it will catch up to you," she says.

Here are nine habits you should adopt.

**1. Always warm up.** A proper warmup will loosen muscles and make your workout less of a stress on your body. You'll be less likely to pull a muscle or otherwise hurt yourself.

**2. Focus on recovery.** The most noticeable impact of aging upon training is the need for more recovery time between workouts. If you are a competitive runner, this might mean a greater number of easy running days between hard workouts; if you are a recreational runner, this might mean fewer actual running days per week. Your total training volume and miles will likely drop. "You might have done three hard workouts a week before, and now it's five every 2 weeks," says Palmason, cofounder and codirector of Women's Running Camps in Denver.

Those numbers shouldn't concern you, though; getting the proper recovery is the important thing. If you ignore your body's request for rest, you could find yourself injured or chronically tired. "Part of running is always paying attention to the signals you are getting," Palmason says. "By the time we're 55 or 60, we should definitely have learned to do that!"

**3. Take easier off days.** Now that you're taking more off days, make sure that they actually give your body a break. A strenuous hike on a day that you don't run, for example, might not allow you to recover. If you want to stay active, do something that is not weight-bearing, such as swimming or cycling. This type of activity will allow your running muscles and joints to rest while developing other parts of your body.

**4. Always stretch after your runs.** Counteracting the tightening effects of running becomes more important with age. Stretch gently, without bouncing, in order to avoid injury.

**5. Do strength training to keep your muscles and bones strong.** Both muscle and bone strength tend to diminish with age. But a strength-training program can slow down this natural process so that you can keep running and stay active in all your other endeavors.

**6. Take a multivitamin and stay hydrated.** As we age, our bodies do not absorb nutrients as efficiently as they once did. And women, in order to protect their bones, have even higher needs for calcium as they age. To ensure that you are getting the proper vitamins and minerals, take a daily supplement. Drink plenty of water and watch your intake of diuretic drinks such as soda and coffee.

**7. Never run in a worn-out pair of shoes.** Replace your shoes about every 400 miles to make sure that they are offering the proper support and cushioning.

**8. Switch from joint-jarring roads to softer trails.** Trails, dirt roads, and grassy parks all cushion the blow to your legs. If you must run on pavement or concrete because of where you live, try to drive to a course with a softer surface at least once a week.

**9. Keep challenging yourself.** As you age, the pace of your steady runs and speedwork will eventually slow. But that doesn't mean that you can't still challenge yourself. Continue to push your limits, in intensity and distance. Your hard training days can still be hard days, they just might not be as fast.

# PERFORMANCE CHANGES

Runners can slow down the aging process, but they can't fool it altogether. Sooner or later, all of us will be looking back on our record times instead of setting new ones.

Women typically hit their years of peak performance somewhere between the ages of 20 and 40. Runners who start training later in life, however, can expect years of improvement, no matter what their age. Mary Kirsling, for example, continued to get faster well into her seventies after starting at age 64; Diane Palmason experienced 8 years of improvement after beginning to run at the age of 38. In general, from the day you start running, you can expect 8 to 10 years of improvement before your times begin to slow.

Slowing times might be inevitable, but that doesn't make them any easier to accept. You may feel frustrated. You may look for excuses: Is it just an off year? "For so long, it's about getting better, getting faster. Then suddenly there's a realization that you won't," says Welzel. "But if you're running because you enjoy it, you will find a way to continue. There are always other things to achieve and other reasons to be running—so much more that you can get from the sport. It's better to focus on those things rather than wishing that you could still do the other stuff."

Here are some alternative focuses for runners who are no longer getting faster.

**Change your goals with your changing age.** As you get older, you can challenge yourself by focusing on your "new PRs," trying to run your best time since turning 50 or 60, for example. "Thank goodness for those 5-year age groups," jokes JoAnn Behm Scott, 44, of Carlsbad, California. Competing on and off as a national-level masters runner, Scott typifies the struggle that comes with changes due to aging. "You have to give yourself permission to back off. After years of training, you may feel that you're letting yourself down if you don't keep progressing. But you get to a point where it's okay. It helps to frame running in terms of new chal-

## IN YOUR OWN WORDS

# The Passing Years

*I'll say this even to the younger ones: If you want to run, you must start out slowly. Don't be worried about anybody else, how fast they are going or what they can do. As I always say, take it telephone pole to telephone pole.*

**Mary, 77, Albuquerque, New Mexico**

*I will probably always run, because I enjoy the act of running. And I will probably always compete, because I like that, too. It's so woven into my life; I've been doing it for the last 25 years. It's always been a metaphor for life, and that will always be there.*

**Jane, 45, Fort Collins, Colorado**

*It's not an easy thing, to go against cultural beliefs, against what you are "supposed" to do at a certain age. Women's masters runners used to be few and far between. Today, it's become quite competitive. And, as more women participate, those old beliefs are changing.*

**Lorraine, 44, Boulder, Colorado**

*My mind wants to go faster than my body, but I still push myself; it's the way I was "raised" in running. I like the sprints because I love the feeling of flying. There aren't many women my age doing the shorter races, but that seems to me to come from the "old" rules of being a woman—like that you have to cut your hair once you're 40. After all, what exactly does it mean to act your age?*

**Colleen, 50, Albuquerque, New Mexico**

lenges. Right now I'm thinking, Yeah, let me turn 45! That way I can set new goals for myself. It gives me new focus."

Race organizers, recognizing the influx of older runners into the sport, have responded by adding more age groups. "When I started racing (in the 1980s) there very rarely were any age groups for older runners—it was just '60 and up,'" recalls Kirsling. "And because there were so few women out there to begin with, I was often racing against myself." Thanks to the greater number of older runners now in the sport, 5- or 10-year age groups can be found up into the eighties and sometimes beyond. (The breakdown typically

---

*A*nyone older than me is an inspiration to me. I need to know that we'll all still be running together in races or out on the trails no matter what our age or health condition. Older women runners always look so strong and healthy and have 20 times the energy of women their age who don't run. And that's where I want to go.

**Shelley**, 39, Boulder, Colorado

*D*on't stop. Whatever you are doing, keep on doing it at a rate you can maintain without being injured. Do not think about your age; just keep on trucking.

**Eve**, 63, Mill Valley, California

*T*he thing is to stay in love with running, with being outside and in good shape and seeing friends. Those parts of it are never-ending. And being at a certain age and still being in the shape of a 20-year-old woman is pretty nice, too!

**JoAnn**, 44, Carlsbad, California

*B*ecause I can see the benefits over the course of my life, I'm much clearer now than at the age of 40 that even if I never enter another competition in my life, I will keep running. It's crucial to feeling good and having my body function properly. It's who I am.

**Diane**, 61, Blaine, Washington

depends on the size of the race.) Naturally, the "youngsters" in each bracket will have an advantage; thus the sweet irony of looking forward to growing older in order to enter a new age group.

**Run a different type of race.** If you're used to focusing on your time in a 5-K or 10-K, choose a challenge that you can't compare with those. Try a trail race, a relay race with friends, or a duathlon, which combines running and bicycling.

**Run for your health.** Instead of trying to lower your times, try to lower your blood pressure or your cholesterol level.

**Run for someone else.** More running events now focus on charity. Consider using your running to raise money for an organization by entering one of these races. Or dedicate a race to the memory of a loved one. Or encourage a daughter or granddaughter—or grandson—to start running with you.

**Run to see the world.** Many younger runners don't have time to travel to races. Pick a major race in a city you've wanted to see, and create a vacation around it.

# MENOPAUSE

Few studies have looked at the relationship between running and menopause. Research has generated intriguing theories but little in the way of definitive answers. "Until recently," as Palmason puts it, "we have all been experiments of one."

Evidence does suggest that physical activity can alleviate menopausal symptoms in some women. Several studies report fewer mood disturbances, hot flashes, and sweating among women who are active than among their sedentary counterparts. One study of female runners showed that they were less likely to experience the weight gain that typically follows menopause. And a 1998 survey of 625 women readers of *Runner's World* magazine that was analyzed and reported by the Melpomene Institute found that 74 percent of women runners felt that running improved their overall menopausal and postmenopausal experience.

An interesting finding of the study is that, running may make you hit menopause sooner. According to the *Runner's World* survey, the average menopausal age for the runners was 47.6; the national average for all women is 51. Melpomene program director

Jaffee says that the questionnaire results corroborate anecdotal evidence that women runners have been reporting for years. Until further studies are done, researchers can only theorize as to the reason for such early menopause, but they believe it might be related to the typically lower hormone levels in active women.

## TRAINING LOG

*When people ask me who my running inspiration is, one woman comes to mind: Mary Kirsling. When I met Mary, she was 73 years old. She was training on the track once a week in the same group that included her two daughters and her grandson. As Mary would complete her 400s and 800s, the rest of the group would shout encouragement with whichever familiar moniker seemed most appropriate given their own age: "Go, Mom!" Or, "Go, Grandma!" Mary, it seems, had become every runner's adopted matriarch.*

*Over the years, Mary has become a minicelebrity of sorts in her hometown of Albuquerque. Runners one-third her age stop her on the bike path to talk. They tell her what an inspiration she is to them, how they hope to be as fit and strong and confident and happy as she is when they reach her age. And I have told her the same thing.*

*Several years back, Mary and I were both in a group of runners that had gone to the mountains for a camping trip/training retreat. Over the weekend, I caught a glimpse of Mary running by herself, several miles out from the campground, and heading up the steep mountain road that pointed the way back. I marveled: How many women her age would be on that camping trip? How many women her age would even be walking in those mountains, much less running? How many Marys will it take before this scene seems ordinary?*

*Women traditionally have more fears than men do about growing old. We live longer; thus, the statistics say, we are more likely to be left alone, or to be left in ill health. To see Mary—or to see any of her increasingly growing number of female cohorts—on that mountain road, on that track, on that bike path, is to see the realm of possibility that each of our futures hold. Thanks to Mary and the others, the future is looking good.*

Whether women experience an accelerated decrease in performance during menopause is also yet to be proved. "Some women do complain that their pace drops dramatically while they are going through menopause," Jaffee says. "While everybody's pace drops eventually due to aging, it seems that women experience a more pronounced impact than men." However, it's still unknown whether slowing in women runners is due more to the effects of aging or to the effects of menopause. If it's menopause, then those performance fluctuations might reverse themselves when menopause is complete, as many runners report.

The impact of hormone replacement therapy (HRT) on running performance is also uncertain. Experts agree that the primary basis for deciding whether to undergo HRT should be your personal and family medical history. More than half of the women responding to the *Runner's World*/Melpomene questionnaire reported taking some form of HRT. Of these women, 22 percent felt that taking the hormones made a difference in their running. About one-quarter reported a reduction in symptoms that made running difficult, 21 percent reported an increase in energy, and 17 percent said they could run longer and faster. Nineteen percent, however, said that HRT had a negative impact on their running.

# Index

Boldface page references indicate photographs. Underlined references indicate boxed text.

Anorexia nervosa, 184–85, <u>184</u>
Arch supports, in shoes, <u>8–9</u>
Arm stretch, 235, **235**
Arthritis, <u>23</u>
Asthma, 196
Attire. *See* Clothing
Attitude
  confident, 218–19
  positive, 104, 150–52
Avon Running-Global Women's
  Circuit, <u>89</u>

# B
Babysitting co-ops, 142
Back extension, 244, **244**
Backpacks, 20
Back pain, 196–97
Back stretch, 235, **235**
Balance, of running and life
  changing roles and, 144–45
  child-care issues, 141–42
  commitment and, 140–41
  "magnificent obsession" and, 145,
    <u>146</u>, 147
  reasons for, 138–39
  Training Log entry about, <u>146</u>
  travel schedules and, 142–44
  unsupportive partners and, 139–40
Base building, 70
Bathroom breaks, 27–28
Beginner marathon training
  schedule, <u>115</u>
Beginner training program
  challenges, 41, <u>47</u>
  going beyond, 49
  marathon, <u>115</u>
  pace and, 43–46

6-week schedule, 46–48
style of running and, 42–43
suggestions for, additional, <u>43</u>
Beginning competitor training
  schedule, 81, <u>81</u>, 84
Biceps curl, 241, **241**
Biomechanics, 4, 42–43, <u>117</u>
Birth control pills, side effects of,
  197–98
Black toenails, 198
Bladder problems, 205
Blisters, 198–99
Body, listening to,
  at beginning stage of running, 45
  health issues and, 190–91
  importance of, 34
  marathon training and, 116
  mental readiness and, 88
  pregnancy and, 253, 259–62,
    266–67
  race toughness and, 103
Body image
  acceptance of body and, 178–82
  best and worst scenarios, 177
  disordered eating, <u>186–87</u>,
    188–89
  dissatisfaction with body, 179
  eating disorders, 184–88, <u>184</u>
  messages about body, 177–78
  reasons for running and, 182–84
  sub-elite runners and, 180–82
  tips for improving, <u>183</u>
  women runners' personal
    comments about, <u>180–81</u>
  younger runners and, 271,
    279–81
Bonding, of women runners, 1

---

**Boldface** page references indicate photographs. <u>Underlined</u> references indicate boxed text.

**Boldface** page references indicate photographs. <u>Underlined</u> references indicate boxed text.

Boldface page references indicate photographs. Underlined references indicate boxed text.

**Boldface** page references indicate photographs. Underlined references indicate boxed text.

**Health issues**

Achilles tendon pain, 194
acne, 195
allergies, 195–96
arthritis, <u>23</u>
asthma, 196
back pain, 196–97
birth control pills, side effects of,
    197–98
black toenails, 198
blisters, 198–99
bone bruises, 199
breasts, aching and sagging, <u>23</u>,
    199–200
calluses, 201
chafing, 200
colds, 200–201
corns, 201
dehydration, 201–2
diarrhea, 202
disordered eating, <u>186–87</u>, 188–89
eating disorders, 184–88, <u>184</u>
flu, 200–201
frostbite, 203
hair, damaged, 201
heat cramps, 203
heat exhaustion, 203–4
heat rash, 204
heatstroke, 204
hyperthermia, 203–4
hypothermia, 203
iliotibial band friction syndrome,
    204–5
incontinence, 205
injury prevention, 191–93
listening to your body and,
    190–91
medications, side effects of, 205–6
menopause, 290–92
menstrual problems, 206–8
muscle cramps, 208–9
osteoporosis, 207, 209–10
physical examination, 21–22, <u>284</u>
physicians, selecting, 191
plantar fasciitis, 210–11
razor bumps, 211
runner's knee, 211–12
shinsplints, 212, 214
side stitches, 25, 214
skin damage, 214–15
sore knees, <u>23</u>
stomach upset, 215
stress fractures, 215–16
vaginal itching, 216
wrinkles, 214–15
younger runners and, 270–71,
    <u>274</u>
**Heart-rate monitors,** 18, <u>34</u>, <u>45</u>, 261
**Heat illness,** 203–4
**Heat rash,** 204
**Heel cups, for shoes,** <u>9</u>
**Heredity, running and,** 31–35
**High-knee drill,** 246–47, **246–47**
**High school years, physical activity
    during,** 273–75
**Hill running,** 60–61
**Hip and waist stretch,** 234, **234**
**Hopping drill,** 248–49, **248–49**
**Hormones,** 4, 29, 292
**Hormone replacement therapy
    (HRT),** 292
**Hot weather**
    clothing for, 204
    problems in, 203–4

---

Boldface page references indicate photographs. <u>Underlined</u> references indicate boxed text.

**Boldface** page references indicate photographs. <u>Underlined</u> references indicate boxed text.

Boldface page references indicate photographs. Underlined references indicate boxed text.

Boldface page references indicate photographs. Underlined references indicate boxed text.

Boldface page references indicate photographs. <u>Underlined</u> references indicate boxed text.

**Boldface** page references indicate photographs. Underlined references indicate boxed text.

**Boldface** page references indicate photographs. <u>Underlined</u> references indicate boxed text.

**Boldface** page references indicate photographs. <u>Underlined</u> references indicate boxed text.

Boldface page references indicate photographs. Underlined references indicate boxed text.

Triceps extension, 242, **242**
T-shirts, 16
Two-a-days, 75–76

# U

Upper abdominal crunch, 243, **243**

# V

Vaginal itching, 216
Visualization, 88–90
Vitamin supplements, 169, 171

# W

Waist belt, 20
Walk-to-jog transition program,
    44, 46–48
Warmup, 95–97, 285
Watches, sports, 15–16
Water intake. *See* Hydration
Weather
    cold, 16 –17, 103, 203
    hot, 203–4
    safety issues and, 224
Weight loss
    calories burned, calculating, 173
    consistency and, 172
    dining out and, 175
    food choices and, 175
    indulging in food and, 175
    maintaining, 175, 182
    motivation and, 182
    resistance training and, 176
    tips for, 172–76
Well-rounded runners
    benefits for, 225–28
    cross-training and, 226, 228–29
    drills and, 226, 244–49, **244–49**

massage and, 226, 250–52
pool running and, 226, 250
resistance training and, 226,
    236–44, **238–44**
stretching and, 226, 229–36,
    **229–36**
Women runners. *See also*
    Frequently asked questions
    benefits for, physical and
        emotional, 1–3, 156–58
    bonding of, 1
    evolution of running and, 2–4
    gender differences and, 1, 4–5
    increase in, 2–4
    marathon and, 106–8
    myths about, debunking, 23
    personal comments from
        becoming a more serious
            runner, 52
        beginner's challenge, 47
        body image issues, 180–81
        lifetime of running, 288–89
        memories of first running, 26–27
        pregnancy and running, 256
        racing, 91
        social vs. solo running, 126
        time for running, making, 140
    racing events for, premier, 89
    reasons for running and, 30, 52,
        151, 182–84
Women's Sports Foundation, 270
Wrinkles, 214–15

# Y

Younger runners
    age for starting physical activity,
        271

---

**Boldface** page references indicate photographs. <u>Underlined</u> references indicate boxed text.

**Younger runners *(continued)***

---

**Boldface** page references indicate photographs. <u>Underlined</u> references indicate boxed text.